Enjoying Old Parish Churches

Volume I

By the same author

Essex Fonts and Font Covers

Enjoying Old Parish Churches

Volume I

W. N. Paul F. INST L. EX.

The Pentland Press
Edinburgh – Cambridge – Durham – USA

First published in 1996 by
The Pentland Press Ltd
1 Hutton Close,
South Church
Bishop Auckland
Durham

ISBN 1-85821-361-4

Typeset by Carnegie Publishing, 18 Maynard St, Preston
Printed and bound in Great Britain by
Bookcraft (Bath) Ltd., Midsomer Norton, Somerset

To my late wife, Pauline, who often patiently waited while I photographed architectural and other features, taking notes, and for allowing me to spend so much time in my study and in research.

Acknowledgements

I would like to thank my old friend David Phillips who accompanied me on many of my visits to parish churches and also to my friends and former students, Ken Feline for his line drawings and Marcus Dain for his line drawings, advice and encouragement.

Contents

Illustrations

Introduction

A nation which has forgotten its past will never have a future.

Churchill

The parish church is our main link with the past centuries and though most village churches contain museum-worthy features of local and national historical interest a church is by no means a museum. The church was built for prayer and worship, perhaps some eight hundred years ago and prayer and worship has continued continuously since then and still continues.

Entering an old church is a great spiritual experience with its feeling of solitude, emptiness, smell, the beauty of the workmanship of different periods of its history, and, of course the atmosphere brought about by the worship of many thousands of people over the centuries. A medieval church is something which, like our great historical houses, can never be replaced.

Many people when on holiday or out for a drive during the weekend visit an old church but to many, however, they generally see only the tombstones and read the wall plaques. These tell us something about the people in the past who attended the church or were its benefactors but nothing about the builders of the church or how it grew. It is hoped that this book will help to increase the number of people visiting old churches, give them pleasure and deepen their understanding.

We may not discover all the evidence of how it grew but by exploring the building we will not miss the visible marks which are all part of the past. Looking for these marks and being able to understand them helps to time the history of the church and the events which affected it and led to it being as it is now. Doorways and windows which have changed from round-headed to pointed, together with their decorations and pillars are perhaps so different in style from the remainder of the building that they must have been added later. Types of pews, some having beautiful carving, fonts, pulpits, misericords, sedilia, piscina, wall-paintings, hatchments and brasses, all these things have much to tell us and it is when we know what to look for and to understand what we are looking at that our visit becomes so much more interesting and worthwhile; it becomes an adventure into the past. Each addition to the structure has been an occasion of personal satisfaction to those who made it and every memorial expresses pride or pious affection. The beautiful things to be found were an expression by men and women of their love of God and their will to adorn the place where they worshipped Him.

There are some ten thousand medieval churches in England and each one is worth a visit. It is usually around the church that the best part of any village or small town is to be found. Many, however, are situated some way from the village and it is certain that looking for them will take one down lanes and byways which one would never, otherwise, have visited. These churches are rich in individuality and charm and the extent to which these buildings have been altered is an indication of the fluctuating prosperity and social conditions of the parishioners at various periods and reflect the changes in religion, the architecture of the church and its furnishings and fittings as well as the despoliation during the Reformation, dissolution of the monasteries, the Puritan onslaught and the Civil War.

The interest in old churches is a growing one, but many are rarely visited either because people do not know how many there are or what to look for and interpret on arrival. For this reason the enormous wealth of interest remains hidden and unknown and, as a result, is often neglected and eventually lost.

It is hoped that this book will help your to understand our old parish churches and so make your visits more interesting and provide a deep insight into the past.

Architectural Periods

Period	Dates	Style
Saxon	600–1066	ROMANESQUE
Norman	1066–1189	
Transitional	1145–1189	
Early English	1189–1280	
Transitional	1250–1280	GOTHIC
Decorated	1280–1377	
Transitional	1350–1377	
Perpendicular	1377–1547	
Early Tudor	1500–1547	
Late Tudor	1547–1603	RENAISSANCE
Jacobean (or Early Stuart)	1603–1625	
Carolian (or Late Stuart to 1689)	1625–1649	
Hanoverian (William & Mary, Anne and Georgian)	1689–1837	CLASSICAL (From 1689)

I

The Origin of Parish Churches and Their Development

The diocese was, from the beginning, the principal unit of church administration. The bishop was in charge and the cathedral was his headquarters. The whole area was controlled by the bishop with the assistance of a staff of priests who he sent out into the country to preach and teach and provide the services. It will be seen that before long the distances to be travelled and the amount of work involved became too much of a burden for the diocese and it was divided up and subsidiary churches called minsters were established serving smaller areas in a similar manner to the diocese. A minster, derived from the Latin word *monasterium*, was either a monastery or a mother church staffed by monks and secular priests, that is those not belonging to a monastic order, living as a community.

The commonest method of creating parishes under Saxon rule in the tenth century was the one whereby the local chieftain who had been converted to Christianity built a church to serve his own estate. Before conversion he would have been accustomed to build a place of worship as well as providing a priest for his pagan followers and now, after conversion, would provide the church for the new worship, probably installing the priest from the old benefice to the new. It was, therefore, from the lay patronage that he received his appointment but his spiritual charge was committed to him by the Bishop.

It is very possible that he used the site of the old ceremonies and it is therefore possible that the graveyard of an old church is older that the church itself. So many churches either stand in or near prehistoric earthworks or stone circles that it seems clear that such sites were deliberately chosen for Christian worship. In fact the policy of the early church does much to confirm this. This policy was to encourage the continual occupation of a sacred site and this was expressed in the instructions which Pope Gregory sent to St Augustine in 601.

> Do not pull down the fanes. Destroy the idols; purify the temples with holy water; set relics there; and let them become temples of the true God. So the people will have no need to change their places of concourse, and where of old they were wont to sacrifice cattle to demons, thither let them continue to resort on the day

of the saint to whom the church is dedicated, and slay their beasts, no longer as a sacrifice, but for a social meal in honour of Him whom they now worship.

This probably accounts for many churches being found on high ground often apart from the village.

Gregory the Great was wise in his forecast of what happened; the annual fairs in the churchyard, the church ales and other joyous festivals continued but all memory of their pagan origin was lost.

It has been contended by one authority that the ancient churches lie on the lines of the ancient straight tracks which were sited across the country and frequently having the 'mark' points, either stone, tree groups or mound, on the highest points touched.

Beauchamp Roding church in Essex was built in the fourteenth century on a much earlier site and on a hill outside the village where there is a mark stone in the churchyard. Legend has it that the villagers were told to build a church by the side of the stone on top of the hill but it was so far away from the village that they decided to drag the stone down the hill towards the village. However, on the following morning, the stone was found back in its original position on the hill. Again it was moved down to the village and once more super-natural forces took it back. Once again the stone was moved only to return to its original position. The struggle was given up and the church was built where it is today, beside the stone on top of the hill!

The ecclesiastical laws of the period forbade people to indulge in the worship of fountains, necromancy (evil magic), auguries (prediction), and enchantments, or to bow down to idols and heathen gods or to the sun and the moon, or to resort to special stones or trees as holy places.

Christianity was growing in strength and the tenth century was, on the whole, a period of peace and progress for the people of England.

Towards the end of the tenth century Edward the young King of Wessex was assassinated, leaving the throne to the incompetent Ethelred. The Vikings took this opportunity to renew their raids on the south coast and in 1011 Canterbury was sacked, its cathedral burnt and a large number of its citizens with the Archbishop, Alphege, were taken prisoners. Alphege was held to ransom because he refused to burden the poor with raising the ransom for him and so he was murdered by being clubbed or stoned to death by the Vikings near Greenwich on the 19th April 1012.

It seemed as though God had deserted his people and the country would once more fall into barbarism.

By 1016 the second Viking invasion had been so successful that the Danish King, Cnut, had made himself master of England. Cnut, was, however, a Christian and his distinction as a ruler was that from the beginning of his reign he set out to gain the respect of the English Church and he soon made his mark, not as a tyrant and oppressor but as the protector of the Church.

Cnut's reign from 1016 to 1035 was, on the whole, a time of peace and prosperity for the country and encouragement and growth of the Church.

The death of Cnut was followed by eight troubled years after which the English monarchy was restored and Edward son of Ethelred the Unready was crowned in 1043.

At this time the country was divided into two parties. On party consisted of Edward at the Court with his Norman clerks and the other party represented by the great earls like Godwin and Harold. These men bitterly resented the intrusion of foreigners into England.

Edward, known as the Confessor, in spite of his personal holiness allowed the Church to deteriorate during his reign. The clergy were poor and ignorant and little was done for their improvement. The one positive monument to Edward's reign was the building of the Abbey at Westminster which was consecrated in 1065 but the King was too ill to attend the ceremony and died six days later.

On the death of Edward, Harold became King. Before his death Edward had promised the crown to William, Duke of Normandy and on the crowning of Harold, William decided to invade England.

With the defeat and death of Harold at Hastings in 1066 after having been on the throne for only a few months the Church in England entered upon a new stage in its history.

The Saxon Church did much for the people of England and produced some of the greatest men who have been honoured by the Church which included the holiness of Cuthbert, the zeal of Wilfred as an evangelist, the courage of Boniface in his work in converting the pagan hordes in Germany and the learning of Bede.

When the actual Norman Conquest took place it seems to have had little effect on the architecture of this country and although some of the great churches built in England after the Conquest show a French influence in their planning many more retain the plan which was common to Anglo-Saxon England. It was not until some years after the conquest that the architecture began to show traces of French influence, for example, the pointed arch.

The Norman barons drew up the plans of their castles and the Norman abbots their great churches but the actual building was carried out by Anglo-Saxon masons in the style which they had developed throughout many generations. The Saxons were fond of decoration and although the early Norman buildings were austere many of the later Anglo-Norman buildings from about 1090 onward show Anglo-Saxon influences.

When it is remembered that the net result of the Conquest on the population of England added about one per cent to a native population of some two millions it will be seen that although Norman masons were used a vast number of Saxon masons, equipped with their hereditary skill, would have been drawn from the native population.

One very important step was taken by King William in 1075 when he ordered the abolition of the vague rural Saxon dioceses and founded in their place proper episcopal sees in the cities which were being established throughout the country. From this period the secular Church, that is whose members were not bound by monastic vows, and its bishops, began to be established and so they were able to compete with the old established Benedictine monasteries in the building of cathedral churches which would compare with the great monastic churches.

Soon after the Conquest there was a spate of building which did much to enhance the art of masoncraft, an art about which the Saxons knew little as most of their buildings were timber, a material with which they were well acquainted.

Most of the Saxon churches were small and built of timber. They belonged to the local lord who built them. He claimed the right of appointing the parish priest and this right continued through the medieval period and in some cases continues today. The lord also claimed the right to remove his church or even to use it for some secular purpose, for example, a mill or a barn.

In many villages today we can observe how near the manor house is to the church and often has its own gate into the churchyard.

The early churches were primarily shelters for altars. The early Christians gathered round the wayside altars or crosses to see and hear priests celebrate Mass. Later, for their own convenience, they built shelters which developed into the nave of the parish church. All medieval churches were designed with one idea, that the alter and celebrant should be seen and so the services were rather seen than heard. Blind walls and pillars were pierced by 'squints', a hole cut through so that the eye should miss nothing.

2

Builders and Their Buildings

Who were the men who built the parish churches? It was a popular notion that they were monks or even the parishioners themselves and that they worked for the love of it without hope of reward. This is now thought to be wrong. The builders were paid craftsmen but they were craftsmen who put all their skill into their work in an effort to produce the best work possible to the glory of God.

Two systems were in use just as they are today. The first was by direct labour the employer providing the materials, engaging workmen and a master craftsman as overseer and paying each expense separately. The master craftsman who would provide the design and undertake to complete the building for a definite sum or at least that portion of the building for which his particular trade was responsible as there were usually separate contracts for each trade. It was usual to employ a master mason to complete the foundations, walls and floors and then a master carpenter contracted to roof the building.

The builders of medieval village homes were the 'wrights' or carpenters as we would call them today. Every village had its wright who was required to make carts, ploughs and agricultural and domestic items. On the coast he would build ships but everywhere he built houses.

Later the carpenter, so far as craftsmanship with his particular material was concerned, was eventually superseded by the joiner who specialised in methods whereby timbers could be joined together and thereby able to construct lofty timber roofs, screens and many other parts of the church using strong joints some of which were cunningly hidden. Together with the carvers, the joiners provided the great medieval craftsmanship we find in our greater churches and cathedrals especially in the glorious screens, stalls, bench-ends and roof work.

When stone walls first came into use they were mainly built by unskilled hands and consisted of assorted-sized rubble roughly piled up. Sometimes the walls were roughly coursed or herring-bone masonry was used. Another method of laying rubble stone is to fit the pieces carefully together in what is known as 'ragstone' technique. This method was common throughout the Middle Ages in Kent but is also found in districts where flint is used. Rubble walling is raised evenly along its length and has no core as in a true masonry wall which was built up of square blocks of freestone known as ashlar and laid in more or less

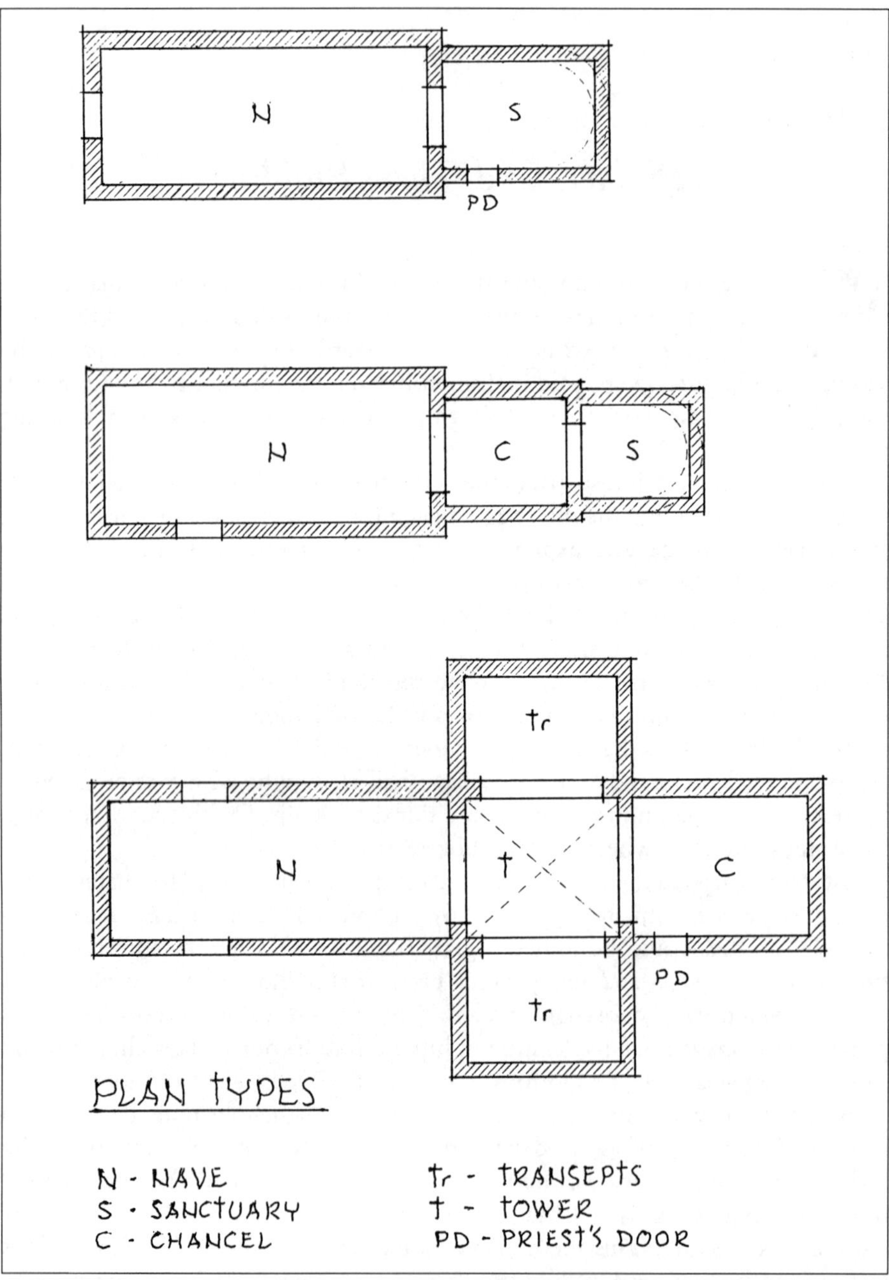

FIGURE 1.
Church plan types

regular courses having a central core of rubble. The whole being set in lime mortar which was the usual method employed where freestone was plentiful. Freestone is a fine-grained stone which can be cut into square or rectangular blocks for walling and decorative features.

Typical Plan Types

Nearly all parish church plans can be traced back to one of three fundamental types:

1. Nave and Chancel
2. Nave, Chancel and Sanctuary
3. Cruciform or transeptal church with Nave, Transepts, Chancel and Central tower.

Saxon Period, circa 600–1066

Nave with square ended chancel plan is the most common and usually the nave is longer, narrower and more lofty that the Norman. The chancel is shorter narrower and more lofty. Transeptal chapels were sometimes added to the nave and entered from inside the church. Entrance was generally from the west end and side porches were uncommon though western porches were constructed and were often later carried up to become western towers, as at Deerhurst, Gloucesteshire. Aisles were rarely employed.

The earliest Saxon churches, as Bede tells us were, as a rule, built of wood and have, therefore, long since disappeared. Only one has survived at Greensted-juxta-Ongar, Essex. Later rubble and ashlar were used in which the stonework of the towers and windows show that the builders imitated in stone the wooden constructions with which they were familiar, a good example of which may

GREENSTED CHURCH, ESSEX.
Saxon nave wall timbers.

been seen at Earls Barton, Northamptonshire. Stone churches were built by the Saxons before the Conquest and it is now beginning to be apparent that many of these churches were retained by the Normans but were given, windows, doorways, roofs and other features of the period.

Due to the difficulties of quarrying and transporting stone considerable use was made, especially in stoneless districts such as East Anglia, of the Roman bricks that were still to be found in large quantities about the country in their decaying buildings, together with flints and pebble-rubble.

During the latter part of the Roman occupation Christianity began to take hold and the Romans built some fine churches. St Martin's, Canterbury, Kent is an old Roman church but it has been so thoroughly rebuilt over some fifteen hundred years that it no longer looks Roman.

When the Saxons began to be converted to Christianity they did not have the skill or experience to build anything like the churches of the Romans and so they followed a style of their own. On a small scale they copied some of the details of a Roman shrine and so the style has been called 'Romanesque' or 'after the Roman manner' and this style was continued into the Norman period.

ESCOMBE, DURHAM.
Long and short work.

The principal clue to Saxon architecture is a peculiar custom known as 'long and short work' which is composed of large stones with their longer axis vertical with smaller stones laid flat in between. This work appears at the angles of walls and forms the quoins of their towers and main buildings. Examples of stone churches with this work are to be found at Earls Barton, Northamptonshire and Wareham in Dorset.

Theodore of Tarsus became Archibishop of Canterbury in AD 668 and took in hand the more effective organisation of the church in England, carved out dioceses, increased the number of bishoprics from seven to fourteen and established a more orderly system of ecclesiastical government. He also encouraged Saxon landowners, the thegns, to build churches on their estates either for themselves as private chapels, or for the use of the peasants on their land. A church would be put in charge of a cleric who gained a living from the produce of the glebe given to him together with fees from baptisms, marriages selling holy water for cures as well as supervising trials by ordeal. The patronage of these churches was also granted to the founders by the Archbishop.

Anglo-Saxon England grew wealthier through the centuries due to the considerable trade with Flanders and into this expanding civilisation Anglo-Saxon England was forced to suffer the devastating attacks of the Scandinavian pirates, the Danes.

Alfred was responsible for bringing peace between the Saxons and the Danes and on Alfred's death was ushered in the Golden Age of Anglo-Saxon England, the tenth century, and by the time of the Norman Conquest in 1066 the Anglican masons had developed a style of architecture as fine as anywhere in western Europe.

Norman Period 1066–c1189

Many Norman churches stand on the sites of Saxon buildings as the Normans either made a clean sweep of the old buildings and started afresh or, if the structure was in good condition, they used the structure and refashioned the doorways, windows, roofs, fittings and furnishings. During the century following the Conquest there was a period of extraordinary activity and the severe style which had predominated on the other side of the channel was developed, improved and adorned and became known generally as the Norman style. This century was a period of unyielding energy with almost inexhaustible resources which were combined with religious zeal so that their work was devoted to the honour and glory of God.

The exterior of the Norman church had about it an impression of solemnity while the interior had a sense of grandeur however small the church might be, as at Kilpeck, Herefordshire.

The plan type, in the main, differs only in detail from the Saxon but in more important churches a third space was added between the nave and the chancel for those singing the offices and that space was the 'choir'.

The population of Norman England was absurdly small in comparison with the enormous number of parish churches and it was not often found necessary to provide more space for the worshippers than a good sized nave could provide. Only in a few instances were churches build from the beginning with aisles to the nave.

Later in this period the addition of aisles became popular and naves were lengthened and in some instances porches were built.

It is very probable that few Norman parishes had more than one resident priest but in larger places there were more and it was necessary to provide additional altars to enable them to perform the daily mass. These additional altars were usually accommodated by adding transepts to the choir space so producing the cruciform plan.

This style was imported from the Continent where it evolved in an attempt to copy the ruins of Roman buildings. The transition from Saxon to Norman may be described as a good example of the overlap in dates and periods and it would be wrong to assume that Saxon work came to an abrupt halt in 1066 and thereafter all architecture was Norman. Edward the Confessor received a great deal of his early training at the Norman court and under his patronage Norman fashions were copied and were in vogue before the Normans themselves began to supersede the earlier style. Both in Edward's own Abbey of Westminster and in Harold's church at Waltham, Essex, the Saxon style was abandoned in favour of the Norman. It can be said, therefore, that in pre-Conquest Britain there was an appreciable amount of Norman work but that after 1075 there was very little Saxon work. The next result of the Norman Conquest on the population of England was to add about one per cent of Normans to a native population of some two million and it was from this population that the whole of the craftsman, equipped with their hereditary skill, would have been drawn.

The chief influences arriving from the influx of the colonists originated from the Benedictines. Wealthy monasteries, still further enriched with the spoils of vanquished England, grew more and more powerful. Once again the fine monastic churches were rebuilt vaster and more magnificent than before. New monasteries were also being founded throughout the countryside. The medieval church was taking a firm hold on England.

All this monastic development having been instituted for the benefit of the Benedictine Order was contributing little to the ecclesiastical organisation of the country. Lanfranc, Archibishop of Canterbury, however, a loyal servant of the Conqueror worked together to bring the English Church into the main stream of Continental church life but it was to remain under the leadership of the king. English prelates were gradually replaced by Normans.

The Conquest brought to an end not only the line of English bishops but the whole Anglo-Saxon culture. The English language went underground for three centuries. Norman French being spoken during this period. English art and architecture were replaced by continental styles and no Englishman had the slightest hope of promotion for many years to come. The effect of this on the Church was quickly seen in the new styles of architecture. The Normans were enthusiastic builders and lost no time in pulling down many of the Saxon churches and replacing them with new buildings of their own design.

The wave of buildings following the Conquest, was mostly directed to the erection of castles, abbeys and cathedrals which enabled the art of masoncraft to expand itself enormously so that by the end of the building boom about the middle of the twelfth century, the Anglo-Saxons were able to turn to the task or rebuilding their wooden churches in a fine masonry style and to a scale commensurate with the population they served.

Generally we find the building work of the Normans, after 1075, which survives today, is very massive which is why it has survived. Youlgreave church in Derbyshire is a good example. Enormous mass was employed with great effect, the church tower having the look of a castle keep. The exteriors of Norman churches have the look of solemnity and the interior a sense of grandeur although the whole structure may be on a small scale.

Before a building is begun it is necessary to work out the weight of the roof and whether the walls will be strong enough to support it. This, however, was extremely difficult in the Middle Ages when our modern Arabic numerals were unknown. It was extremely difficult to do sums in writing. When you know how, it is simple to multiply 625 by 48 and get it right, but if you want to multiply DCXXV by XLVIII you must do it all in your head! Because they got their sums wrong the Normans often built too lightly and when the building fell down they built it again with stronger piers and thicker walls. This frequently happened with their central towers.

When commencing a building, the foundation lines have to be set out from the plan, pegs and string being used at all dates. The early buildings were inclined to be roughly set out without true right-angles, (Chichester Cathedral has no two walls at right-angles), but from the early twelfth century geometrical accuracy became the rule. It is probable that this was due indirectly to the re-discovery of Euclidian geometry about 1120 but also because of the knowledge gained by masons who had served as military engineers with the Crusades. The method used for obtaining a ninety degree angle was by erecting a triangle having sides in the proportion of 3, 4 and 5 on the base line using pegs and string. This method would have been passed on from generation to generation.

William the Conqueror reigned as king of England for twenty-one years and during that time he and his followers made England a force in continental affairs and established a system of government that in the next century made her the greatest empire in the then known western world. England had been given a national identity and endowed with military strength, religious drive, art and architecture and a new level of learning which made the Norman achievement all the more remarkable. The creation of his new kingdom and the establishment of Norman rule made it possible for him to bring about the greatest administrative triumph of the Domesday Survey.

The Period of Transition

The latter half of the twelfth century was, in architectural development, the time of transition which witnessed the passage of the Romanesque into the pointed Gothic style.

The returning crusaders brought back with them a wider outlook and new ideas. The latter part of the twelfth century marked the change from the old order of feudalism and the beginnings of modern progress, the change from tyranny to the growth of liberalism, slow though those changes were. With these changes coincided a momentous change in architectural detail which was to have far reaching effects in the Christian architecture of the west; the introduction of the pointed arch in place of the round arch.

The introduction of the pointed arch brought in new elements that became dominant in the buildings of the following centuries. The change was, however, very gradual, for Gothic architecture was not a complete style which took the place of an earlier style. One new development led to another and the builders experimented and tried out new ideas. The pointed arch was the first important feature introduced and is to be found in churches which are otherwise Romanesque and contain no other Gothic feature as Malmesbury Abbey, Wiltshire.

All through the period of transition there was some overlapping of the two forms. How exactly the builders came to build the pointed arch is not certain but it is very likely that knowledge of the pointed arch was brought back by returning Crusaders who had studied the architecture of the Saracens. The appearance of the semicircular form was greatly improved by the Gothic pointed arch, a form of which had been in use since Anglo-Saxon days in timber buildings using pairs of braces and so English architecture was not averse to accepting the masonry style. Pointed arches were used in Armenia by the latter half of the seventh century and it is probable that the Armenian architects introduced this form of arch into Syria so reaching this country as a result of the Crusades. A good example may be seen at Furness Abbey, Lancashire (1127–1537).

Early English Period, circa 1200–1272

The Early English style was not a development of the Romanesque but a complete break-away brought about by the introduction of the pointed arch.

Whereas in the Saxon and Norman periods strength had been dependent upon the massiveness of the building as a whole, now the strength lay in the gathering together of weights which were partially carried to the ground by distribution through piers and buttresses. Thus, it was no longer necessary for walls to be of very great thickness, it was the buttresses which took the pressures of the structure through the arches down to the ground. The walls were thinner, the piers more slender, stones smaller and windows larger.

Decorative features played a large part and the masons handled their chisels with supreme skill in the deep and varied mouldings around archheads, the foliaged capitals and the shafting, often in Purbeck marble, grouped around piers.

From the barrel vault of the previous century groined vaulting now came into general use often with diagonal ribs and sometimes with longitudinal and transverse ribs.

The great bulk of parish church buildings during this period was in additions and alterations to existing fabrics, for example, the removal of the apse or east wall and the lengthening of the chancel. There was little new building partly due to England being placed under an Interdict by Pope Innocent III in 1208. This was caused by the monks of Canterbury electing their superior Reginald as Archbishop of Canterbury in place of Hubert Walter on his death in 1205.

King John was annoyed and he quickly nominated one of his friends John de Grey, Bishop of Norwich. Both sides appealed to Rome and Pope Innocent solved the problem by choosing Stephen Langton. King John was furious declaring that his rights had been ignored and refused to allow Langton to set foot in England. Langton, like Anselm and Becket, was obliged to live abroad for the next six years while the Church in England suffered from lack of any real leadership. What John failed to realise was that he was pitting his strength and wit against one of the most courageous and cautious Popes who had ever lived and Pope Innocent soon made it clear to John that he had no intention of allowing him any concessions and, as John continued to defy him, he used his most powerful weapon and on March 23rd 1208 England was placed under an Interdict and in 1209 John was excommunicated.

Immediately following the excommunication the churches were closed, Mass ceased to be said and congregations of the faithful were forbidden to gather together for worship. Only the barest essentials of infant baptism and confessions of the young were allowed to continue. Christian burial was suspended, bodies being disposed of in bogs, woods and ditches. Marriages and the churching of women took place in church porches.

In 1213 John accepted Langton's election to Canterbury and Langton absolved the King and re-admitted him to the Church.

The introduction of the pointed arch was to herald in a style of architecture known as 'gothic' which, in turn ushered in the splendid ecclesiastical buildings of the thirteenth and fourteenth centuries. England was becoming more settled, the distinction between Norman and Saxon was becoming less marked and the complete autocracy of the sovereign destroyed by the nobles who, by this time, must have begun to think of themselves as English. King John was an erratic and moody tyrant using the legal and administrative machinery inherited by him to subject the landowners to intolerable and arbitrary taxation. He exploited every means to extract greater revenues and trained the elaborate fiscal and legal system into a merciless machine for extortion. Despite growing opposition John persisted in his tyranny and alienated a large part of the baronage who went into rebellion. Finally, following John's renewal of his financial demands the extremists of the baronial party resorted to force. They mustered at Stamford and sent their formal defiance to the King and began operations against royal castles in the Midlands. John was ultimately brought with his opponents, by Langton to Runnymede in 1215 where the terms incorporated in Magna Carta were agreed.

The main part of Magna Carta comprised more than sixty articles commencing with John's Confirmation of the Liberties of the Church in England. Many of the articles met the particular grievances of the baronial class arising from John's exploitation of their feudal obligations.

Langton's wisdom failed to save England from the civil war he feared and the reconciliation effected at Runnymede was short lived. The barons were distrustful of John's intentions and John was obviously not prepared to accept Magna Carta as permanently binding. After John's death in 1216 further revisions were made by Henry IV in 1225 but in 1258 Henry rather unwittingly, assented and took an oath to observe the provisions for the future government of England made by the committee of twenty-four at the Oxford Parliament in June 1258. These provisions became known as the Provisions of Oxford.

Following Magna Carta and later the Provisions of Oxford, the barons had been increasingly critical of Henry III's policy from 1237 onwards. Magna Carta had only taken them part of the way, now their endeavour was to get Henry to rule responsibly and to appoint responsible men approved by the *Curia Regis*, the inner standing court of the Great Council and further, that he would swear to govern by the advice of the Privy Council and by no other.

In 1258 the Pope flung Henry to the mercy of his barons on a threat of excommunication. The barons realised that it was necessary to take the government out of his incapable hands and so under the guise of helping Henry to rule the Provisions of Oxford became the effective constitution of England for a time and gave England a written constitution in which the king reigned and the Council ruled.

The Crusades of the twelfth century had enabled the Normans to learn much of easter architecture in which the Saracens excelled. Communication with Europe was constant and new ideas emanating there were immediately adopted at home. It was during this period that the medieval Church became fully developed. The desire for salvation and fear of damnation gave rise to a pre-occupation with life after death that probably had not been equalled since the days of ancient Egypt.

Outside the body of the Church few could read or write so the medieval builders symbolised their religious beliefs in wood and stone making their churches dramatised representations of their ideals and incorporating in them such incidental and picturesque stories from the Bible as could be rendered in carving and stained glass.

Medieval society below the King was essentially considered to be divided into three distinct and separate classes; the men who prayed (those who had taken religious vows), the men who fought (the feudal nobility and knights), and the men who worked (the peasantry).

The organisation and administration of the Church in the thirteenth century was complex. Above the two Archbishops of Canterbury and York was the Pope and below the Archbishops there were bishops who were responsible for twenty-one dioceses, three in York and eighteen in Canterbury.

By the thirteenth century the smaller churches were really becoming what we understand by 'parish' churches. The limits of parishes were now not only defined but emphasised at regular intervals by the ceremony of 'beating the bounds', still performed in some parishes. Bishops who were responsible for the cure of souls in their dioceses were beginning to offer 'indulgences' to lay lords to persuade them to erect churches on their lands, or at least to contribute towards the cost of erection. The lords considered themselves the owners of the churches they had built near their halls in positions which suited their own convenience, a practice which for some country churches exists today being on the outskirts of the village or even a little distance away from it. It was not only a single landowner who erected and endowed a church on his land but sometimes a group of landowners or wealthy merchants collaborated in building and endowing a church. They sometimes even changed the site or gave the church to a monastic establishment together with the profits of the obligatory tithes and offerings to a monastic establishment without consulting the parishioners. An example of this attitude by some landowners took place in the thirteen century when the local landowners gave the profits of the church of Sutton-in-Holland, Lincolnshire to Castle Acre Priory and allowing the church to be demolished and a new one built on a different site provided by them.

When the village had grown up at the gates of a monastery and the monks were the overlords they would have been responsible for the provision of a place of worship for those people on the monastic lands. The monks, would, therefore, either allow the villagers to use the nave of the church, or part of it, an arrangement which often caused friction between the religious and the laity, or build a separate, independent church for them within the monastic precincts apart from the monastic church. This explains why we find a number of parish churches adjacent to abbeys e.g. St Margaret adjacent to Westminster Abbey and Tilty church adjacent to the ruins of Tilty Abbey, Essex.

The manor lord of the monastic chapter held the advowson of the church and would appoint a mass priest to serve the church. This priest would not be obedient to monastic rule and was known as the 'secular' priest. Thus the parish system grew out of village life and through the centuries it has worked satisfactorily.

A parish church in the thirteenth century was a busy place especially on special days, holidays, church ales, festivals and on market days when the nave was full of stalls and stall-holders. The church was a social centre and not just used on Sundays. There were, prior to the late fourteenth century, no benches or pews in the nave except, in some churches, stone benches which ran round the walls or some of the nave piers for the use of the old and infirm. The congregation walked about, talked, gossiped and sometimes even came to blows as well as coming and going all through the service.

When services were not being held the nave was used for singing and dancing, eating and drinking on feast days, as well as for business transactions and preparation of contracts. Later, business transactions were transferred to the porch and at Lechlade, Gloucestershire, there is a bargaining stone just outside the porch on which bargains were struck.

The use of the nave for these purposes was not approved by the ecclesiastical authorities and in 1285 the Statute of Westminster forbade the use of churchyards for fairs, dancing, markets and the grazing of cattle.

The peasant used his church for purposes other than devotional and his spiritual and secular lives were closely bound together, religion being an inseparable part of his everyday life. The church was to the peasant like a palace, with its colour, spaciousness and sweet smelling rushes on the floor, compared to his squalid hut which he shared with his pig, goat or cow and with a pile of dung, used for fuel, by the door. It is easy to see why he was only too pleased to get away from the squalor of his hut and enter the comparatively clean, sweet church.

During this century, the lengthening of the chancel or its re-building on a larger scale, as well as the addition of aisles and transeptal chapels, was usual. Old apses and short single-bay chancels were swept away and long graceful eastern arms, two or three bays in length, were erected in their stead, some were even vaulted.

The chancel extensions of the thirteenth century, however, had the result of removing the altar so far away from the congregation that they could not possibly see what was going on so openings were often made beside the chancel arch to assist them. These openings are called squints. They were also used to allow a priest celebrating at a minor altar to observe the High Altar in order that he did not begin his own celebration before the Elevation of the Host.

The wider chancel arches destroyed much of the effect of mystery so it became customary to place a Rood beam across from side to side and fill up the arch with a wooden partition serving as a background for the Rood mounted on the beam. From this developed the Rood-screen enclosing the chancel and having a Rood loft with its gallery passing before the Rood in order to enable the candles which lighted it to be lit and renewed as well as enabling the Rood to be cleaned. In order to reach the gallery, entrance was obtained by a small newel stair within the chancel wall. Sometimes a staircase may be found on both sides of the chancel arch. Although most of these features disappeared at the Reformation the newel stair remains in a large number of old parish churches.

The reign of Edward II (1307–1327) though one of great political upheaval culminating in the deposition and murder of the King, was also one of the most brilliantly inventive periods for English medieval architecture.

The style of architecture in use between the latter part of the twelfth century and the near middle of the sixteenth century was known as Gothic. This Gothic style has been said to be the true definition of pure architecture as it is the only architecture where ornament is structure and structure ornament. A Roman or Greek temple or a church of the sixteenth, seventeenth or eighteenth centuries stripped to its bare walls is still a building, but a Gothic church cannot be stripped. If any part of it is removed it is mutilated and loses part of its being. Architecture, other than Gothic, requires clothing in the form of ornamentation but Gothic does not require clothing. Every part has beauty in its form and this can only exist in an object which performs a particular function and is specially used in the performance of it. It is not possible to separate the construction and the enrichment of medieval buildings incorporating structural and aesthetic components serving as part of the whole. Once the mason or carpenter had cut mouldings or carved forms of decoration on structural features, for example, arches, capitals and corbels a beautiful feature had been deliberately introduced and later development of such details was an artistic progress which arose from individual creativity.

In the late fourteenth and fifteenth centuries when Gothic architecture had reached its apogee there was almost no wall, only numbers of buttresses and large traceried windows. Gothic is full of exuberance and lively fancy which gives so much individuality to the work which is shown in the nature of the carving.

The medieval carpenters have gone, taking with them their craftsmanship with successes as well as errors but they have left us the results of the craftsmanship carried out with adoration because they believed what everyone believed.

From ancient buildings we can gain insight into the lives and mode of thought of our ancestors. The building of Gothic churches was no mere decorative accessory or diversion but an essential part of the expression of worship which was held to be man's highest function. The churches of the Middle Ages were not a picturesque background in people's lives as were the later churches of the Renaissance period, but were the very centre of their lives.

Medieval architecture was democratic in its inner significance, its masterpieces were not the work of individual geniuses, many of the names of architects are unknown, they were the expression of the life and thought of the people. In a letter written by Harmon, Abbot of St Pierre-sur-Dives in the fourteenth century he describes the popular enthusiasm and co-operation in the building of churches as the outcome of a religious revival.

No effort was too great, no toil too difficult to accomplish if it was required to complete the structure that was to be the resplendent beauty of a city and a lasting monument of the piety of the community and its love for God.

The Decorated Period, circa 1273–1349

This period has been called the Golden Age of Architecture when the Christian development of architecture reached its peak. The religious structures of this period portray a time of spiritual freedom when there was devotion to what was beautiful and true and which arose out of a deep-rooted religious faith.

When the Early English style took the place of the Norman there was a great advance made in architecture, the introduction of the pointed arch. When the Decorated period followed the Early English no new advance was introduced; there was only a continuation and development of the impulse which had been given in the preceding period.

The builder and the sculptor had increased their skill and mastery over both building construction and materials; there is balance, proportion and dignity. There is much more space in the arches, the aisles are more lofty and the piers more slender and varied.

This was a period of parish church building mainly brought about by wealthy benefactors who, for various reasons, built with a faith which could only provide something which excelled and which in itself was the bringing to perfection of that faith. This was emphasised by the rise of the guilds which taught the ordinary man to sanctify work impressing upon him self-respect and the dignity of labour.

About the end of the Decorated period the splendid architectural development was brought to a halt by a devastating blow caused by the outbreak of a terrible pestilence which we know as the Black Death. The plague started in 1348 and quickly spread causing so much death that for many years activity was paralysed.

It is difficult, so long afterwards, to realise that appalling disaster which the Black Death proved to this country during the years 1348 and 1349. It is believed that about one third of the total population of some four millions died.

Manors were left ungoverned, monasteries were depopulated and merchants fled the country. Peasants died like flies so that labour was almost non-existent and the race of English craftsmen almost perished, as did the leaders, lay and ecclesiastical. The mortality rate was heaviest among the clergy both lay and monastic. The parish clergy were brought closely into contact with the dead and dying in the execution of their everyday duties. The friars lived in more populated districts of the towns where infection spread rapidly and the monks lived in close proximity and sometimes in unhealthy surroundings.

Inside the tower of Ashwell church, Hertfordshire is an inscription carved with deeply cut letters two or three inches in height. The words are in Latin and read:

> 1350. Wretched, wild and distracted. The dregs of the people survive as witnesses.

These words show us how the ordinary people were feeling following the death and destruction which had hit them. All believed it was the end of the world!

And so, in the space of a few months, leaders, wealth, labour and craftsmanship were also swept away and a cloud of anarchy, social and economic settled upon the stricken land. Peasants, their power enhanced through the labour shortage, revolted. The loss of leadership hastened the breakdown of the old feudal system which had been the backbone of medieval England.

No more great churches were built in the land. Those that needed rehabilitation performed this by carrying out repairs and not, as of old, by sweeping away and rebuilding. The new method was to encase an older structure within a new skin in an endeavour to make it look as if it had been rebuilt. The cathedrals of Gloucester, Winchester and Norwich are evidence of this.

It was the merchants who saved the country, aided by the now firmly established sheep-farming industry which had not been so badly hit as labour-employing agriculture.

Following the Black Death Parliament in 1351 passed the Statute of Labourers which prohibited wages being paid above the pre-plague rates. The policy was dictated by the new agricultural middle classes rather than by the old-fashioned feudal magnates though the great landlords supported the demands of their tenants because high wages were indirectly a danger to the payment of rents. Direct contention, however, grew between two classes of peasants, the small farmer and the landless labourer whom he hired and out of this general resentment built up over the next thirty years.

The parliamentary laws in restraint of wages began the gradual change from a society based on local custom of personal service to a money economy. Heavy taxes were levied to carry on the Hundred Year War with France and there was a rapid increase in population. As the families of the villeins multiplied the number of strips in the open fields allocated to a single farmer grew less. The peasantry became divided among themselves as employers and employees and so the battle of the landless labourers against the farmers, backed by Parliament, went on.

In 1380/1 the unpopular Poll Tax of a shilling per head was levied. It was a personal tax collected locally by special officers and created a worse burden for the poor who found themselves and their families counted and made to pay no less than the rich and was a major contributory cause of the astonishing Peasants Revolt in 1381. In this revolt, mainly by the men of Essex and Kent the King, Richard II, was almost overthrown and one of the most remarkable incidents of this country's long social history took place in the capture of London, even the impregnable royal fortress of the Tower was surrendered to the rebels and unpopular characters like Simon Sudbury, Archibishop of Canterbury and Chancellor of England, Sir John Cavendish, Chief Justice of England, Sir Robert Hales, Treasurer of the Kingdom, lawyers, sheriffs, foresters, tax-collectors, lords and others were murdered.

Following all this there was a great prosperity in the country brought about by the spoils of the Hundred Years War and the rapid expansion of the wool and cloth industries. Tenants or employees were substituted for serfs and wages rose to their economic level.

Towards the end of the period churches began to be rebuilt, the plan type normally being unaisled chancel, aisled nave and western tower. The only relic of the former church may be the dimensions of the nave, the old foundations being usually employed as a base for the new arcade.

In small churches the nave and chancel plan is often found with the chancel almost or quite as wide as the nave.

Aisle widening and lengthening was a feature of this period many narrow lean-to aisles of Norman and Early English date being swept away to give place to the new fashion of wide and lofty aisles.

Flat roofs began to be general over naves and aisles and these led to the use of parapets, previously almost unknown in parish churches. These parapets were used to hide lead box gutters provided to collect the rain-water from the now much flatter roofs.

Spires now began to be slanted from the inner instead of the outer face of the tower which was surrounded by a parapet. Before this the base of the spire was usually made to oversail the top of the tower.

Pinnacles were often built at the four angles of the tower their function being to load down and so render immobile masonry below. Previously they had been low and massive but now they had become tall and spiky and were used for decorative purposes producing a mass of ornament comprising pedimented or ogee niches and crockets terminating in a finial, both the crockets and the finial being carved with the fashionable foliage of the day.

From the time of the narrow lancets of the twelfth and thirteenth centuries there had been a constant demand for larger windows. By the introduction of the horizontal transom in the tracery of the window it was discovered that the area of glass would be enormously increased and the goal for which the designers had been striving for two hundred years or more had been reached.

Porches were now regarded as a necessity and medieval England was in full swing.

In this fashion England began, for the first time in her medieval history, to develop a social class of 'yeomen' who were midway between the lord and the poverty-stricken peasantry who had hitherto formed the bulk of the population. The improvement in the financial status of the middle-class villagers resulted in their giving financial aid to their parish place of worship and so we come to the fifteenth century the era of fine rural churches as well as the huge churches in the rich mercantile towns, built from the profits of wool, like Lavenham, Suffolk and Dedham, Essex.

Before we turn to the fifteenth century perhaps we should have a brief look at the work of the parish priest and conditions in the parish during the fourteenth century.

The parish priest had a certain amount of administration. A rector had to see to the collection of all the tithes, a vicar had the right to the lesser tithes excluding the 'great tithe' of corn. The medieval church was not run on a system of voluntary finance, the parish priest could excommunicate for non-payment of tithe and the secular courts would enforce the obligation. The parish priest also tilled or let out the glebe land of his church. He was bound to keep the chancel of his church in repair and to see that the churchwardens repaired the nave. He was also bound to see that no fairs or morris dancing were held in the churchyard and that it was not otherwise profaned.

It was his duty to relieve the poor and strangers as far as he could himself, though his stipend was usually too small to permit of much almsgiving. As there was no state system of poor relief it was the priest's especial duty to exhort his parishioners to care for the poor and induce the dying to leave alms for this purpose. He would also help with the miracle and mystery plays which were held fairly frequently and were indeed the only drama in fourteenth century England. The priest would be required to bless the sick children, animals or horses for which divine protection was desired and would exorcise evil spirits and ghosts and it was his duty to warn his people not to use spells and incantations or gather herbs by moonlight.

The spiritual work of the parish priest consisted of the instruction of his people and the administration of the Sacraments. He was supposed to preach on the Sunday Gospel at the parish Mass or to instruct his people in the Creed, Commandments, Sacraments, Works of Mercy, Seven Virtues and Seven

Deadly sins. The education of the parish clergy had not been sufficient to allow the preaching of sermons but by the end of the fourteenth century clerical education was better and Sunday sermons were becoming common in parish churches.

Some peasants had become wealthy and had accumulated land. This was usually accomplished by conspiring against their neighbours, especially the poor and causing them to be disinherited in the courts of their lords. These peasants often deceitfully accused their neighbours to their lords of fictitious crimes and so lost their goods.

The lord could be much worse exacting and extorting both from villeins and free tenants many goods beyond what the tenants ought to pay. Often this was done with violence the tenants being reduced to poverty and scarcely able to provide enough food for themselves and their families.

The priest had his part to play in all this and the role of the Church as mediator had much to commend it. Even at the priest's level it could correct and chastise the oppressor. This could never have been allowed to happen had the parish churches remained as they were before the twelfth century when they were the private property of the local landowner. Neither could it have happened if the bishops had not been successful in their efforts to improve the learning, income and social status of their clergy.

The parish priest was a busy person, the church was a busy place used, and known intimately, by every villager.

Perhaps the most distinctive development in parochial life of the fourteenth and fifteen centuries was the growth of chantries, the saying of the daily requiem. Before this, those who wished for the prayers of the Church after their death normally obtained them by endowing or giving money to a monastery or other religious foundation. In exchange for such gifts the monks inscribed the names of the benefactors in their 'book of life' and saw that they were remembered in their prayers. As man's confidence in the monastic orders began to wane their benefactions were transferred to the foundation of chantries or endowment of priests to say daily Masses for the souls of the benefactors and their families. By the fifteenth century all the larger churches contained a number of chantry chapels often signified by a separate altar or chapel and there were probably few parish churches in England without some such foundation.

Fixed seats or simple benches came into use during this century. Prior to this seating was not considered necessary although some churches had stone benches at the base of the walls or piers for those unable to stand during the lengthy services.

The fourteenth century was a period which suffered many perils and adversities, plague, war, taxes, brigandage, bad government, insurrection and by division and disagreement in the Church. It was a violent, tormented, bewildered, suffering and disintegrating age, a time, as many thought, of Satan triumphant.

Perhaps we can see something similar today with our economic chaos, high prices, profiteering, depraved morals, lack of production, industrial indolence, wild expenditure, luxury, social hysteria, greed, maladministration, and decay of manners. Voltaire said that 'History never repeats itself. Man always does.'

Near the end of the fourteenth century the Reformers were gathering strength. They deplored the conditions of the time with people failing to keep the Church feast days and the falling-off of religious observance. 'Churches were empty and mass meagrely attended'. So said Clamanges in his great tract *'The Ruin and Reform of the Church'*.

The young, according to Nicholas de Clamanges (d. 1437), rarely went to church except on feast days and then only to see the painted faces and immodest gowns of the ladies with their headdresses like immense towers with horns hung with pearls. People kept vigils in church not with prayer but with lascivious songs and dances while the priest played dice as they watched.

Jean Gerson (d. 1429), another Reformer, deployed the same laxity. 'Men left church in the midst of the services to have a drink and when they hear the bell announcing the consecration they rush back into the church like bulls. Card playing, swearing and blasphemy,' he wrote, 'occurred during the most sacred festivals and obscene pictures were hawked in church, corrupting the young. Pilgrimages were the occasion for debauchery, adultery and profane pleasures,' 'Men slept in indifference and closed their eyes to the scandal,' mourned the Monk of St Denis, 'It was a waste of time to talk of ways to reform the Church.'

The Church during the last half of the century was suffering schism by reason that there were two Popes, Urban VI followed by Bonniface IX in Rome and Clement VI in France and this grave disagreement made itself felt throughout the whole church.

Indifference is not, however, a national condition of human affairs and new devotional movements were afoot and change was taking place to culminate in the Reformation some one hundred years later.

Perpendicular Period, circa 1350–1539

The final development of medieval gothic architecture in this country known as Perpendicular arose out of the Abbey church of Gloucester. King Edward II who was murdered at Berkeley Castle in 1327 was buried in the Abbey church and his tomb became a shrine for pilgrims whose offerings greatly enriched the Abbey enabling the reconstruction of the choir of the church to be planned.

As the old Norman piers were sound the Gloucester workmen did not demolish them but transformed them by covering over the great round arches and massive piers with stone screen-work of open tracery with mullions running up from the floor to the vault and immediately there had come into being a new style. This style was suitable for doorways, windows, buttresses and towers. All that was necessary was to rule the space into parallelograms by vertical and horizonal lines and add cusped arches to the heads. The Decorated style had passed to the Perpendicular. The work at Gloucester was finished by 1350 but the Black Death was at its height and due to the scarcity of workmen masons were sent out from centres like Gloucester and so the new style was carried throughout the kingdom and for this reason did much to account for the uniformity in building detail to be found in our parish churches from about 1380 onwards. Gloucester Cathedral may, therefore be regarded as the cradle of the Perpendicular style of architecture.

As the Decorated period is known as the Golden Age of architecture the Perpendicular period is the Golden Age of Church Furniture and Fittings. Specialised craftsmanship greatly increased. The sculptor became distinct from the mason, the art of stained glass was in the hands of specialised workers and so the church of this period tended to become a setting for the craftsmen's work in glass, sculpture and wood-carving. We see their results in the beautiful stained glass windows, wonderfully carved rood-screens, stalls, bench-ends, pulpits, font covers and sepulchral monuments.

We can sense, however, that the compelling force of their faith, which had previously inspired the work of craftsmen, had now gone, the work is much more detailed and fitting for the worship of the people but the feeling of being lifted up by the faith which had inspired the work of the craftsmen of previous centuries has been lost as the builders had become mathematicians trying to make everything perfect down to minor constructive features and ornaments.

The planning necessities for the period were primarily a large nave, wide aisles for processions and a multitude of chapels for the altars of guilds or chantries. The chancels seemed, as a rule, to matter little and were often poor compared with the rest of the fabric but this was not surprising as the repair of the nave was the responsibility of the people whereas the chancel was the responsibility of the priest who usually had little money to spare for repairs or rebuilding. The guilds were wealthy and were able to provide additional altars and in many cases to build chapels on to the existing fabric.

Money being plentiful in this period the builders were often able to sweep away an earlier building or at least everything west of the chancel arch and rebuild on a new plan thus satisfying the conflicting demands for a large nave and many chapels which could be provided, not as separate buildings, but by screening off bays of the wide aisles.

Innumerable towers, spires and porches were also a feature of this period.

Much of the oak forests had been wastefully used up in early medieval days but now East Anglia was becoming the richest part of England by pouring wool into Flanders. The ships came back in ballast which was Flemish brick and so brick came into general use and we can see the result in the beautiful red Tudor brick buildings which we have throughout the countryside. Chignal Smealey church in Essex is a good example.

More and more light was being demanded by the clergy. The architecture of the church, the piers, the enlarged windows and towers appear to reach up to heaven, the lines of the composition carrying the eye upwards from floor to roof. The vast windows with their rectangular divisions and straighter lines of tracery greatly encouraged the art of the glazier, the windows lending themselves either to large pictures occupying the whole window or to a series of scenes from the Bible or from the lives of the Saints.

In all parts of the church the tendency was ever more and more towards greater richness and elaboration. Stone and wooden screens with rich carving or paintings, effigies in wood or stone or bronze canopied tombs, heavily carved sedilia niches, stalls and bosses, all worked out in the most intricate and elaborate designs, contributed to a splendour of decoration far surpassing anything which the country had so far seen.

Let us picture what the church would have looked like in this period.

The church is by far the most prominent building, with perhaps the exception of the manor house, because the equivalent of cottages in the villages, were mostly 'cruck houses', that is tent-like buildings with roofs coming down almost to the ground, most of them being mere hovels.

The approaches to the village were by way of grassy tracks which were extremely muddy in winter with great water-filled ruts.

Near to the entrance to the churchyard would be the church house where the churchwardens stored beer ready for the 'church ale', the feast which was held on the anniversary of the consecration of the church. This feast was used to raise money for repairs to the church. The church house is the origin of so many old inns in England beside the churchyard some of which still exist on a six-day licence like the one attached to Hackington church just outside Canterbury.

The graveyard had no tombstones. The dead were buried there and were remembered, not in stone but in the prayers of the priest at the altar at Mass. Everyone went to church travelling in from outlying farms and villages and stabling their horses outside the churchyard. Not only did everyone go to church on Sunday but also on weekdays too, for it was impossible to say daily prayers in the little hovels in which most of the villagers lived. School was taught in the porch and business was carried out by the cross in the market square where the stalls were, there being no shops.

In the nave of the church on a weekday there would probably be some people standing about gossiping while other people were praying. There was no privacy in the medieval period. The nave belonged to the people and they used it as today we use a village hall or social club. No one thought of not going to church: they believed that men had souls and that their souls must be exercised in worship and the Sacraments used regularly.

The builders were chiefly concerned with making the interior of the church as rich and splendid as possible, something which would bring the people to their knees.

Most parish churches, even the smallest, had three altars, one in the chancel and one on either side of the chancel arch.

On entering we would find at the door a stoup made of stone containing holy water and somewhere near, in a prominent position, would be the font. Over it there would be a painted wooden cover rising like a church steeple and securely clasped down to the basin and locked. The font was kept locked because it contained baptismal water which had been solemnly blessed and which was retained in the font and not thrown away as it is today. Up to the Reformation this water was valued for its intrinsic virtue and the fonts were lidded and locked to prevent the water being taken for making up into prescriptions in sorcery, witchcraft and charm medicine. After the Reformation, when the virtues of christening water had been exploded, font covers were prised away by the new Evangelists and hasps and hinges broken off. The scars caused by the wrenching away of the hasps and hinges from the font rims may still be seen on nearly all medieval fonts.

The plastered walls were covered with paintings, mostly of a dull brick-red with occasional blues, greens and blacks. Chiefly the paintings were pictures of the life of the Virgin Mary, scenes from the Bible stories as well as a large painting of St Christopher, the travellers' saint. Medieval art was used by the Church to stress moral contrast, good and evil, doom and redemption were portrayed in dramatic opposition and the contrast between those safe within Holy Church and the awful fate awaiting all others met those entering through the doors of the early churches. The pictures on the church walls reminded people of how to live while on earth if they wished to avoid Hell when they died.

The wooden chancel roofs had their beams painted red, green, white, gold and blue. The nave roof may not be painted but over the rood-beam, just above the chancel arch, it was probably more richly carved and painted than elsewhere. This part of the roof is called a celure.

It was over the rood-beam, painted on a wooden panel over the chancel arch, that the Doom picture was seen, the Last Judgement which should decide whether the soul might pass into eternal life. Most of these painted Dooms are now half obliterated but even if we can see little more than the horns and tail of a dragon; or the vast jaws and teeth in the bottom right hand corner of the mouth of Hell, we should remember that once the whole picture presented to the fearful congregation a terrifying forecast of a sinner's fate. Above the screen, however, would be their hope, the great Crucifix as the symbol of salvation.

The floor of the church was frequently of beaten earth often covered with yew boughs or sweet smelling herbs whose aroma was stronger when crushed underfoot. People did not wash much or change their clothes very often and the stink of piles of refuse must have made villages unpleasant places in hot weather. The crushed yew and rosemary must have been a welcome contrast in the cool brightness of the church.

By the end of the century fixed seats became general and they were often richly decorated with carving on the ends and in Norfolk many of the backs were beautifully traceried.

In this period the building of a clerestory stage over the aisle arcades took place and which would be lit with windows thus providing more light to the interior of the church.

3

The Dissolution of the Monasteries

Monasticism in England came to a sudden halt. This was brought about by King Henry VIII in the Dissolution of the Monasteries by a process which was spread over some four years and which was completed in 1540. Henry was a powerful king and was ably served by such men as Thomas Cromwell, the Kings's Secretary, Thomas Howard, Duke of Norfolk and Sir Thomas Audley, but they would have been unable to push the dissolution through if there had been determined national opposition rooted in loyalty and devotion to the religious orders. It would appear that lay society, in the main, accepted the dissolution, more being in favour than against.

In 1536 there were, in England and Wales, some eight hundred or more religious houses, monasteries, nunneries and friaries with something like 10,000 monks, nuns, cannons and friars. By 1540 there was none. Buildings, land, plate, stock, property and anything of value was seized by the crown and sold or leased to new lay occupiers. There were many different orders of monks and nuns, for example, Carthusians, Augustinians, and Cistercians and they all, in theory, lived in apostolic poverty though in practice this meant that no individual had any personal property but many of the communities were very wealthy. Although there is some difference of opinion it is thought that they possessed between one-third and one-quarter of all the land in England. The prime function of the religious was to ensure the daily round of prayer throughout the day with its daily offices and mass.

During the two centuries before the dissolution there was a steady decline in the number of the religious and many of its great houses were half empty. The enthusiasm of the twelfth and thirteenth centuries had wained and this was not helped by the ravages of the Black Death in the fourteenth century. The monastic ideal had lost much of its appeal, only eight new houses having been founded since 1400.

From the reports of visitations which survive it would seem that there were grave financial irregularities, indiscipline and immorality and that standards were low. The inhabitants of the larger religious houses were inevitably deeply involved in the problems of management and administration which necessitated the supervision of the affairs of tenants and engaging in litigation in defence of rights and privileges. So for a variety of reasons the abbots of the more important houses found themselves involved with the gentry and the Crown which they served in a number of ways. All this caused them to adopt a life-style similar to the gentry.

Lay people were employed as servants and retainers as well as performing work on the land and gardens formerly carried out by the religious. The smaller houses were not so fortunate, the routine housekeeping and farming having to be carried out by the religious themselves.

All was not well with English monasticism in the early years of Henry VIII and it was recognised that it needed some pruning. Various bishops from time to time secured papal permission to close down certain houses, for example, St Radegund's nunnery in Cambridge. Selborne Priory, Hampshire and Bromhall (Broomhall) nunnery, Berkshire. Although this was not an attack on monasticism it was not many years afterward that the dissolution began in 1536 with the Act of Suppression of the Lesser Monasteries which was presented as a measure of reform rather than confiscation.

This act was, however, an act of expropriation despite its disguise as an act of reform and soon the government agents were visiting the larger houses conducting negotiations for their surrender. In 1536 there was a rebellion in the northern shires known as the Pilgrimage of Grace. The northern rebels were not solely concerned with the Dissolution of the Monasteries but with many other grievances, economic, social and political as well as religious. The permanent restoration of the suppressed religious houses was high on the rebels' list of demands. Although the rebellion created a threatening situation for some moths it was, in the end, a total failure.

In the last eighteen months of the dissolution Cromwell sent his commissioners across England to procure the surrender of all surviving houses. A new Act of Parliament in 1539 vested in the Crown all the properties of monasteries which had been surrendered and all those which might be surrendered. The Act did not compel or authorise the final dissolution but gave royal title to all the spoils. One by one the great abbeys surrendered and early in 1540 the last, the Augustinian Abbey of Waltham, Essex, went down.

Following the dissolution of most of the houses the monks and nuns were granted subsistence pensions which declined in real value as inflation increased. Many of them turned to secular occupations and some died in poverty.

As soon as a monastery had surrendered it was ransacked and reduced to ruins by the royal agents who showed no sensitivity to the sacred and beautiful furnishings and objects, but only vandalism and greed with the purpose that the monastery should not be re-occupied by monks or nuns to revive its religious life.

In a short time the finest creations of medieval designers and craftsmen disappeared. The valuable lead was stripped from the roofs and gutters and melted into pigs over fires built in the monastic chancels from the stalls which had so recently dignified those structures. Soaring towers which had been the glory of the English countryside for centuries were destroyed by mines used to blow up the walls as though they were enemy fortifications. Stained glass windows, statues, the Great Rood, altar pieces, paintings, vestments and many other items were destroyed or sold. The gold and silver plate was sent to London to be turned into bullion for the King. The stripping of the lead from the roofs deprived the buildings of their protection from the weather and so the great churches soon suffered from neglect and quickly fell into decay. They were a good source of building stone and soon plundered by the local people to build dwellings. Much of the monastic land was sold and the purchaser would build himself a magnificent mansion using the ruined monastery as a quarry. An example of this is Fountains Hall, Yorkshire, which is built of Fountains Abbey stone. Richard Rich, Chancellor of the Court of Augmentations bought Leighs Priory, Essex, as a residence.

There is no doubt that the long-term consequences, religious and social, of such a wholesale extraction of a way of life as well as such a vast transference of property must have, indeed, been great.

On the spiritual level the ending of the monasteries was not of itself a catastrophe but their disappearance had considerable consequences. The suppression of the Carthusians, the Bridgettines and the best of the nunneries removed a way and practice of life which had always attracted some of the best people who had a value which, however many of the inferior there might be, could not compare. Even a reasonably observant religious house could have had a great influence for good upon people of the neighbourhood as well as having practical uses as a school, almshouse, inn and employer of labour.

Following the destruction of the monasteries and colleges there disappeared from the country that rich ritualistic life of chant and ceremony which formed a large part of medieval religious life. There remained only the parish church and the cathedral, reduced in position, and there was nothing left to take the impact of the reforming iconoclastic zeal which followed.

Perhaps the most important result was that, good or bad, the monasteries were an important and integral part of the traditional church life of the medieval ages and their disappearance, especially when their lands and wealth were held by a great number of the upper classes, rendered any complete revival of the old ways extremely difficult. Without their support, Mary, had she lived to an old age, would have had an extremely difficult time to re-establish Catholicism and any vast restitution would have met with great hostility on the part of the country's landowners. Probably neither Henry VIII nor Cromwell fully realised what they were doing in this respect; they thought of the religious orders as a source of wealth.

The social changes are more difficult to assess. A few great families with their new found wealth emerged, but those who really gained from the change were the large numbers of men of small or moderate wealth who bought themselves a small estate or added to an existing one. Everywhere it was the laymen who were in possession having taken the place of the religious. Now there are only the ruined houses scattered throughout the countryside like ghosts of the medieval monastic past and leaving, between then and now, a depth of mystery which will never be fully understood.

The brightness of a Gothic cathedral with its painted walls and jewelled shrines is hard to visualise from the bare grey stone interiors of today. The noble skeleton is seen, but not the flesh and blood with which our forefathers clothed it.

4

The Reformation

It would take too much space to go into understanding how the English Reformation came about but it is generally recognised that the dissolution of the monasteries was the principal event. Henry VIII became persuaded that his marriage to Catherine of Aragon, widow of his brother, Prince Arthur, was met with divine disapproval in its failure to provide a satisfactory heir and so he found a biblical text in Leviticus 20 & 21, 'If a man shall take his brother's wife, it is an unclean thing . . . they shall be childless' Although Henry's stubborn fight with Rome to secure an annulment was a wonderful opportunity for the theologians and lawyers to assert themselves, particularly under Wolsey's direction, compliance with Rome could not be secured. After much discussion and audiences with Pope Clement, Henry's 'great matter', as it was known, came to a head in 1527.

Henry had, by this time, fallen in love with Anne Boleyn whom he married in 1533. In 1534 Parliament, in the Act of Supremacy, declared him to be Head of the English Church.

No doctrinal or ecclesiastical dispute set off the Reformation in England, but a national and constitutional revolution paved the way for the Puritan reformation in the next century, but now the new Church of England had been brought into being by Parliament.

Following the Dissolution of the Monasteries there was a rising in 1536 of the Roman Catholics in the northern counties against dissolution. This was the Pilgrimage of Grace and the Catholics demanded the removal of Thomas Cromell, Henry's chief minister, an end to the dissolution and restoration of papal authority. A further rising took place in 1537 when many of the leaders were executed. The resings were, however, of no avail and the Dissolution of the Monasteries was completed by 1540.

Henry VIII died in 1547 and was succeeded by his son Edward VI. The political reformation of Henry was succeeded by a doctrinal reformation by Edward and England turned from Roman Catholic religion to complete Protestantism and a Church with a congregation of participants rather than spectators and with services and ceremonies in English rather than Latin. Many changes were made,the new liturgy of the church tending to ignore the chancel using the nave only with the altar being replaced by a communion table.

Orders in Council appeared in 1547 whereby all images remaining in any church or chapel were condemned to be removed and utterly 'extincted and destroyed'. Holy water, confessions, candles and incense were declared illegal. Roods were torn down and replaced by royal coats of arms, the rood-screens and lofts suffering in consequence. Wall paintings were whitewashed over, statues of saints were defaced and stained glass windows smashed. Chantry chapels were wrecked because they represented the Catholic belief in purgatory and their endowments were seized.

Edward died in 1553 being succeeded by his half-sister Mary Tudor, an ardent Catholic, who reversed the Protestant reforms, brought back Catholic bishops, restored the laws against heresy, including the professing of Protestantism, and burned hundreds at the stake. The result of all this was that many more people became Protestant.

Elizabeth I succeeded Mary in 1558 and took a middle course in an endeavour to resolve the misery of rebellion, sedition and division which was affecting the whole country. Not only Catholics had to be curbed but so did the growing number of Puritans; England was sufficiently Protestant in 1559 to produce a Parliament which passed two Acts of Supremacy and Uniformity in England and severed England from Rome. The new creed was one of liberation from the tyranny of popish 'works' such as the many Saints' days, votive masses, purgatory, pardons and indulgences, pilgrimages, monks and friars, holy water, oils and wells, scapulars and tonsures, incense and ashes, trentals and relics. All this was condemned by Protestantism as idolatry, magic, irrelevance and pagan or semi-pagan practice which did not allow men and women to progress spiritually but even to become subverted.

Under the Elizabethan settlement preachers were only allowed to preach four sermons a year unless a licence for more was obtained. The reason for this was to counter the danger of dissenting propaganda and Elizabeth went further by insisting on an oath of allegiance from the Church. Elizabeth, like her father, was excommunicated by Rome.

The Book of Common Prayer, which had first been issued by Thomas Cranmer, Archbishop of Canterbury, in 1549 and modified in 1552, was authorised once again in Elizabeth's reign joining the English Bible to form the foundation for the development of the Anglican Church. The reign of James I saw two strands of religion, Puritanism which was a verbal rather than a visual religion and was not interested in the building or repair of churches and so few were built between the Reformation and the Civil Wars 1640–1649. During the latter half of the sixteenth century the Church of England had grown and become more confident but a middle way had to be found between Puritanism whose devotees practised a sense of godliness which with their plain churches, long sermons and objections to the Book of Common Prayer, abolition of the sign of the cross in Baptism, the wearing of the surplice and bowing at the name of Jesus, set them apart from the Anglicans who wished to restore beauty to churches and the services, as well as emphasising the Sacraments, rather than preaching long sermons. Under James I these two religious schools of thought co-existed but the Puritans had hoped for great things from James who had come from a Presbyterian country. Their demands were placed before the King, who listened, but referred them to a conference at Hampton Court in 1604. This conference was a great disappointment to the Puritans and led to many of their number emigrating to the New World.

During the reign of Charles I and his Archbishop of Canterbury, William Laud, the co-existence which had existed under James, turned to conflict and rivalry. Charles dissolved Parliament in 1629 and ruled personally by Royal Prerogative for the next eleven years. Secular affairs were administered by the Earl of Strafford and ecclesiastical matters were entrusted to William Laud, Bishop of London, who in 1633 became Archbishop of Canterbury. Criticism or opposition was not allowed and Charles's judges dealt heavily with any who did not comply. Puritans who opposed the High Church rulings of Laud were pilloried by order of the Court of High Commission or had their ears cut off. Charles was forced to summon Parliament in 1640 because of his need for revenue from taxes to put down a Scottish rebellion against Anglican episcopacy. This Parliament, the 'Short Parliament', only lasted three months and was dissolved by Charles because it refused to grant funds until certain grievances were redressed.

Months later Charles had to summon a new parliament which became known as the 'Long Parliament' because it lasted until 1660. Those in opposition to the King quickily rose to power and in 1641 effected a constitutional revolution. It was deemed unlawful for more than three years to elapse without calling Parliament and for Parliament to be dissolved without its own consent.

The Star Chamber and High Commission were abolished and the King's two chief ministers, Earl Strafford and Archbishop Laud were impeached and imprisoned, later to be executed in 1641 and 1645 respectively.

The 'Long Parliament' deprived the Crown of all the prerogative powers enjoyed by Tudor monarchs although it professed to be simply restoring ancient liberties. But affairs between King and Parliament reached their lowest point when it tried to take command of the army from Charles who countered by demanding the arrest of five of its members. The issues of the control of the army and the Church divided the King and Parliament into 'root-and-branch' reformers, the parliamentarians and the moderates, the royalists. By 1642 the King and his opponents were so divided that the issue could only be decided by war; the King and the Church, who could count on the rural regions and market towns furthest from the capital and Parliament and the Puritans gaining sympathy where recent economic change had been strongest, as in London under the influence of the great trading companies, seaports and manufacturing towns. After much skirmishing and with 'up and downs' on both sides Charles was captured in 1647 and in the following year a decision was made to try him before a special High Court of Justice. In 1649 Charles was tried and executed, the Monarchy and Lords being abolished and England proclaimed as Commonwealth.

On the death of Oliver Cromwell in 1658 his son Richard became Lord Protector of England but he proved to be a weak ruler and the country was in danger of sinking into anarchy. In order to prevent this happening General George Monck used the army to force the Long Parliament to dissolve itself in 1660 and a new elected parliament invited the exiled Charles II to return as King in return for promises which included full liberty of religious conscience. The Stuart line was thus restored and the brief spell of republicanism came to an end.

Despite all the despoliation which had taken place during the dissolution of the Monasteries, the Puritan period in Elizabeth's reign, and the Reformation, the Civil War and Commonwealth saw the destruction of any remaining 'superstitious images and inscriptions' in churches. A parliamentary decree of 1540 ordered the destruction of all stained-glass windows as many still depicted saints and the Holy Family and were regarded by the Puritans as the work of the Devil.

In Herbert Read's book, *English Stained Glass*, he quotes that the women of Middlesex in 1642 declared, 'We desire that profane glass windows whose superstitious paint make many idolaters, may be humbled and dashed in pieces against the ground, For our conscience tells us that they are diabolical and the father of Darkness was the inventor of them, being the chief patron of damnable pride!'

In addition, the appalling damage included defaced figures of angels, evangelists, saints and other works, timber stalls burnt, plate melted down, pictures and crosses, sculpture, monuments and brasses defaced, vestments and organs destroyed and shooting both at the church and the carved angels in the roof. In Mildenhall, Suffolk earlier this century, the angels in the roof were found peppered with buck shot as well as two iron arrow heads. (Blythburgh, Suffolk, also has angels which have been shot at with buck shot).

In Suffolk and Cambridgeshire, William Dowsing, a Parliamentary Visitor, was a particularly nasty type who had a very bad record of his destructive work which began in 1643. On Innocents' Day 1643 Dowsing's records for King's College, Cambridge, show that, 'Steps to be taken and 1000 superstitious pictures, the ladder of Christ and thieves to go, many crosses, Jesus writ on them.' At Haverhill in Suffolk Dowsing recorded, 'At Haverhill we tooke down about an hundred supersititious pictures, and seven Friars hugging a Nun; and the picture of God and Christ, and divers others very superstitious. And 200 had been broken down before I came. And we beat down a great stoning cross on top of the church.'

This devastation went on throughout the whole land, from Yorkshire to Cornwall, with many Visitors giving orders to others to carry out these works of destruction creating a loss which it will never be possible to measure. Few parish churches escaped and consequently little in the way of additions either to furnishings or buildings were made.

With the Restoration of the Monarchy in 1660 the Puritans lost their grip on the national Church and the Anglican spirit was restored. The altar, which had been set in the middle of the chancel, was now returned to the east end but the pulpit remained in a prominent position in the nave.

Renaissance Period, circa 1547–1688

This period introduced churches which were in imitation of the style of buildings practised in Italy and western Europe.

The style applies sometimes to the earliest works only and sometimes to the more later ones. The phases are distinguished also by separate names such as 'Elizabethan' and 'Jacobean'. The word 'renaisance' comes from the French 're' – again and *'naissance'* – birth. It was by no means a re-birth of the old and true craft spirit but merely a widening of knowledge in which the art was degraded into a mere supply of style as demanded by the whim of fancy and patronage. Intuition was pushed out by intellect and intuition has not returned.

In the reign of James I (1603–1625) the professional architect arose with Inigo Jones who made a clean sweep of the old Gothic forms and designed every part of his building in the Renaissance style which soon carried everything before it.

In the fourteenth century this country, as well as much of the then known world, suffered from plague. Once again, in 1665, some three hundred years later, the country suffered another major epidemic. London was particularly affected as evidenced by a correspondent who wrote,

'If you be taken away by this dreadful pestilence you have had a fair warning and a very long time to prepare yourself for Heaven. It seems that every day at London is now a day of judgement and that all our thoughts are placed on death, on Hell, on Heaven and upon eternity. Thy will be done on earth as it is in Heaven is the balsam that cureth all.'

Sir Thomas Browne, a Norwich physician, wrote in 1665, 'For the world I count it not an inn but a hospital, not a place to live but to die in.' Death still seemed to be the climax of man's existence, the time when he reaped what he had sown. The total deaths in London are estimated at 100,000.

In 1666 fire broke out in Pudding Lane and fanned by high winds quickly spread among the timber buildings in the narrow streets of London. All the City from the Tower of London to the Temple and from the Thames to Smithfield was destroyed including eighty-nine churches and St Paul's Cathedral as well as many public buildings. Some 436 acres were devastated and yet it did little to bring the plague to an end as most of the slum districts survived.

Out of all the devastation caused by the plague and fire another architect came to the fore, Sir Christopher Wren who followed Inigo Jones and who took full advantage of the unique opportunity which fell to him after the Great Fire.

The great difference between the Gothic churches, pre-Reformation and those of Sir Christopher Wren and his successors is the difference between the romanticism of medieval faith and the austere Puritanism of the seventeenth century.

The first post-Reformation churches differed little in plan from those of medieval times. Wren in some of his churches in the City of London seems to have tried to build uncompartmented churches where Baptism, Morning and Evening Prayer and Holy Communion could all be conducted in an undivided space without the priest and his assistants moving out of sight or earshot. Usually the plan was of nave with a three-decker pulpit dominating Mattins, Litany and Evensong and a screen through which the congregation passed for Communion and a Baptistry at the west end. The earliest post-Reformation churches usually had west galleries for organ and choir as well as side galleries.

The style of tracery, decoration and wood carving changed, windows were square-headed in the sixteenth century later becoming round-headed. Grapes, cherubs and a cornucopia of fruit cascaded down the sides of the altar-pieces, wreathed round the panelling of pulpits and flattened themselves into patterns on the ceiling.

Before leaving the sixteenth and seventeenth centuries perhaps the most striking of all the differences between the life and activity which centred around the pre-Reformation parish churches and their role in community life, after the Elizabethan Settlement, whereby the Marian exiles returned and the Puritans in Parliament pressed for a Protestant religious settlement and Elizabeth assented to the Act of Supremacy in 1559 thus renewing the breach with Rome, is the changed attitude of the parishioners towards the church buildings. Before the Reformation parishioners eagerly lavished money on the fabric, furnishings and decorations of their churches, the constant stream of bequests and gifts is shown in the pre-Reformation churchwardens' accounts. Churchwardens were obliged to obtain money from compulsory church rates or from pew rents and other charges levied upon churchgoers. Church building virtually ceased and the disembowelled, whitewashed church interiors of decency and order no longer attracted the generous donations of the laity. Churchwardens were constantly involved in a struggle to ensure enough money to maintain the fabric and provide the essentials for the services.

The Sunday services were the only regular occasions on which the whole parish met together and were, therefore, important in the life of the community. Attendance was compulsory and the churchwardens were charged with the duty of reporting regular absentees at the archdeacon's or bishop's visitations.

The Elizabethan Act of Uniformity of 1559 ordered the clergy, under the pain of severe penalties, to use the book of Common Prayer and no other and that all persons should attend their parish church regularly upon Sunday and other days ordained to be kept as Holy Days and these to be orderly and soberly. Failure to attend was punished by the church courts.

Because people were obliged to attend church the behaviour of the congregations during the services was not always what would be desired. George Herbert, the Rector of Bemerton in Wiltshire, had several times in the 1630s to exhort his congregation to attend carefully to the service and to say the responses clearly, 'not in a huddling or slubbering fashion, gaping or scratching the head or spitting even in the midst of their answer'.

While it is easy to find examples of disputes and ill-behaviour during the seventeenth century few services were enlived by such events and it would be wrong to suppose that in most churches the congregations behaved other than soberly and reverently.

One reason for absenteeism was the fact that many parishes were very large and people were obliged to undertake a journey of several miles in order to reach their parish church. The evidence of this may still be seen in the multitude of hat-pegs which still adorn the walls of a few churches which have escaped the hands of the restorers as well as the notices exhorting women to take off their pattens or over-shoes which they used for walking across muddy fields. The pattens were left on the stone benches which still remain in many church porches.

In the Civil War of the seventeenth century many of the Parliamentarians saw the Church and the Monarchy as just enemies and were eager to purge the parish churches of what they considered the surviving relics of popery so that works of art and things of great beauty which had escaped destruction during the sixteenth century fell victim to Puritan zeal during the 1640s. Stained glass was smashed, statues defaced or destroyed, vestments cut up or torn to pieces and organs, service books and woodwork burnt.

In 1645 an Act was passed whereby the use of the Book of Common Prayer was strictly forbidden and in its place a Directory for public worship was issued which left considerable latitude for individual ministers. Under the act any person using the Book of Common Prayer was fined £5 for the first offence,

£10 for the second offence and for the third offence given a year's imprisonment. the impact of the changes in the services in parish churches consequently varied from place to place and most congregations experienced not only new services but other changes as the Puritans unleashed another orgy of destruction.

With the return of the king in 1660 came the return of the Anglican Church. The Puritan ministers were removed and in many parishes those they had replaced resumed their offices and their rights to tithes and other dues. The use of the Book of Common Prayer was revived and re-issued with a few minor changes in 1662.

The interior arrangement of parish churches was restored with the altar in the east end of the church. The essential link between the Monarchy and the Church was emphasised by the erection of the Royal Arms in parish churches throughout the country and appropriate texts also appeared on the walls drawing attention to the Christian duty of obedience, to establishing authority and to the wickedness of rebellion, for example, '*The powers that be are ordained by God,*' and '*My son, fear God and the king and meddle not with them that are given to change.*'

The changes and upheavals of the past twenty years had been too far reaching to allow total restoration. Nonconformity had now to be recognised in almost every parish as an established fact of religious life and no longer could the Anglican Church claim to include all Christians within each parish. It is from the Restoration of 1660 that the real beginning of the deep and significant division of English social life between 'Church' and 'Chapel' can be dated and this gulf was to remain until the twentieth century. This division touched all aspects of life and affected attitudes to society, politics, education and economic life and had an immeasurable impact upon the development of the nation.

The eighteenth century church depended upon whitewash for interior decoration, it was cheap and effective and made for a light and airy building in which to hear the sermons which formed such an important part of the services. Further decoration was provided at the east end of the chancel by the Ten Commandments the Creed and the Lord's Prayer either painted directly on the wall or upon boards arranged around the altar. Texts could easily be applied to the nave walls with the Royal Arms as a prominent feature symbolising the essential link between Church and State and the role of the Established Church in the life of the nation.

Sermons were a much more regular feature of the services than was the Holy Communion service and the pulpit occupied a correspondingly more important place in the interior arrangement of the church. It was the main focus of attention in the eighteen-century parish church and consisted of a pulpit and reading desk often combined with a desk for the parish clerk. Many of these three-decker pulpits complete with their large sounding-boards and elaborate pulpit cushions survive and provide, perhaps more clearly than anything else, a reminder of the atmosphere and priorities of eighteenth-century Anglicanism.

It was also during this period that the splendid brass chandeliers were installed and still form an attractive feature of many parish churches.

Square box pews filled the nave with the private pew of the squire occupying a favoured and prominent place often elaborately furnished with a fireplace, table, chairs and sofas and having a separate entrance.

In the nineteenth century there was a great boom in church building and restoration and a great number of Anglican churches were built or restored. The Camden Society (later known as the Ecclesiological Society) was founded in 1839 by two Cambridge students, J.M.Neale and Benjamin Webb, who urged the return of a medieval architectural and artistic setting for Anglican worship and so we find churches of this period built in the style of the thirteenth and fourteenth centuries. The fittings and furnishings included encaustic floor tiles, particularly the brown tiles with their yellow patterns known as 'Minton' tiles, which replaced thousands of grave slabs levered up from the floors of medieval churches, brass altar rails, brass candlesticks and eagle lecterns. The three-decker pulpit was either disposed of or cut down to a less prominent size and the altar, covered with fine linen cloths and a woven or embroidered frontal, surmounted with either a stone or wooden reredos, was now again in full use. The old box pews were largely swept away and replaced with pine seating, the windows were adorned with brightly coloured modern stained glass and the galleries were nearly all swept away. The church had now devoted itself to the Eucharist and the preaching of the Word had been relegated to an equal if not second place.

5

Building Materials

Though certain criteria of date, such as mouldings, were constant throughout England there is still at all dates a great variety in the churches of different areas, for example a fifteenth-century church in East Anglia may be a very different building from one of the same date in north Oxfordshire.

The differences may be due to various causes, historical, economic and geological, the last perhaps being the most important.

The builders of the great abbey churches had resources that made them independent of local conditions; if good building stone was not locally available they could, and did, import it. All but a few parish churches however, had to cut their coat according to the cloth and make the best of local materials. Our best native building material is the colite limestone of which a broad band stretches diagonally across the country from Somerset to Yorkshire. Along this line are found the noblest churches and innumerable parish churches for which they served as models. The stoneless fen, however, is almost equally rich in fine churches for its numerous water-ways made the transport of building materials a comparatively easy matter.

The west had its quarries of warm red sandstone but this stone is soon eroded by wind and rain and is, therefore, a poor material for external moulding and sculpture. On the other hand the granite of Cornwall is too intractable for fine carving. The flint of the chalk districts in Berkshire, Sussex and East Anglia cannot be carved and in these districts the necessary freestone for quoins, tracery and other architectural features had to be imported and because of this it was used with the utmost economy. The most important English medieval quarries were Taynton, Oxfordshire, Barnack, Northamptonshire and Huddleston, Yorkshire. Throughout the thirteenth century deposits of dark shelly limestone called Purbeck marble were quarried in the Isle of Corfe in Dorset and were much used for shafts and piers, wall arcading and making tombs and effigies. This stone was so popular that quarries of similar 'marbles' were worked at Petworth, Sussex, Bethersden, Kent and Frosterley, Durham. When polished this non-crystalline stone had the appearance of marble although it is not geologically marble.

Much of the masonry was worked at the quarries and supplied ready for fixing in buildings perhaps many miles distant.

When stone walls came into use they were merely roughly piled up by unskilled hands in rubble of assorted sizes either roughly coursed or utilizing the principle of herring-bone masonry. Another method of laying rubble stones is to fit the pieces carefully together in what is known as 'ragstone' technique. This was common throughout the Middle Ages in Kent and is also met with in the districts where flint is used. Rubble walling is raised evenly and has no core as in a true masonry wall. The difficulty of constructing the angles of walling in rubble was probably originally countered by utilizing stones from ruined Roman buildings: possibly in many cases such valuable material would have been transported from some distance if necessary. In many instances bricks from ruined Roman buildings in the vicinity were used, for example, at Chipping Ongar, Essex.

The advent of the first true mason with his mysterious knowledge of how to construct walls of hewn freestone must have been a great experience to many primitive village community in Anglo-Saxon days.

Let us consider the significance of the craft of mason and the all-important part it played in medieval architecture. The first principle of masonry is to extract from the earth stone of such a nature, that, after various operations have been performed upon it, it can be, as it were, rebuilt to form the walls of a building.

The method of quarrying freestone varied little with the district, the principle was to cut the stone into sections subsequently levering each portion off its bed with wedges. The size of the stones, as a general rule, increased as the years went by due to the improvement of the devices employed for hoisting the stone up to the scaffolds.

The actual method used in building a wall was to construct its two faces separately filling in the space between with a rough concrete made of mortar mixed with the 'spalls' hewn from the stones when they were squared up.

The term 'mason' is apt to be loosely applied to any tradesman connected with the erection of masonry. Masons were of varying grades performing entirely different operations and working independently of each other at their various tasks. Obviously there had to be someone who could organise and direct the operations connected with the erection of a building. This individual on whom practically the whole responsibility for designing and constructing the building rested was known as the 'master mason'.

In order to get the stone prepared for the master mason each mason had to employ a team of perhaps up to a dozen stone-cutters or hewers. They would have been of varying grades of skill from the axe-man who cut plain blocks of walling-stone to the experienced dresser who could, under the master mason's directions, prepare stones of any shape required.

The stone was split with wedges and levered out of its bed. To use it to the best advantage from the point of view of strength and resistance to weathering it was customary to lay the stone on its natural bed or set its natural bed at right angles to the direction of thrust. For example, voussoirs of an arch were cut and placed so that their natural bedding planes would be laid radially. Great accuracy was needed or the result would have been a clumsily built wall or arch.

From the 'lodges' occupied by the stone cutters gangs of labourers carried the dressed stone to the position in which it was to be laid. Here other masons would be found, known as 'setters', who would carefully place the stones on their new beds and set them in mortar.

The reason for the stone cutting and carving being carried out at the quarry and the setting of the stone carried out by other masons on the site was that the weight of the stone which had to be transported was reduced. If the stone was carried overland in carts its price would be doubled in twenty-five miles but water transport, where possible, was cheaper. It was for this reason that stone was prepared at the Caen quarries in Normandy for use in Canterbury Cathedral and many buildings in London. When stone was brought from Caen in 1287 for Norwich Cathedral it cost £1.33 but it cost a further £3.10 to transport it.

It will be seen that the master mason was not, as is sometimes supposed, a man whose work is of the same nature as that of a bricklayer. He was, in fact, the director of the labours of a considerable number of men. It may be said that he represented the medieval equivalent of a building contractor. When the wright was needed to erect the roof timbers, the plumber to cover these with lead or the smith to hang the doors on the 'hooks and bands' which were the medieval equivalent of hinges, all these tradesmen would come under the direction of the master mason. In the architectural world of his day the mason was the most important tradesmen in the medieval economy.

To reconstruct a picture of the scene of operations on a building site in the Middle Ages one can imagine the walls and pillars at all stages of erection with scaffolds rising to the highest parts. In sheltered angles the lean-to lodges of the masons, each surrounded by scattered heaps of newly delivered stone, indicate where the hewers are cutting on their 'bankers' or stone benches, the stones which are being called for, from time to time, by the masons directing operations. Pairs of labourers carry the dressed stones, suspended from a pole resting on their shoulders, from the lodges to the working site. Other labourers carry cauldrons of lime mortar to the men who are setting the stones in place.

Behind the scenes were many other people who contributed towards the building. The most important were those who quarried the stone. Another was the man who burnt the limestone for making the lime used in mixing mortar.

The earliest walls were laid dry. Later, when it was desired to fill the interstices between the stones this was done simply with earth or mud and sometimes cow or horse dung and chopped straw were added to make it more cohesive. If the mud was chalky this was to the good for lime is a valuable binder. The first hard-setting mortar was the cement used by the Romans. For internal marble work plaster of Paris, derived from burning gypsum, was used.

The two basic ingredients of good mortar are sand and slaked lime. During the medieval period other ingredients were introduced from time to time to make them harder, such as ox-blood and wood ash. Other ingredients included at various times were the silt-like mud from the primitive roads brought about by the wheels of wagons or later, coaches, to which was added lime. Dust from the sawing and working of stone mixed with lime was also used.

It would appear that the early builders made their jointing material out of whatever could conveniently be found near at hand and this led to some of the materials being more durable that others.

The preparation of lime for the making of mortar was no easy task. It may be obtained from all kinds of limestone including chalk which is used in about a third of the lime used in the building trade today but which is not considered to be as good as 'stone lime'.

Firstly, it was necessary to convert the lime into quicklime which was done by burning the lime in a kiln. The old kilns were merely circular holes in the ground covered with timber and brushwood. Sometimes a layer of coke was also used. Over this was placed broken up pieces of limestone then more coke or timber, more limestone and more coke or timber alternatively until the kilns were about ten feet deep. When the kiln was completed the fire was lit and as the layers of firing were consumed the burnt lime dropped to the bottom of the kiln. The burnt lime which was in an unstable state and thus rendered difficult to transport, was removed from the kiln, in order that it may be slaked.

Most heavy loads, like stone for building, could only be carried long distances by water but it was not possible to put quicklime into barges because any dampness would start it to heat and slake and so cause damage, by burning, to the vessel. To overcome this the limestone had to be shipped unburnt and there is evidence that kilns were erected close to the building sites or sometimes even on the quayside where the limestone was disembarked. Later this difficulty was overcome with the development of hydrated lime.

There were two methods of slaking lime, the liquid and the semi-dry. In the liquid method lumps of burnt lime were carefully put into a large tub or tank half-filled with water and stirred. As the water was absorbed the lime became hotter and with more stirring it would boil without any form of additional heat. At this stage the lime would be dangerous and those looking after the production needed to take care especially protecting the eyes from the bubbling liquid. At this point more lime would be added together with more stirring when the liquid became thicker developing into a creamy consistency. It was then ladled out and poured through a sieve into a pan which was either a shallow hole in the ground or a container on the ground built up with sand to a height of approximately eighteen inches and lined with sand at the bottom. The liquid was then left to cool for seven to fourteen days during which time the water gradually evaporated. When it had reached the consistency of butter it was called 'putty lime' and was then ready for making into mortar. Some people thought, however, that if it was kept for a time it was of better quality since any pieces of lime which have managed to pass through the sieve would have had time to 'blow'. This would be serious if it occurred when the work was finished when 'blowing' might cause a mortar bed to 'lift' or swell and so dislodge a block of stone. It was, therefore, necessary to let the putty-lime stand for at least a year when all that was then necessary was to mix it with sand.

The second method was the semi-dry process. A layer of sand was spread out on which were placed alternate layers of quicklime and sand with the quicklime layers being lightly watered. Gradually a conical heap was made having a base some six or seven feet across. The whole was finally watered and covered with a layer of sand. This whole was then left to heat up and expand and blow. The final result was a dry powder which, after being passed through a fine screen, was ready to be made into mortar by the addition of more water and sand.

Most limestones are not of themselves hydraulic and will not harden when wet which explains the variety of strange ingredients which were added in the Middle Ages to make the sand and lime mixes harder.

From Saxon times mechanical mortar mixers were used and in 1974 a Saxon mixer was found near the east end of St Peters Church, Northampton. A circular bowl between two and three metres in diameter was cut into the ground or constructed on its surface and lined with wattle. Paddles were suspended from a beam pivoting a central post and rotated to mix the mortar.

An important point to bear in mind is that the mortar mix must not be stronger or harder that the stone which is being bonded and preferably it should be softer. Most of our old churches are built of ashlar or rubblestone and from time to time require re-pointing. Ashlar requires little pointing because as the shape of each block has to be true the joints rarely exceed one-eighth of an inch and so all that is necessary is for their joints to be filled flushed with the wall-face. Where the church has been built of uncoursed stones perhaps ribbon pointing is used for repair. This form of pointing always detracts from the natural beauty of the stone and if used on rubblestone, which it often is, looks disastrous. It is easily recognised as it takes the form of wide bands of cement mortar with the surface kept forward about one eighth of an inch. The ribbons are trimmed at the edges so leaving a heavy looking ribbon of hard mortar which may be as much as an inch wide. Not only does this form of pointing look unsightly but technically it is unsound as the ledges formed by the projecting mortar stop the flow of rain water down the wall and channel it into the joints behind the hard pointing.

The transport of heavy stone could easily cost more than the stone itself and so many churches were built of whatever material could be found locally, for example, pebble-rubble, Roman bricks, puddingstone, ironstone, clunch or flint. To build walls composed of a mixture of these materials which were all irregular in shape, although clunch could be shaped into blocks but was usually found irregularly shaped when used in walls, required a great deal of mortar. Some of this material is non-absorbent and lacks suction which causes the mortar only to adhere with difficulty. In addition the lime mortar would not be as durable as the stone. In an effort to strengthen these large amounts of mortar little stone wedges were introduced to help stabilize the stones and counteract rocking. These wedges might consist of chippings from the quarry or the masons' workshops, flakes of flints or just small pebbles. This process became known as 'galletting' from the French *galet* meaning small smooth pebbles found on the sea-shore and in beds of streams. Although this practice, which goes back to medieval times, was originally structural it is now mostly used for decorative purposes. (Dunsfold, Surrey).

The walls of churches which were built of uncoursed rubblestone were not acceptable as they were considered uncouth for the House of God. This type of walling was invariably covered with a thin coat of rendering internally and frequently externally too. Whether or not the exterior was rendered it would certainly have been concealed by a coat of whitewash.

From quarry to quarry, the endless steams of transport of all kinds made their way to the building site year in and year out. Where the source of material was close to the site pack-ponies or horse drawn sledges would be used for the whole journey. More frequently, however, the stone would be brought from a distant quarry by water, unloaded at the nearest convenient spot, and then taken overland. Behind the actual building workers there was, in addition, a host of drovers, shipmen and labourers supplying materials.

The two tradesmen mostly concerned were the wright and the mason. The 'quarries' of the wrights were the oak forests of England. English timber building differs from much of the Continental work in the same material in that the hardwood employed in this country necessitated much harder work. The material, as well as being much tougher than the softer coniferous timber, is inclined to be very irregular in shape and a more finished technique was required in order to make use of the timber available and counteract its awkward tendency to bow and warp.

The English wright used only the heart of the tree for building, rejecting the less desirable sapwood. Their principal tool, which was also employed by the mason, was the axe, held in both hands and employed hatchet fashion in short chops. The axe was also used by the wrights with great accuracy to cut and smooth timber.

Later, timber would have been squared with the saw which was a long two-handed saw used with a saw pit, one man in the pit and the other at ground level. This is where the terms 'top dog' and 'under dog' came from. The under dog was the sawyer who was always smothered in saw-dust!

Two further tools were also used known as the 'celt' or chisel used for cutting mortices and the 'wimble' or auger for drilling the holes through which were driven the wooden pegs holding the joints in position. Steel tipped tools had been known since the thirteenth century, the steel being imported from Sweden and Spain and was called 'osmonds'. Because of the high price of steel it was used sparingly for tips of wedges, edges of axes, point of picks and other tools.

It is no exaggeration to say that without wood the English parish churches could not have been built at all. Wood provided all the scaffolding, the centring essential to the construction of every stone or brick arch or vault, porches, belfries, roofs, the timber foundation of spires together with the vast amount of woodwork used inside the church for benches, pulpits, lecterns, stalls, communion rails, doors and many other items.

All this timber in the medieval church was oak and despite the splendid qualities of English oak, with its immense strength and remarkable durability, it is safe to say that, from the Norman period onwards, wherever stone of almost

AYTHORPE RODING, ESSEX.
C13 Plastered wall and lancet windows.

any kind was readily available church builders used it. Even when the only stone available was either soft or intractable, for example, sandstone or granite, it was still generally preferred to wood for church walls, apart from some towers. There are, accordingly, many churches in East Anglia and the south-east which look as if they had been built of 'any old thing', lumps of stone of various kinds including chalk and conglomerates like puddingstone, unknapped flints, boulders, pebbles and later patchings of brick held together with large quantities of mortar. It must be remember that this rough masonry was always either plastered over or whitewashed. Unfortunately after years of wear and tear parts of this covering have rotted away or the whole has been removed and has not been replaced.

6

Orientation of Churches

The English word orientation comes from the classical Latin word *oriri*, 'to rise' the reference being to the sun but there was also a Latin word *orientare* which specifically meant 'to set towards the East'. From the medieval term comes the verb 'to orientate' which implies the setting out of a church east to west with the altar towards the east.

In 472 the Apostolic Constitutions ordained that churches were to be built according to a rectangular plan but with the 'head' to the east.The congregations were literally directed to pray eastward, which fixed the orientation until the rule was defied at the Reformation. In the thirteenth century Gulielmus Durandus cites the custom dating back to primitive Christian days, 'The foundations must be disposed in such a manner that the head of the church lies exactly to the east that is to the part of the sky in which the sun rises at the equinox.'

The majority of churches are true to the cardinal points of the compass with the chancel in the east end.If however, a careful compass bearing is taken it will be noticed that the major axis deviates from due east and west, the tendency being for the eastern part of the structure to incline to the north from five to ten degrees and in some cases as much as twenty or thirty degrees out of true orientation. It has also been found that a similar inclination is to be seen in the south.

There are a number of reasons which may account for this.

In the 1950s the Reverend Hugh Benson compared the evidence of several writers with the orientation of churches in relation to their dedicatory saints and sunrise alignments. His work was based on churches in Oxfordshire and he found that most were orientated on the sunrise of important church festivals, having taken into account the alteration in the calendar and any changes in dedication.

It has been thought, that apart from orientation by means of the sun, the magnetic compass may have been used to determine the orientation of some sacred buildings and the medieval Freemasons are believed to have used this means.

The use of the compass was known from the early thirteenth century but it is doubtful whether the builders were aware of its variable field whose poles wander within an area close to the axial poles and of the necessity of making adjustments accordingly. This variation gives an angular difference between true north and magnetic north and varies from year to year. As an early example in the year 1580 the variation was eleven degrees fifteen seconds east but in 1622 the angle was six degrees east.

A study by Sidney Searle of the orientation of a number of churches, including Chichester Cathedral, noticed a correlation between their angles or orientations and their dates of construction. At Chichester Cathedral where the best materials and craftsmen would have been used, there is hardly a line that is straight, any two lines that are parallel or any angle that is a right-angle.

Searle's studies showed that the angles were correct for the magnetic variation at their respective building periods. He claimed that the different parts of the church were built at different times and as they were orientated by the magnetic compass their alignments would differ with the wandering of the magnetic pole. The masons were part of an art directly related to the earth and so would not go against the compass bearing as it registered an actual flow of current, the magnetic field of the earth. It is authoritively stated that the variation which we know today was discovered by Stephen Burrowes when voyaging between the North Cape of Finmark and Voigatch about the year 1553.

It is known from manuscripts stolen by a Parliamentary Army captain named Taylor, during the Civil War, from Hereford and Worcester Cathedrals, that when a church was to be built the ecclesiastics, mason and others watched and prayed on the vigil of the dedication and took note of the point on the horizon where the sun rose in the east. A survey of many churches found that the east-west axis line points to that point of the horizon where the sun rises on the day of the Saint to whom the church is dedicated.

The method used was to place a pillar or gnomon on the proposed site of the church. Using the gnomon as centre a circle, with a diameter having a width of the proposed church, was then marked on the ground. The shadow-lines at dawn and dusk from the gnomon were marked off on the circle, giving a true east-west axis. The east and west points were then used as centres for marking out two circles which intersect to form an almond shape or vesica piscis. A line drawn between the vertices of the vesica gave north-south axis. Again using each of the four points as centres circles were described and where they intersected the four corners of a square were established, which was orientated to the true cardinal points.

Apart from the orientation of the church as a whole there is also the curious example of churches in which the axes of nave and chancel do not correspond but point to different points of the horizon. Usually the subject treated is the chancel which is said to be 'deflected', 'skew chancel' or 'weeping'. These expressions, however, beg the question, because unless it can be proved that nave and chancel are of the same age and that the chancel was purposely deflected or that it was deflected at some subsequent re-building it is possible that the nave is the part of the building which has been mis-aligned. The important thing to bear in mind is whether either the nave or chancel has been re-built.

It is admitted that there exist many examples of skew chancels and reason have been put forward by the symbolists and rationalists to account for this. The rationalists consider the deflection is the result either of carelessness or differences in the dates of building the nave and the chancel respectively. It is generally believed that the choir of a church is often consecrated as soon as it was completed, the consecration of the nave being held over until that part of the building was, in turn, ready for use.

If the various reasons already mentioned, are removed we should consider the suggestion which has been put forward by one or two writers. They submit that the axis of the nave or the choir, whichever portion was already standing, would probably be hidden from the mason's view through the temporary blocking up of the chancel arch and so make the task of alignment difficult.

In many cases the deflections were discovered only when the rood-screen was, for one reason or another, taken down. Where there was a screen the mason would have his line concealed while setting out the new section of the building.

If we accept the Saint's Day theory there remains the possibility of error caused by re-dedication or plural dedication. This difference might originate without any re-building of the fabric.

Let us consider Whitby Abbey which, as a whole, is dedicated to St Peter and St Hilda jointly. St Peter's Day is on the 29th June and St Hilda's Day on the 25th August.Originally the Saxon Abbey was dedicated to St Peter only, the dedication of St Hilda having taken place subsequently at one or the other of the re-buildings of the Abbey. This does not imply acceptance of the Saint's Day theory as explaining the variation from true east and west for if it did we would expect to find many more cases of deflection among churches with double dedications. Neither does re-dedication support the conception that the builder was incapable of setting out a straight line or right-angle. It does, however, show the real difficulties which exist in arriving at a true conclusion as to how the medievalists obtained their axial line.

It must be remembered, when considering the Saint's day theory, that the Gregorian Calendar (devised by Gregory XIII, 1582) was not introduced into the United Kingdom until 1752. The introduction of this calendar made a difference of eleven days and in that year 3rd September was reckoned to be 14th September, dating being carried on from that date.

A further explanation is claimed by the symbolists for the deviation of the chancel toward the north which, they say, typifies Our Lord upon the Cross whose head, when he died, bowed towards the right in the direction of the

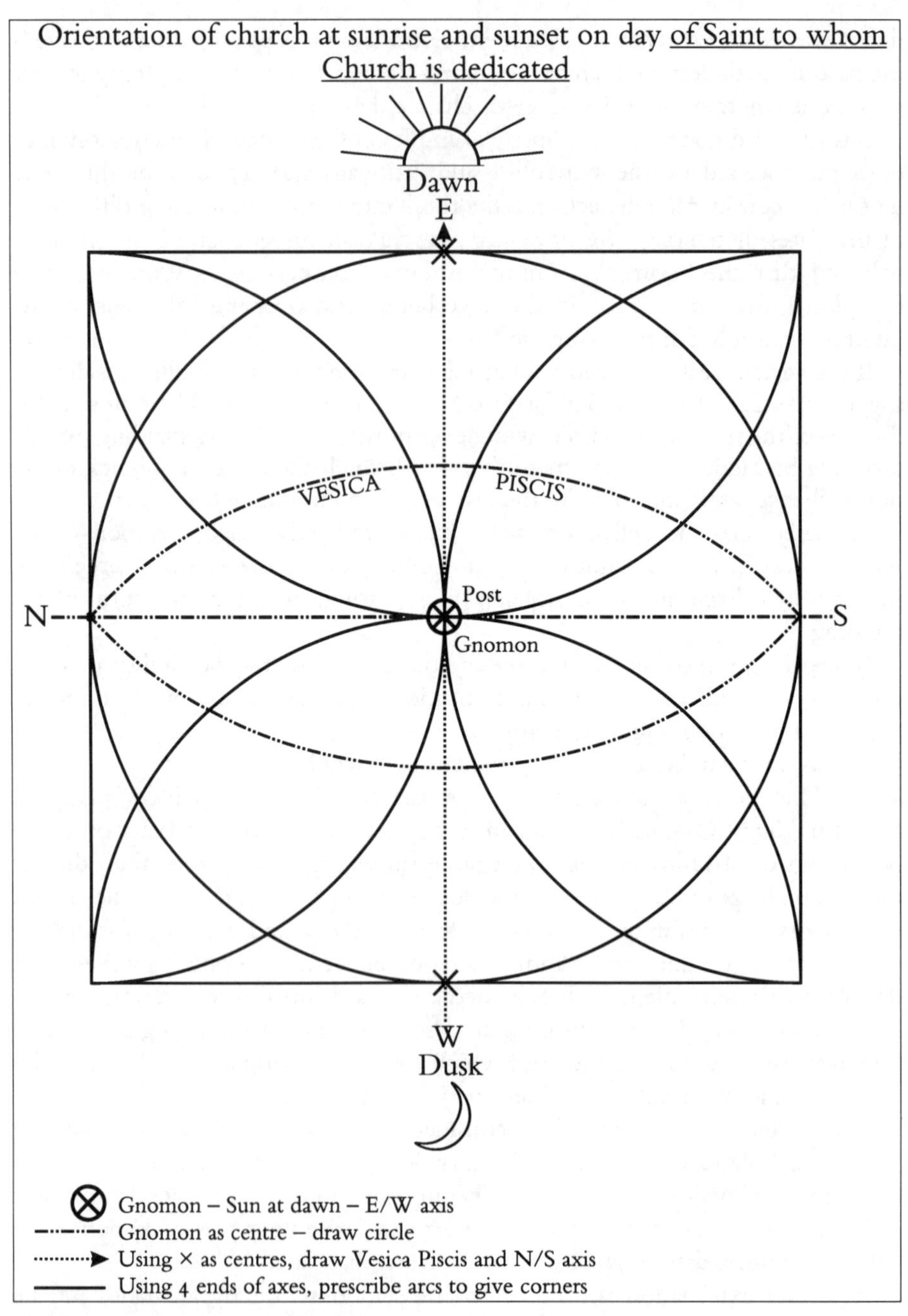

FIGURE 2.
Orientation of a church

penitent thief. There are, however, churches where the inclination is towards the south!

It is said that when Pugin, the great Victorian architect was viewing a skew-chancel in Leicestershire he remarked, 'Pack of nonsense, it was because they didn't know how to build straight'. The same architect was also heard to give an opposite opinion when asked about the bend in the nave at Whitby Abbey when he declared that it signified that the debt of redemption had been paid 'for after the Saviour had expired on the Cross his head would naturally lean or incline to one side'. Which of Pugins's two opinions is the earlier is not known but even if his disbelief of the 'leaning head' theory was his matured judgement he could not really believe that the deflection was due to carelessness and bad building.

It is difficult to understand how the architects who built our magnificent Gothic cathedrals which exhibit such skill and design in workmanship were unable to build straight.

To sum up, skew-chancels were in some cases due to carelessness or unskilfulness and some caused by the architect being loathe to build on old foundations, a dislike shared by Christopher Wren in the re-building of St Paul's Cathedral. The Saint's Day theory certainly holds good for a number of examples where positive instances of observance can be produced. Although the symbolism of the leaning head may not be readily accepted it cannot be dismissed entirely. Medieval symbolism is visible in many guises in our churches and we may therefore assume that it was also embodied into architecture. The deflection does cause an agreeable optical illusion and it was probable that this was intended.

The search continues for some early documents or other evidence which will throw light on this subject but until then it is only possible to go on searching.

7

The Churchyard

The usual entrance to the churchyard is through a gate which may be a 'lych-gate' or 'corpse-gate', 'lic' or 'lich' being a Saxon word for a dead body or corpse. The roof served to shelter the body which, in medieval times, was generally brought in its shroud without a coffin or, perhaps, in the parish coffin from which the body was taken out and placed on a wooden or stone table within the gate while the priest said part of the burial service. The body was then transferred to the parish bier and taken for burial direct into the ground. Few lych-gates of a date earlier than the seventeenth century remain. Many have been restored or rebuilt.

MINSTEAD, HAMPSHIRE.
Lych-gate with coffin slab

Only rich people were buried in coffins in medieval days, the poor being wrapped in a sheet or shroud. In England, coffins did not come into general use until the end of the seventeenth century, the poor being carried on a bier with the body wrapped in a winding sheet. In the terrier of the vicarage of Caistor, Lincolnshire, for 1717 is this item, 'For every grave in the churchyard and without coffin, fourpence, if with coffin, one shilling'. In London it appears that biers went out of fashion at a much earlier date, toward the end of the sixteenth century when the Vestry of St Helen's, Bishopgate ruled 'that none shall be buried within the church unless the dead corpse is coffined in wood'. A parish coffin for the general use of the poor parishioners was often provided and examples still exist at Easingwold in Yorkshire and Howden in Humberside.

From the year 1666 to 1814 it was illegal to clothe any body for burial in anything not manufactured of wool but the Burial in Wool Act 1666 was disregarded for some years and because it was so ineffective a second Act was passed in 1678. Under this act it was decreed that,

> 'No corpse of any person or persons shall be buried in any Shirt, Shift, Sheet or Shroud, or anything whatsoever made or mingled with Flax, Hempe, Silke, Haire, Gold or Silver, or any stuff or thing other than what is made of Sheep's Wool only, or be put in a coffin lined or faced with any sort of Cloath or Stuffe or any thing whatsoever that is made of any Material but Sheep's Wool only, upon paine of the forfeiture of five pounds of lawful money of England.'

This all gave impetus to the wool trade of the country and its provisions also required that an affidavit was to be made in each case before a Justice of the Peace or some other authorised person and that a register of the fact that all had been carried out as required should be kept by the parish priest.Examples of such entries may be found in old parish registers. In the Fyfield, Essex, parish registers, 1538–1700, may be found the following examples:

> 1686. John Sidney, Rectr. of Beauchamp Roding, Certified that affidavit was made before him that Robert Curch of Fyfield was buryed according to the two Acts of Parliament for burying in woolen. March 31, 1686.

> 1690. Mr John Holsester, Rectr. of Little Laver certified concerning the burying of Wm. Cousins, a child, that it was according to ye Acts of Parliament for burying in woollen. May 17, 1690.

The Acts were repealed in 1814.

Uncoffined burials took place up to the nineteenth century and when the marks of the burial had disappeared fresh corpses were buried in the same plot of ground. Any bones which were disturbed and remained when the burial had taken place were preserved in a Bone-hole under the church. Examples may be seen at Stanton Morley Norfolk and Mitcheldean, Gloucestershire.

In the early days, churchyards were usually circular or sub-circular a shape derived from the unfenced tumulous or barrow of pre-Norman or Celtic times. With the introduction of Roman influence the square or rectangular form was introduced. The Norman clerics carried on the continental tradition of the rectangular form with the customary area of an acre.

In medieval days 'God's Acre' as it was known, was a busy place. On feast day there were dancing and games called 'Church Ales'. This was started by

BARFRESTON, KENT.
Groove caused by arrow sharpening.

Pope Gregory VII in the eleventh century to take the place of the sacrifice of cattle and horses, accompanied by feasting and dancing which was common in pagan Britain. The game of fives was played between the buttresses, fairs were held and travelling merchants set up their booths and stalls in the churchyard and, in troubled times, it was a refuge and men took their few chattels and drove their stock there.

Churchyards were also used for archery practice, particularly during the fourteenth century. One of the commonest proofs is the occurrence throughout all parts of the country of grooves made on suitable stones in the church walls, especially near the porch and sometimes in ancient churchyard walls by the sharpening of arrow heads on them. Wherever there was suitable freestone in the walls of the church it became a whetstone for arrow heads.

William Fitzstephen writing in 1180 speaks of his popularity of religious drama in the London churches of his day. The crowds thronging the churches to see their performances became so great that there was difficulty in accommodating them and the plays were therefore transferred to the churchyards and open fields and afterwards to the streets and squares.

A Synod held at Exeter in 1287 commanded that parish priests should forbid the use of churchyards for dances, combats or stage plays especially on Saints' days. Perhaps this prohibition was enforced in the diocese of Exeter but elsewhere churches and churchyards continued to be put to secular use.

Feast days, and sometimes on Sundays, fairs and markets were held in parish churchyards and probably in bad weather the stalls were set up in the church nave. In 1416 the churchwardens of St Michael-le-Belfry, Petergate York, Yorkshire, complained of the noise and tumult of Sundays and Holy days when 'divers things and goods and rushes were exposed for sale' at the common market in the churchyard. In a poor parish the rents paid by the stall-holders were a most acceptable source of income.

On many occasions the bishop strove to suppress the holding of fairs in God's Acre and forbade buying and selling in the precincts of parish churches. In 1285 the Statute of Winchester prohibited the use of churchyards for fairs and markets but apparently the practice continued in various places for in 1368 Archbishop Langham of Canterbury issued a mandate forbidding Sunday markets in churchyards in the Isle of Sheppey because Divine Offices were disturbed by the clamour of the traders.

In places, the parish churchyards were the parish cemeteries and the responsibility for enclosing them with fences and keeping them in proper condition rested upon the parishioners. Bishop Peter Quivil of Exeter decreed in 1267 that all churchyards in his diocese should be enclosed and neither the laity nor the clergy were to allow their cattle to graze there nor were any trees to be felled as these things were intended to ornament and protect God's house from damage by gales. Visitations made by bishops or their representatives revealed much that called for redress in the use of churchyards. In 1348 Bishop John Trilleck of Hereford threatened parish priests with excommunication if they allowed their churches or the precincts to be put to any but religious purposes. This ban was probably not unconnected with the Bishop's fear of the plague.

It seems, however, that these episcopal injunctions failed to suppress dancing, wrestling and the playing of balls games in churchyards. In 1472 the parishioners of Salton, Yorkshire, who indulged in 'improper and prohibitive sports in the churchyard' were made liable to a fine of twopence for each offence. This was so ineffectual that many years later transgressors were threatened with excommunication.

As we have seen this state of affairs continued through the centuries and did not finally come to an end until the seventeenth century when gravestones were introduced and the churchyard became a more orderly place.

It is said that the largest part of the churchyard is always on the southside and consequently the oldest graves are found there so that the shadow of the church should not fall on them. but an equally good reason would be that the church was built to the north of the new Cross so that its shaft might remain in sunlight and throw a shadow of the Cross, which was, no doubt, considered an essential function. The first graves would then be grouped around the Cross as this part of the churchyard would be considered of greater sanctity. A further reason that most burials took place on the south side of the church was that the north side was supposed to belong to the Devil and so people were reluctant to be buried on that side which was mostly used for the burial of unbaptised children, suicides and felons.

At the beginning of the present century there were many churchyards in which the south side was so crowded with graves that enlargement had become necessary although hardly a mound marked the ground to the north. When

Parliament made it obligatory for ground to be reserved in the churchyards, though unhallowed, for the burial of criminals, suicides and unbaptised infants, these plots were always situated to the north of the church. Such was its ill-repute that an unexplained burial there might have been considered an implication of guilt and a gravestone of 1807 at Epworth, Yorkshire, bears the inscription, 'That I might longer undisturbed abide, I choose' to be laid on this northern side'.

The results of burying people on top of one another may be seen in many churchyards where the level of the earth outside the church is above that of the church floor, sometimes almost up to the sills of the windows.

In William Cobbett's *Rural Rides* (1830), he comments on the churchyard in the village of Rogate near Petersfield, Hampshire, where he says, 'the churchyard was on the other side of the road; surrounded by a low wall. The earth of the churchyard was about four feet and a half higher that the common level of the ground round about it, and you may see, by the nearness of the church windows to the ground, that this bed of earth has been made by the innumerable burials that have taken place in it'. Cobbett speaking to a group of three or four others said, 'It has taken a pretty many thousands of your forefathers to raise that ground as high'.

Important people were originally buried under the floor of the church, the poor being buried in the churchyard. In time, however, there was no more room for the important people inside the church so it became necessary to add extension, as it were, by interring them immediately outside the church walls, though there was always keen competition for a place as near the building as possible.

There were no tombstones or monuments and those we now find in our country churches date from the seventeenth and eighteenth centuries. Inside the church, in the aisles, we may find massive floor slabs of the seventeenth and eighteenth centuries made from bluish-grey stone or, if a wealthy person, perhaps of alabaster. These slabs are known as 'ledger stones'. The earliest tombs were simply slabs of stone carved with a cross to show that a Christian was buried below and these may be found inside the church or occasionally outside as at Greenstead, Essex.

By the twelfth century figures began to appear on the tombs inside the church showing the dead man lying in state. It is doubtful whether he looked as shown on his tomb, but the effigy will usually show all the emblems of his rank, for example, the spurs of a knight, the vestments of a priest or the crozier of a bishop.

Sometimes we see tall tombs which look like stone altars. These are table tombs which follow the form of the altar tombs we find inside the church. The tops were raised above ground and so, more often than not, did not get overgrown with weeds although they can be found with perhaps an elderberry tree growing up through a broken top.

The tops of the table tombs nearest the porch were often used for the distribution of bread and beer to the poor left by the wills of charitable persons. The eighteenth and nineteenth century copies of these old table tombs are often heavy and clumsy in appearance.

As the floor of the church filled with tombs and burials took place in the churchyard, those members of a family who wished to remember the deceased erected a head-stone the material of which varied according to the locality. For example, in the Home Counties where stone was scarce wooden head-stones can be found or, where stone was available or the family was rich enough to have stone sent, it would be of stone and in the Midlands head-stones were later made of cast iron many of which still exist.The erection of gravestones did not take place until about the seventeenth century.

Some of the head-stones of the eighteenth and nineteenth centuries were carved with classical emblems, such as, skull, crossbones, hour glass, scythe and others. These emblems have symbolical meanings, the scythe represented 'Death the Reaper', hour glass 'the sands of time run out fast', torch, inverted, 'Death, darkness and night', torch, upright, 'Life, light and day'. These pictorial devices were intended to serve as reminders of human mortality.

Interesting and amusing inscriptions are often to be found. Anthony Childs buried in Ramsden Bellhouse churchyard, near Billericay, Essex died in 1726 aged 81. He had lived through the Civil War, the beheading of Charles I, the short lived dictatorship of Oliver Cromwell, then Charles II, James II, William and Mary, Anne, George I, and George II! Martha Blewitt of the Swan Inn at Baythorn End at Birdbrook, Essex, who had nine husbands in succession has the following tombstone 'Martha Blewitt of the Swan Inn at Baythorn End in this parish; buried May 7 1681: was the wife of nine husbands successively but the ninth outlived her'. The text at her funeral sermon was 'last of all the woman died also'. At Margaretting, Essex, this verse may be found on a tombstone,

> She on this clayen pillow laid her head,
> As brides doe use, the first to go to bed.
> He mist her soon, and yet ten months he trys
> To live apart, but lyks it not, and dys.

At Flamstead in Hertfordshire, carved on a pillar is an inscription which brings us nearer to the humbler folk of the sixteenth century and which was said of someone they obviously loved, 'In this middle space and at this seat's end There lieth buried our neighbour frind Olde John Grigge of Cheverill's End.'

Occupations are frequently given and naturally have a close relationship with local trade and industry. A grave-stone may have a carved representation of the tools or implements used in life by the person concerned, a palette and brushes in the case of an artist, a spade for a gardener or a bale of wool for a seventeenth-century wool merchant.

Even physical peculiarities are occasionally mentioned as in the case of Benjamin Cromack buried in Calverly churchyard between Leeds and Bradford who died in 1826 aged 25 who took a coffin seven feet eleven inches long!

At Greenstead churchyard there is a wooden cross. The lettering on the cross is almost obscured but it tells a sad story. It is about Edward Edwards who fell on his scythe while sharpening it and died within the hour.

Sometimes graves are protected by iron railings or grilles. These were to prevent the body snatchers of the nineteenth century digging up the corpses in order to sell them to anatomists for dissection. Sometimes a watch-house to give shelter to a night-watchman on the look out for body snatchers may be found, as at Wanstead churchyard in the London Borough of Redbridge.

In and around the churchyard there may be found a pillory (Little Wakering, Essex), whipping post (Canewdon, Essex), ducking stool, lock-up and stocks (Candewden, Essex), or steps used as a mounting block (Bradwell-on-Sea, Essex). There may also be an old tithe barn (Abbotsbury, Dorset), alsmshouses (Stock, Essex), school, (Felstead, Essex), holy well, (Runwell, Essex), churchyard crosses (Castle Hedingham, Essex) or perhaps a bargaining stone to which people came to strike a bargain (Lechlade, Gloucestershire).

Yew Trees

Many churchyards have yew trees. In early times they were about the only evergreen trees in southern England and Wales and before the conversion of Britain to Christianity were considered sacred. They were probably originally on religious sites and are invariably found on the south side of the church.

There is no doubt, however, that these trees were frequently planted during the Norman period and it would appear evident that the practice of planting churchyard yews was general among the clergy in England after the Conquest.The two Archbishops of Canterbury, Lanfranc (1070) amd Anselm (1093) both came from north Italy where the cypress had been planted in graveyards since Roman times and this may have influenced the adoption of the yew in Britain as its equivalent.

Giraldus Cambrensis, Archdeacon of Brecknock, Wales and a historian, writing c 1184 said that yews 'were planted by the hands of holy men', and that Henry II when in Ireland, 'sacrilegiously laid hands on a group of yews in a most irreverent and atrocious manner'. This suggests that sanctity was attributed to the yew by the Christian Church.

All over Europe the yew has been associated with death and its seeds are said to be poisonous though birds eat the berries. Pliny describes its shade as 'mortiferous'; Shakespeare in Hamlet refers to the 'double fatal yew' and Graves states that it produced 'Hebenon' the juice used by Hamlet's uncle to poison the King. In Macbeth the witches cauldron contained 'slips of yew, slivered on the moon's eclipse'.

Another reason for the planting of yews in churchyards was that they were considered to be protection against witches.

The idea of protecting the fabric of the church by means of surrounding it with trees occurs in one of the decrees of the Synod of Exeter held in 1287 which runs,

> 'Since trees are often planted in the churchyard to prevent the church from being injured by storms, we strictly forbid the rector to fell them unless the chancel shall stand in need of repair, or unless, when the nave requires to be repaired, the rector, on account of the poverty of the parishioners, shall think proper, out of charity, to grant them some of the trees for that purpose.'

The observance of Palm Sunday has been traced to the fifth and fourth centuries. Palms are not grown in cold climates so substitutes had to be found and in the London area it was customary to carry the sallow with its catkin bloom or the willow in north, south England and Scotland. When the symbolism of the yew derived from Pagan times faded the supply of evergreens needed for Palm Sunday contributed to the care taken of yews in churchyards.

The churchyard being the parson's freehold, the yews in the sixteenth century were a source of revenue, the branches being sold for making bows although the wood of the British yew was not so suitable for this purpose as that from Spain or Portugal and in the Middle Ages bows made from imported wood were worth three times as much as native yews.

From the time of Edward I until Charles I the practice of archery was encouraged by Parliament. An Act of 1466 directed that every able-bodied Englishman should have a long-bow of his own height and should practice on Sundays and Feast days at butts set up in all townships and villages. Churchyards were used for archery practice and marks may be found on stone window sills or jambs of windows showing where arrow heads have been sharpened.

One of the oldest and largest yew trees in the country is in the churchyard at Much Marcle, Herefordshire. The hollow trunk is so large that inside it contains several seats.

Churchyard Crosses

Prior to the Reformation in the sixteenth century every church had its Cross on the south side some of which were of great beauty. Unfortunately, owing to the wrath of the Reformers few are left intact though there are many bases and headless shafts.

The Cross was often, in the first instance, erected on or near a pagan shrine and was a centre of worship before any church was built. A number were set up by the preaching friars from Italy and used as preaching positions. Some of the Crosses had a niche in the shaft for a pyx which was a receptacle containing the Host.

8

Consecration Crosses and Apsidal End

When a church was dedicated twelve crosses were carved or painted both on the outside and on the inside of the walls of the church, usually seven to eight feet above the ground to preserve them. There may be above or below each cross a hole for a bracket to hold a candle used in the ceremony of anointing with holy oil by the bishop who used a short ladder to enable him to reach.

The ceremony comprised the marking of the walls both inside and out with consecration crosses. All persons, except the deacon, then withdrew and the doors of the building were made fast. The bishop, ecclesiastics and the laity passed in procession three times round the outside of the church during which the bishop anointed with holy oil the twelve crosses which had been placed on the exterior wall. The bishop then struck the threshold of the main entrance to the church with his crozier three times, in response to which the deacon flung open the door to admit the bishop and his attendants, the clergy and laity staying outside.

After the recitation of the litany inside the church a cross of ashes and sand was sprinkled on the floor and the alphabet in Greek and Latin was traced in it. The bishop then proceeded to consecrate the altar, anointing it with hallowed water and wine and sprinkling the crosses on the walls.

Amid the ringing of the bells the general public was admitted to the newly consecrated church and the celebration of Mass at the High Altar followed immediately. This was the ceremony used in the early sixteenth century.

FAIRSTEAD, ESSEX.
Painted consecration cross.

Apsidal End

When the teutonic tribes, that is the German, Dutch, Swedish, Danish, Norwegian and others came overland into the western Roman Empire they adopted, in a short time, the religious fashions, speech and civil administration of the Romanised indiginous people.

The Angles, Jutes, Saxons and Frisians, however, who came across the North Sea and the Channel to what was to become England, pushed the indiginous Celtic Christianity with them. The Celtic Church was then insulated from Rome.

The invaders laid the foundations of a new 'England' east of a line from Berwick-upon-Tweed to Exmouth and preserved their language and heathen gods for two dark centuries between the Roman evacuation and the coming of Augustine's mission. They inter-married so little with the Romano-British Celts that the old Celtic tongue did not survive in their English lands except in a few place names and personal names. In fact, the various Celtic kingdoms and their folk refused to have any social communication or dealings with the invaders.

So insulated from the Continent and the changes in the Roman rites and practices had the Celtic Church become by the time Augustine and his missionaries began their work in 597 that it rejected his negotiation for a compromise of Christian doctrines and rites. Thus there arose two distinctive and rival streams of Christian thought and teaching in England, firstly that of the Roman Church of Pope Gregory and Augustine in the south and east and secondly that of the old Celtic Church of the north and west in Ireland.

The two streams of thought met for a final confrontation at the famous Sunod of Whitby in 664 summoned by Oswi, King of Northumbria who, under the influence of Paulinus who had been sent to England by Gregory in 601 and who had become a bishop at Canterbury, had rejected the Celtic Church in favour of that of Rome. Arising from a resolution of the Synod to follow the teaching and rites of Rome the old Celtic Church retired from the English kingdoms.

The ancient disparities between the forms of Christian teaching, however, had a lasting effect on the physical aspect of the English parish church.

In one particular the old-fashioned, overcome Celtic Church retreating from England, achieved a notable and paradoxical victory, a victory which is visible everywhere in the rectangular eastern ends of English parish churches.

The continental churches had, and to this day have, semi-circular or apsidal ends and this plan was the one re-introduced into Kent by Augustine and his followers. But the English obstinately preferred the square-ended chancel.

The earliest churches of Rome had an apse or sanctuary at the western end and an entrance at the eastern end. It is likely that the change or orientation was due to pre-Christian pagan influence not unconnected with the worship of the sun, particularly as St Augustine in 597 was counselled by St Gregory to deal gently with the heathen practices which were not directly opposed to Christianity. Certainly, henceforth, all English churches were built with the altar at the east end so that the altar and celebrant should be bathed in the full light of the morning sun through the east window. For thirteen centuries this has constituted the dominant feature of the distinctive English style.

Despite the obstinacy of the English in preferring the square-ended chancel there was another introduction of the apsidal end as the result of the Conquest by way of France, particularly through Normandy. The construction of apsidal ended chancels by the Normans was, without doubt, due to their preference in church building and this preference lasted some seventy-five years in the major churches.

This alternation between the apse and the square-end seems to have carried on through the various periods sometimes with the apse predominating and sometimes the square-end asserting itself.

The survival of apsidal ends is probably due to the slow growth of churches in East Anglia and Essex particularly as building materials were difficult to collect and transport. The reason for destruction, which occurred mainly in small churches, was because, although the nave might be sufficiently large, the apse was considered to cramp the liturgical arrangements of the east end. In the thirteenth century there was considerable enlargement of chancels which accounted for the scanty survival of the apsidal end.

9

Buttresses

The weight of a roof is always trying to push outwards the supporting walls and when the roof is very high and the walls very thin this force will be considerable. To counter this force buttresses were built against the walls on the outside. Sometimes they were built at the same time as the walls or added afterwards when the walls showed signs that they were being thrust outwards by the weight of the roof.

In a church, height was the primary effect at which the builders aimed. As walls rose higher so they had to be increased in thickness in order to support, not only the weight above, but also the thrusts of spreading roofs and vaulting.

The Saxons were good builders and we find little supporting work. Where they considered a wall needed supporting they used pilaster strips of masonry

COPFORD, ESSEX.
Apsidal End and C12.Pilaster strips.

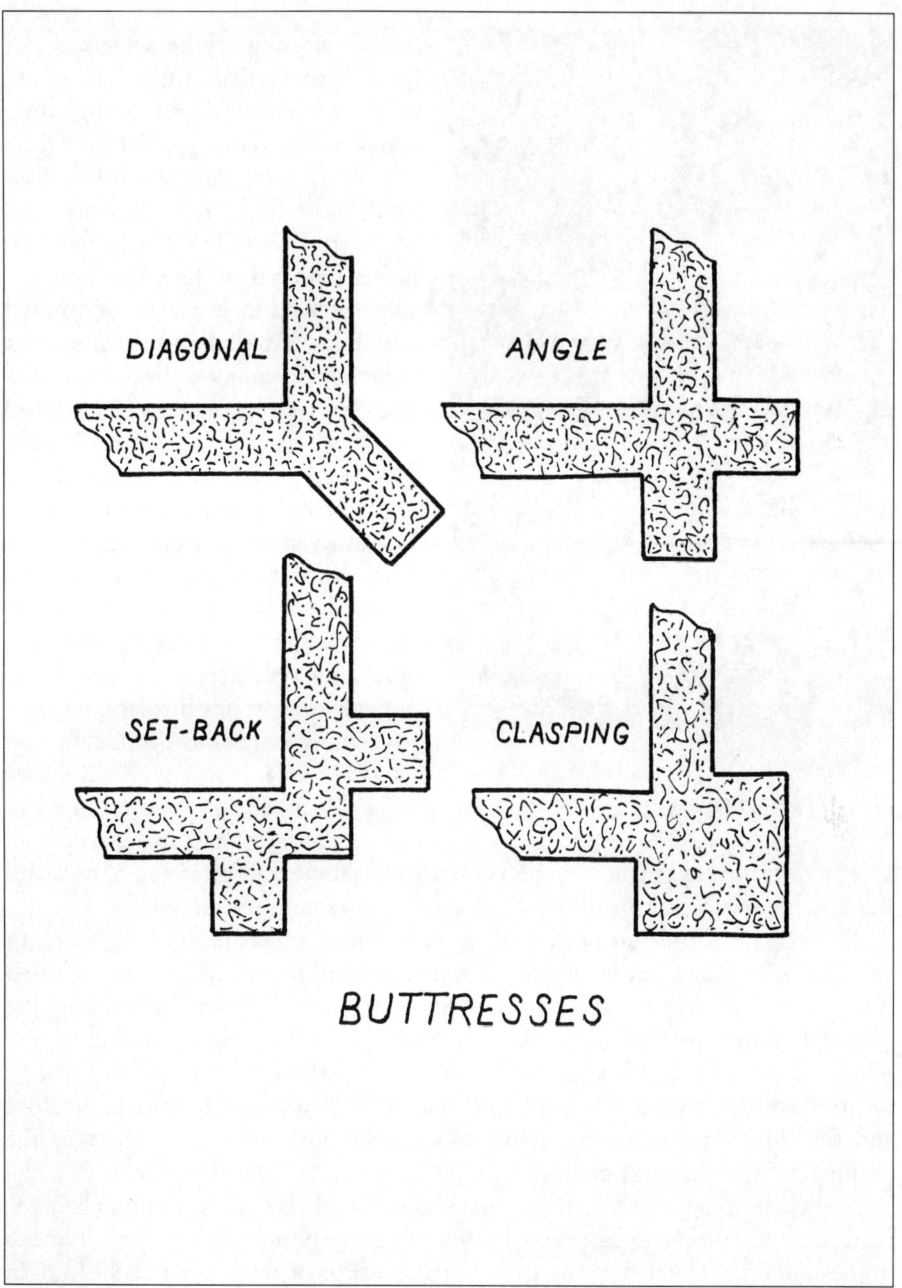

FIGURE 3.
Diagrams of various buttresses.

ICKLETON, CAMBRIDGESHIRE
Early C14 pointed buttress.

which although quite wide did not project more than a few inches and were of equal depth along their length and were, therefore, of little use as supports. Pilaster work is dealt with more fully under Towers.

In small buildings the gable walls being higher than the others are usually thicker. In the case of vaulted buildings, especially the barrel vault which was simply a tunnel and was the first type of vaulting introduced by the Normans, the lateral walls often had to be increased enormously to oppose the overturning thrust.

When two barrel vaults were joined together at right angles the groined cross vault was achieved. This was built of thick masonry requiring a very strong wooden frame to hold the stones in place while it was being built thus producing two equally wide passageways. If however, a vaulted roof was required to an arcade of arches, for example an aisle, it was possible to repeat the central motif alone and omit the barrels and this is what the Normans did in their crypts, aisles and passageways.

The Normans met many difficulties in building a pleasing looking shape to this type of vaulting but eventually overcame them, one of which was to lessen the amount of timber support required during the building by making the diagonal arches, or ribs, first, quite separately as self-supporting members and filling in between the diagonal and side arches with comparatively thin panels of stonework known as the web. This type of arch was never really satisfactory and the difficulties experienced were not overcome until the advent of the pointed arch in the next century.

As soon as the groined arch was introduced the thrust of the vaulting became concentrated upon definite points in the wall corresponding to the bay divisions of the building. This led to the use of pilaster strips or thickening of the wall in positions where loads occurred. These pilaster strips were slim vertical strips of masonry on the outside of the walls and which indicate the bay lay-out of the building as well as serving a decorative purpose in breaking up the monotony

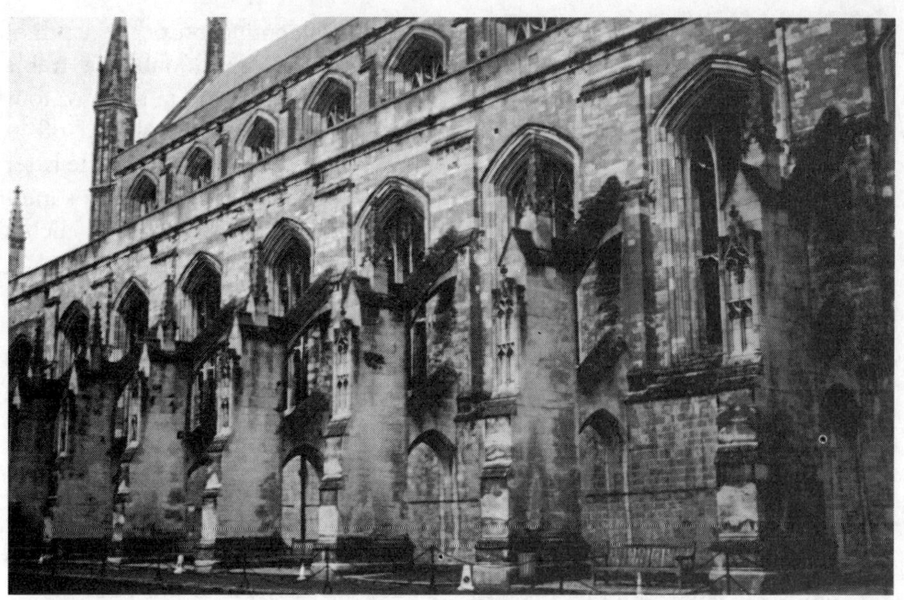

WINCHESTER CATHEDERAL, HAMPSHIRE.

of a plain expanse of wall surface. The externally exposed buttress is a feature which only appears in medieval architecture. By the middle of the twelfth century the pilaster strips began to assume more of the character of the buttress.

Norman wall construction was massive but weak. Walls generally comprised two skins of dressed stone the space between being filled with rubble and stone chippings roughly set in lime mortar. This core tended to remain weak due to the lack of carbon dioxide which was required to complete the chemical reaction necessary to produce hard mortar. Because of this the core frequently shrank away from the dressed stone skin leaving the skin to carry the weight of the structure.

In the Early English period there were further developments due to thinner walls being weakened by larger windows. The higher the building the stronger the overturning thrust and so greater projection was needed for the buttresses which were built in two or three diminishing stages the tops of which were often pointed.

Where buttresses were, as a rule, set at the angles of a building or tower they were set in pairs and were known as angle buttresses.

From about 1377 the pair of buttresses at the angles was abandoned, except in tall structures as in towers, in favour of the single buttress set diagonally in three or four diminishing stages. The diagonal buttress was placed against the right angle formed by the two walls.

WITNEY, OXFORDSHIRE.
C14 Diagonal buttress with niches.

In the fifteenth century the depth of a buttress was often double or treble the width and built up in three or four stages and were usually sloped off at intervals to shed rainwater. In the latter part of the century buttresses sometimes had carved panelling or niches for figures of Saints.

There were also three other kinds of buttress, the 'Set-back' where the buttresses were set back from the angle and 'clasping' where the buttress encases the angle.

The third is the 'flying-buttress' which is, in effect, a prop. If a wall shows signs of falling over a pier may be built some distance away and a prop built from the pier to the wall.

The main use of the flying-buttresses was to stiffen a clerestory wall especially where there was a high vault within. Sometimes wood-roofed churches, without vaults, had flying buttresses when the window area was large. An example of this may be found at Fotheringay church, Norhamptonshire.

In the second half of the twelfth century when attempts were made to vault the main spans of aisled buildings the flying-buttresses were hidden within the roofs of the aisles. Later, when it became necessary to raise the main body of the building so as to obtain better lighting through the clerestory windows the addition of another range of flying-buttresses with their exposure above the roofs became unavoidable. It was discovered that it was necessary for flying-buttresses to be set at an acute angle with the arch of the rib vault describing as complete a semi-circle as possible.

All this work and expense became unnecessary when aisles were raised to a height equal with the nave so that the thrusts from the vaults were equal and opposed and so cancelled one another.

Masons soon discovered that the essential quality of a buttress was weight at the top to ensure downward pressure to counter excessive outward thrust and so pinnacles were used to provide this weight. In addition they helped to throw off the rain and beautify the skyline.

10

Towers and Spires

The primary use of towers was to house bells which, being very heavy, needed strong supports.

Bells were important things in village life not only for calling people to church but in telling the time of day before the clocks came into common use. They were also used for other purposes, to call to arms, to give warning of danger, to drive away witches as well as other uses.

There are three general types of tower to be found in parish churches. The normal position of the parish church tower in this country is in the west end, an arrangement which goes back to pre-conquest church planning. In the Norman period the builders incorporated a central tower many of which are still to be found despite the fact that the towers were often built in a faulty manner causing them to fall down, as can be found at Fyfield church, Essex where the central tower collapsed and has been partially rebuilt and repaired several times. The third type is the detached tower. This was the earliest type and intended to hold the bells and was either wholly detached from the church or only connected with it by some subsidiary part of the building. Such a tower may later become part of the fabric of the church following an extension of the nave aisles The reason for the belfry being detached was almost invariably due to the site problems or bearing of the sub-soil and are found widely distributed throughout the country. A few marshland churches have detached towers some distance from the church due to the desire to avoid settlement of the heavy tower pulling down the main structure.

Sometimes the tower projects externally and is carried on piers with archways on the north and south sides providing a passage for processions so that a complete outdoor circuit of the church may be made whilst remaining on consecrated ground. This arrangement may be seen at Dedham church, Essex.

In Saxon and Medieval times towers were sometimes used for defence purposes and sometimes as guides for travellers by land and sea. At night a beacon fire was lit on the roof, or a lamp was put in one of the openings in an upper story.

The earliest stone towers in English churches are found near the east coast and were probably built as lookouts and refuges during the Viking raids.

FYFIELD, ESSEX.
C12 Central tower – much repaired.

Sometimes the tower was used as a dwelling for the parish priest or guardian of the church and this is frequently evidenced by the provision of an opening looking into the nave from the tower. This allowed the priest to say the night offices without descending to the church. One of these openings may be seen in the east wall of the tower of Deerhurst church, Gloucestershire.

The majority of towers were square but some were round a few rectangular or even triangular, like the thirteenth century tower at Maldon, Essex, which was necessitated by the adjoining road which limited building space. One reason given for round towers was the lack of stone in some areas to form the quoins of the angles. On the other hand it is possible to build a square tower without dressed stone as can be seen at Little Bardfield church, Essex.

Most round towers are of Saxon or Norman origin although one cannot be dogmatic about this as Bardfield Saling church, Essex, has a round tower which was commenced in the early part of the fourteenth century. The building of this church was stopped by the Black Death in 1349 and it was not until after the Black Death that it was completed and the chancel built.

Sometimes towers were enlarged by adding an additional storey or a spire or it may have been impossible to complete it because there was insufficient money or other reasons.

The tower and font are, as a rule, the oldest parts of the church having survived fires, rebuilding and even restoration and will often furnish a clue to the building of the original church. One must beware, however, as it has been known for the font to have been brought from another church.

Saxon

Saxon towers were usually tall and slim with no turret or newel stair.

The round Saxon towers are characteristic of East Anglian church architecture for there are very few in England outside East Anglia. There are only four and the foundations of four others in Essex, two in Cambridgeshire, one in Northants, two in Barkshire, one in Surrey and three in Sussex. There are approximately 170 in East Anglia of which 129 are in Norfolk and 42 in Suffolk.

There being no suitable building stone in East Anglia quoining difficulty was overcome by dispensing with corners and making the towers of circular section. Such towers, especially when they taper upwards as some do, are very strong as is indicated by the great number which have survived the churches to which they were attached.

ROUGHTON, NORFOLK.
Anglo-Saxon round tower.

It is difficult to date these towers unless they have specific Saxon or Norman features such as double or single arched lintel openings, triangular headed openings or round headed Norman window-type openings. The great majority have no specifically Saxon features. Many openings originally cut through the walls were altered in post Saxon or Norman times.

It is not possible to say whether, or to what extent, round towers were built in England specifically for defence purposes. There must have been some, judging by the method of construction. There is, however, a school of thought that it is unlikely that the East Anglican round towers were necessarily used for defence purposes as many were small, some not more than eight to ten feet across and had comparatively thin walls. In addition there was a great risk of fire from timber thatched roofs and timber floors of the towers. It would be easy for the invaders to set fire to the church and roast the defenders out or to their death. It was possible, however, to overcome this by having a vaulted roof to the ground floor which would then allow the tower to be used for defensive purposes. The ground floor of Monkwearmouth church Durham was vaulted in the Saxon period but whether it was vaulted to increase the safety of the tower as a refuge is not known. It is possible that it was used as a refuge as there were no openings on the ground floor, access being obtained by ladder from the nave through an opening fourteen feet above the floor.

On the other hand there are some who are of the opinion that round towers were built for strength and for defensive purposes either as look-outs or to accommodate the villages if there was an attack by the Danes. They are all either near the sea or rivers of East Anglia and, if we ignore any later additions, many have common features which point to a defensive origin. There are no openings low down and none has a western doorway. The entrance to the tower was on the eastern side by means of a narrow arched opening cut straight through the wall and never less than ten feet from the ground access being obtained by a ladder hauled up afterwards. This may be clearly seen in Bosham church, Sussex.

It is known that even as late as the eighteenth century towers were provided for defensive purposes on the turbulent borders of Scotland and Wales and if this was so, how much more necessary would such towers have been on the east coast in pre-Norman days.

There is no doubt that the idea of using church towers as refuges was not foreign to the Saxons. This is evident from the existence of such towers in south Pembrokeshire, in the early twelfth century, which were vaulted in the ground storey and furnished with pigeon-holes in the upper stages and in which the villagers could take refuge when the wild Welshmen made raids into England. Many of these ground storeys are covered with barrell vaults.

A typical tower should have three stages, at least, on the interior, though not always indicated on the exterior by string courses. Of these the top stage would be the belfry, the second stage the ringing chamber and the ground floor a porticus or opening. Such a porticus might be used as a vestry or it might have a subsidiary altar.

Where there are more than three stages to the tower the additional stages must have been built for specific purposes as it is most unlikely that they would have been inserted for decorative purposes, for example, to produce towers of tall slender proportions. It seems likely that the second stage, immediately above

DEERHURST, GLOUCESTERSHIRE.
Gable-headed opening, east side of tower.

the ground floor, was intended for the habitation possibly of the sacristan whose job it was to guard the treasures of the church, for bell-ringing and to keep watch over the altar to prevent theft and profanation. It would be convenient, in fact, necessary for him to live in the tower.

At Deerhurst, Gloucestershire, there is a round-headed doorway about sixteen feet above the floor which would have been reached by a ladder and a small triangular squint to the south through which the sacristan could keep watch. The doorway originally gave access to a gallery long since removed but the stone brackets to the north and south walls close to the west wall were probably part of the gallery supports.

In the third stage is a massive gable-headed double opening, elaborately ornamented, in the east wall overlooking the nave and is almost twenty-eight feet above the nave floor. It is thought that this stage is of later date than those below and specifically built as a chapel. Deerhurst was monastic and the local ealdormen or thegns may well have been generous in their gifts and been granted the special privileges of private chapels in the tower. The fact that the third stage is elaborately ornamented would suggest that the occupiers were people of importance.

There is a further opening of simpler design at a higher level, about forty feet, in the east wall of the fourth stage and now partly above the modern roof of the nave. It is thought that these openings were entrances in the inter-roof spaces. Other examples may be found at Brixworth, Northants, Bosham, Sussex and Earls Barton, Northants.

A belfry is that stage of the tower in which the bell or bells are hung. It is usually, though not always, the top stage, the one below being the ringing chamber. In some cases the original Saxon belfry has been rebuilt or replaced by one of later date, Norman or post Norman. Occasionally a new and additional stage has been added to a belfry in which case it is generally plain that the original belfry was the stage below as at Bosham, Sussex, Skipwith, Yorkshire and Barnack, Northants.

Belfry openings are frequently called windows but they are not windows. All Saxon windows are single or double splayed but belfry openings like the very great majority of doorways are cut straight through the wall. Belfry openings are neither windows nor doorways they are sound holes and are better known as 'belfry openings'. They are frequently double and rectangular in shape. Each half is covered with a round arch the two central meetings ends of which would, as it were, hang in the air if they were not supported from below by a mid-wall shaft, round, square, polygonal or rectangular with rounded edges, earlier types frequently having bulging baluster shafts. Between the shaft and the arch head is a rectangular through-stone the length of the wall thickness, hence its name. This held up the arch and is itself supported by the shaft beneath. The jambs are normally of through-stones two or more to each jamb in vertical arrangement and there are square or rectangular imposts above the jambs, corresponding to the impost above the mid-wall shaft. There may also be similarly square-edged bases or plinths to both jambs and shafts.

EARLS BARTON, NORTHAMPTONSHIRE.
Saxon tower with 'arched lintel' openings with 'bulging balusters' and 'long' and 'short' work.

The arch heads may be cut from one high flat lintel stone or from two half-lengths, laterally disposed lintel stones to provide two apparent arches, one to each half opening. These may be called 'arched lintels' though they are not arches at all but lintels. Earls Barton, Northants. has a quintuple opening of double arched lintels. Account must be taken of local variations and

CORRINGHAM, ESSEX.
Late C11 tower with pyramid roof.

preferences as well as different rates of development in different districts.

A few belfries have heads and jambs to the openings composed of rough rubble work especially in East Anglia where there is a lack of stone. Others were formed of stones cut roughly to shape and different lengths or in a rather more advanced character were made of very few stones of varying lengths, cut to length and to the appropriate curved shape.

Characteristic of double openings is the mid-wall shaft, either a column or bulging baluster. Columns from seven to eight feet in length to three to four feet or less were well known in Roman Britain and the Saxons would have been familiar with both forms and re-expressed the motifs in their own style. The result was the double opening with bulging baluster or straight shaft and is a characteristic Saxon creation. Short bulging balusters were used in Roman Britain for a variety of purposes, for example, supports for hypercausts, legs of furniture, decoration for tombs, altars etc.

The bulging baluster does not occur in the Rhineland of Germany and very rarely in France so it is fair to assume that this motif did not come from Europe and, therefore, the bulging baluster, banded or unbanded and straight columns may be regarded as specific Saxon features inspired by, or perhaps developed from, Roman forms but re-expressed in their own style and used widely for their own specific purposes.

The baluster appears to have been more popular in the North and both kinds, plain and banded, may be found. Both forms were used indiscriminately until balusters gradually disappeared under Norman influence which began before the Conquest.

The banded balusters fall into two groups, the majority being where the bands are raised on the baluster surface, that is where the background has been cut away to leave the bands projecting. Others have the bands formed by two quirks cut fairly deeply round the shaft the intervening strip of surface being rounded off. These bands do not project.

The Saxons also used pilaster strips which were strips of stone varying from four inches in width, as at Earls Barton church, to over twelve inches at Langford, Oxfordshire, and twenty inches at Guildford, Surrey and the projections from two and six inches.

The general opinion is that pilasters were used for decorative purposes to break up the plainness of the outside stone walls in imitation of the struts and beams in the wooden ones where strengthening was not required, for example, in the upper parts of towers. The pilasters in the lower parts may have performed a structural function particularly where the strips penetrate the wall to a foot or more. If they are only 'toothed' in they are for decorative purposes only. Sometimes short lengths were used to make pointed or round arches and 'Y' and 'V' shapes to connect vertical strips. The pilaster strip was a simple but effective way of breaking up a flat surface and was a great favourite in the tenth century.

One wonders why the Saxons thought that their walls needed strengthening. They were magnificent builders better that the Normans, a surprising amount of whose work was shoddy. Saxon foundations were strong and their mortar little inferior to the mortar of the Romans. There is quite an amount of evidence as to the quality of Saxon work. Monkwearmouth, Durham, church tower is an outstanding example, it is only eleven feet square with walls one foot nine inches thick not bonded into the nave walls and sixty feet in height and has continued to stand with no other support than its own good mortar and firm foundations through nine hundred years of neglect and abuse. How many Norman towers have fallen? Many fell soon after they were built, one being the central tower at Rottingdean, Sussex, which was blown down within a century in spite of being supported by nave, chancel and at least one transept. Some Norman piers, such as those at Winchester, were of a thin shell of ashlar filled not with rubble concrete but with any rubbish available, including mud. In contrast to this, compare the Norman south-west crossing pier in Peterborough Cathedral the only foundation of which is the Saxon plaster flooring of the ruined abbey church below. Saxon plaster flooring was indeed good if it could serve as a support for the enormously greater load of the later Norman church.

Norman Period

The Norman towers were usually squat with corbel tables and staircase turret. Sometimes the tower is at the west end but is often situated between the nave and the chancel, a central tower with or without transepts. Occasionally in East Anglia the west tower is round like Tuttington, Norfolk.

In P. J. Helm's book, *Exploring Saxon and Norman England* he says that,

> 'It seems that in the erection of church towers and castle keeps an average growth in height of almost ten feet per season was normal, operations being usually suspended from September to Easter, though when the matter was urgent, work continued as long as possible and even night shifts working by candle-light have been recorded!'

OTHERY, SOMERSET.
C14 Crossing tower.

It is also recorded that Ely tower fell down in the fourteenth century and it took twenty years to rebuild.

The Normans when constructing heavy central towers frequently overreached themselves and the towers collapsed. In fact one might ask of any large Norman church, 'When was the tower re-built?' and so it is not surprising that a thirteenth century petition used at Evensong ran 'And deare Lord, support our roof this night that it may in no wyse fall upon us and styfle us. Amen.'

Early English And Decorated Periods

Except in the East Mercian stone-producing district that is the north-east end of the stone belt around Peterborough where masons were plentiful and the material was at hand, it was not until the beginning of the fifteenth century that the western tower became a general feature of the parish church.

Thirteenth century towers are usually simple unbuttressed structures, occasionally pleasantly ornamented with arcading and good windows but otherwise exhibiting no great richness of design or execution. It must be remembered, of course, that buttresses may have been added at a later date. Where there was a lack of good building stone timber-framed towers were erected.

GREAT BURSTEAD, ESSEX.
Low C14 tower, angle buttresses and timber parapet spire. Note putlog holes.

During the Decorated period there appears to have been even less enthusiasm for western towers as this period was mainly occupied in enlarging the naves of churches.

Perpendicular Period

Although towers were built in the thirteenth century and fourteenth centuries it is to the fifteenth century, the Perpendicular period, that we must turn for our finest towers.

There were two principal areas. One was Somerset at the south-eastern end of the stone belt which likewise possessed an ample supply of masons. The others were Yorkshire, Lincolnshire and East Anglia. The first two of these regions had ample facilities for building, the latter had none.

It so happened that East Anglia with its continental connections was the richest wool district in all England. Nowhere in the country are there such magnificent churches as in the small towns and villages of Norfolk and Suffolk. East Anglia had no masons and building stone was hard to come by.

The local builders devised a technique entirely of their own. The walling was built of flint rubble or anything available and in many cases Flemish brick was used. The whole of the outside of the building including the lofty west tower was covered with a panelling formed of applied stone strips like the tracery of windows. This panelled wall was filled up with what is known as 'flush-work' formed of flint nodules broken in halves to produce two approximately smooth faces. These smooth blank faces of the split flint stone were then set in between the stone strips to form the facing of the wall.

The towers of the wool churches were of the most elaborate design. Their angles were frequently embellished with decorative buttresses, some set diagonally but more often in right-angled pairs known as angled buttresses. The summits of the towers were parapeted and pinnacled.

There were usually three storeys. The lowest formed part of the nave with a wide lofty arch joining the two. In the west wall would be a fine window above

RANWORTH, NORFOLK.
Lofty C15 W. tower with traceried sound holes.

the doorway. The first floor of the tower was the ringing chamber which would probably have good windows in each of the four walls. In Norfolk we find square openings misnamed 'sound holes' but they are actually 'air holes' to allow light and air into the chamber. They are very nicely traceried like the one at Southrepps, Norfolk. The upper belfrey storey was the most elaborate of all, great play being made with the fine louvred openings of each face of the tower to allow the full force of the bells to be heard across the countryside.

Some towers had, instead of buttresses, circular or polygonal turrets passing up each angle or a turret and buttresses.

Where timber was plentiful some towers were built with oak frameworks filled in with a form of cement like the lower storey of Blackmore tower in Essex. This tower contains some of the finest timber framing in the country.

Many of the early towers lack the original roof as frequently battlements or a spire has been added or even another storey.

Top left: BRIGHTLINGSEA, ESSEX.
Late C15 tower with diagonal buttresses, fine windows and large bell openings.

Above: GETHINGTHORPE, ESSEX.
Late C15 brick tower.

Left: BLACKMORE, ESSEX.
Late C15 impressive timber tower, weatherboarded with lean-to roofs and shingle broach spire. One of the most impressive timber towers in England

Spires

The usually accepted origin of the spire is in the pyramid form of roof of the Norman tower which later developed into the most impressive of all Gothic inventions.

Structurally the function of the spire is to wight the tower against the thrusts of the arches that abut upon it. Architecturally it enriches the skyline of the building and emphasises the monumental character of the structure.

The pyramid form of the tower roof of the Normans became taller developing into a spire covered with oak shingles or tiles, lead or copper and during the thirteenth century and early fourteenth century we find 'broach' spires which are octagonal and placed on a square tower rising without an intermediate parapet. Each of the four angles of the tower not covered by base of the spire is filled in with an inclined mass of masonry built into the oblique sides of the spire and carried up to a point of each of the diagonal sides. It is this mass of masonry which is known as the 'broach'. Where stone was scarce wooden spires were common. These were octagonal like the broach spire but each of the four angles were chamfered instead of having broaches.

The broach spire gradually expanded until the base became of equal width to the tower itself and thus absorbed the whole of the tower roof.

The reduction in the pitch of roofs brought about the use of lead and the consequent disappearance of eaves in favour of the lead box gutter concealed behind a parapet caused these latter features, the gutter and the parapet, to become the universal method of capping walls of all buildings including towers.

As the old form of roof disappeared parapet spires crowned many of the great towers of the churches of the wool period of the fourteenth and fifteenth centuries. The parapet spire rose from inside the parapet which was frequently battlemented with pinnacles rising from the angles. This type of spire rose from the centre of the tower allowing a pathway round it so allowed scaffolding and ladders to be erected within the tower top instead of from the ground level and so made repairs to the spire much easier and less costly. Some spires became very slender and are known as 'needle' spires or 'Hertfordshire' spikes.

The box gutter was inside the parapet having gargoyle water spouts to discharge the water. The medieval mind thought that evil forces were always attacking the church so figures guarding the church may be found on the side of church towers. Usually they take the form of giants holding clubs or staves and examples may be seen at High Easter, Essex; Lechlade and Fairford, Gloucestershire.

11

Porches

Apart from the tower the porch is usually the most prominent projection on the exterior of the church. The protection of church doorways from the rain and wind by means of porches can be found in this country as far back as the seventh century when the doorway to the church was frequently in the west end. The doorway was flanked by walls to form an entrance porch and in some cases was later raised to form a bell tower. There are, however, a number of examples of pre-Conquest south porches, one being at Brixworth, Northamptonshire.

It was some centuries, however, before the porch made a general appearance in English architecture. There are a number of porches attached to the larger English parish churches of the twelfth and thirteenth centuries as at Cley, next the sea, Norfolk; Wotton, Surrey, Yapton, Sussex. Where stone was scarce clumsy wooden structures were sometimes built, although in Essex there are some exceptionally good timber porches chiefly of the latter half of the fifteenth century. Among the best are Margaretting; South Benfleet; Doddinghurst and Runwell. When the naves of parish churches began to be reconstructed the porch became a universal feature.

Porches will often be found dated and if there is only one it will usually be found on the south side. If there are two the most important is generally the south porch but where the manor house or the greater part of the village was on the north side then the chief entrance would be assigned to the north porch, an example of which may be seen at Thaxted, Essex. In later times, particularly in the fifteenth century, there were two porches, south and north.

In medieval times porches were very important places and because they had many uses great care was bestowed upon them.

The baptismal service was in three parts, the making of the catechumen (preparation for baptism), the blessing of the font followed by the Sacrament of Baptism. The first part was held in the porch and other two parts being held at the font in the church.

The medieval marriage service was short and the first part, comprising the troth-plight or contract sealed with the ring, being carried out in the porch. This part of the service usually preceded the Nuptial Mass and the feast that

Above: MATCHING, ESSEX.
C15 Timber-framed and plastered marriage feast house.

GREAT MASSINGHAM, NORFOLK.
Fine C13 porch. Tall entrance arch, octagonal buttresses with tall pinnacles and rich arcading on each side.

followed was called 'bride ale'. In Chaucer's 'Wife of Bath's Prologue' the wife says 'of husbands at church door have I had five'.

In late medieval times labourers' cottages were not large enough to hold all the guests invited to a wedding and so there was often a large room in the parish, conveniently near the church, kept for the purpose and sometimes called the 'marriage feast house' but usually 'church house'. Essex still has a marriage feast house which is still used for its original purpose. It is near the west end of Matching church and was built by a Mr Chimney in the fifteenth century. It is a long building with a room filling almost the whole of the upstairs and having four rooms below. One may muse on the different brides and bridegrooms who have climbed the stairs to the upper room during the past five hundred years and still do so. As soon as a parish had a church house, church ales and parish gatherings of all sorts could be held in it instead of the nave of the church which could now be seated and pewed.

Much of the traditional merry-making associated with parish churches was brought to an end by the Reformation and more particularly by the growth of Puritan feeling during the late sixteenth and early seventeenth centuries.

Although many of these church houses survive few are still used for parish purposes most of them being now in private ownership.

The porch was pre-eminently the spot for discussing parish business because it formed a convenient shelter and halting place for the worshippers. It was a focus of attraction to gossips and traders and formed a very convenient rallying point for the transaction of business. There is a record that in 1610 mortgages were paid off in the south porch of Ecclesfield church near Sheffield. In 1601 Thomas Clarke raised money for urgent expenses by mortgaging land in Ham and Oakley Wood, Gloucestershire, to John Crowther, the money to be handed over in the north porch of Cheltenham, Gloucestershire, parish church every 25th March. At Lechlade church, Gloucestershire, there is a bargaining stone just by the porch doorway. Bargains were struck by the parties by putting their hands on top of the stone. Public documents and covenants were frequently signed in church porches. At Eye church, Suffolk there is a tablet in the porch inscribed:

> Seale not to soone lest thou repent to late,
> Yet help thy friend, but hinder not thy state.
> I ought the lende or burrow truly pay,
> Me give, me take advantage though thou may,
> Let conscience be they guid, so helpe they friend,
> With loving peace and concord make thy end
>
> 1601.

Women who had broken marriage vows had to do penance in the porch. A western porch was often called a 'Galilee' porch for its being the final station in the Sunday procession, the priest at the head symbolising Our Lord going before His disciples into Galilee after the Resurrection. An example may be seen at Dedham, Essex.

DEDHAM, ESSEX.
Tall early C16 W. tower with ground floor forming a passageway from N to S with panelled vault. Often referred to as a 'Galilee' porch.

Occasionally the parish church service was enlived by a public penance. For long after the Reformation the Church maintained control of morals and churchwardens were required among their other duties, to report to the church courts all lapses from moral integrity, sexual immorality, failure to attend church or receive Communion or other offences against ecclesiastical law. Persons so reported were brought before the church courts and the sentences imposed ranged from ex-communication and fines to public penance.

Public penance, for the persons involved, must have been an extremely daunting prospect. In a small closely-knit community where each person was well known to all the others, the penitent had to appear before the whole congregation and make public confession of his or her offence. It is not too difficult to imagine the feelings of the unfortunate person compelled to undergo the punishment.

At Charminster, Dorset, in 1631 Ursula Green was ordered by the Dean of Salisbury to come to the parish church before morning prayer covered with a white sheet but the face uncovered and a white rod in her hand where she was to stand until the service began. The parish clerk was then to lead the penitent by the hand and place her in the middle alley of the church or against the pulpit where she shall stand until the second lesson be ended and then in a penitent manner make her confession before the congregation.

Coroners sometimes held their courts in the porch and public notices were exhibited as indeed they are today.

Top left: LECHLADE, GLOUCESTERSHIRE.
Bargaining stone. South porch.

Above: BOXFORD, SUFFOLK.
C14 Timber N. porch with rib-vault with tiercerons. Elaborate tracery in side openings. Possibly one of the earliest timber porches in the country.

Left: SINGLETON, SUSSEX.
Simple C14 porch.

The church porch was often of great size and frequently schools were held in it. John Evelyn referring to the year 1624 said that 'one Friar taught us at the church porch at Wotton' in Surrey. Later, William Bray writing in 1818 stated that the village schoolmaster of Wotton taught in the porch. The porches of Berkeley church, Gloucestershire and Malmesbury, Wiltshire, were used as schools until the 1870s. Even three storeyed porches may be found as at Burford and Cirencester, Oxfordshire. These upper rooms may have been used to house the priest, to store and preserve saintly relics, as a strong room for the books and documents of the parish and as depository for wills with perhaps a custodian living there.

In the fifteenth and sixteenth centuries it was common for the south aisle to be re-built by one of the Guilds who, by this time, had grown very rich, or perhaps by a local benefactor as an act of piety. This re-building would incorporate a south porch many of which were extremely fine and often had two storeys. Sometimes it provided accommodation for a chantry priest and as it was frequently one of the conditions of a charity bequest that the priest should teach boys Latin, the language used for church services up to the Reformation, the room was used as a school. Sometimes a fireplace was installed and windows overlooking the nave. These upper chambers were common by the fourteenth century and may be seen in many East Anglian churches, for example, Eye, Suffolk and St Nicholas, Kings Lynn, Norfolk. Examples of those containing fireplaces may be seen at Crowcombe, Somerset and Northleach, Gloucestershire.

From the time of Edward II (1307–1327) each parish had to furnish and equip soldiers for the Miltia service. The armour was kept in the church for safety and by the time of Henry VIII this obligation was vested primarily in the churchwardens who were required to have it ready when necessary. At Mendlesham church, Suffolk, over the north porch is a room which has been used as an armoury since *c*1470–*c*1610. It is much as it was in medieval times with its helms, breast-plates, pikes and other items and the door is especially strengthened with ironwork and several great locks.

The sixteenth century also saw the provision of a stately porch to the north aisle but this does not mean that earlier north porches cannot be found, for example at Little Sampford and Thaxted, Essex.

Before entering a south porch always look at the stonework of the doorway to see if there is an hour or mass dial or perhaps graffiti such as votive crosses.

A porch may have a holy water stoup either just outside or inside the door into the church. These stoups were abolished at the Reformation and covered over but many have been found and uncovered, some still being in use today. Everyone entering the church dipped his or her finger into the water and made the sign of the Cross, 'to put him in remembrance both of the promise made

Top left: BURFORD, OXFORDSHIRE.
Elaborate S.porch, *c*1450, of three storeys with blind traceried arches and three canopied image niches. Tall crocketed pinnacles. Inside is a fan vault.

Above: LAVENHAM, SUFFOLK.
Spectacular C15 S.porch. The front is panelled and traceried with a central niche and a frieze of six shields of the de Vare family (Earls of Oxford). Fan vault inside.

Left: SANDON, ESSEX.
C16 S.porch of red brick with diaper pattern of blue bricks. Brick windows of two lights, stepped battlements on a trefoiled corbal frieze. Corner buttresses are diagonal. Over outer doorway is an ogee-arched niche. Roof is rib-vaulted.

at the time of baptism and of the shedding and sprinkling of Christ's blood upon the Cross'.

There may be some stone seats; or a niche over the doorway for a figure of the patron saint although many of these were despoiled during the Reformation of the Civil War. Parishioners travelling from far-flung villages would arrive some time before the service began in order to rest on the seats and refresh themselves prior to the commencement of the service.

Do not miss the porch roof. Sometimes it may be of timber or vaulted in stone. If it is vaulted note the bosses at the intersection of the ribs as they are much easier to see than those high up in the roof of the nave. Examples may be seen in the north and south porches of Thaxed church, Essex and at Cley, next the sea, Norfolk. The roof of the Cley porch has some intriging bosses, one of a boy with his trousers down being caned, and another of a woman chasing a fox with her stick.

12

Doors and Doorways

I suppose that in many ways the doorway through which we pass into the church reminds us of the vivid past which is immediately drawn to our attention on entering an old parish church. The quite different and varied periods of building, upheaval at the time of the Reformation, battle, plague and profanity, the social condition of the people, the hustle and bustle of everyday life, all this is summed up in this quotation from the *History and Imagery in British Churches* by M. D. Anderson.

> 'As we climb to hill-top churches, gaze at intriguing altars converted into fonts, or meet the enigmatic eyes of foliate masks which recall both prehistoric sacrifice and medieval jollifications, we can hardly fail to be impressed by a sense of historical continuity. Absorbing rather than destroying, enriched from the strangest variety of sources, the stream of English history flows on steadily, all the stronger because its source has not been marked by the smoking cataracts of sudden, violent change.'

In Saxon times and in the twelfth and thirteenth centuries doors were very strongly built of thick oak boards to resist attacks by robbers or invaders. These doors were greatly increased in strength by the wrought-iron work of the smith.

The church offered sanctuary to a fugitive whether from justice or from the spite of his enemies, until a trial could be arranged. Acknowledgement of the right of sanctuary was included in the laws of King Ina of Wessex in 690 and those of King Alfred in 887. William the Conqueror introduced a scale of penalties for sanctuary breaking such as, 100 shillings for taking a fugitive form an abbey, 20 shillings from a parish church and 10 shillings for a chapel. At first only the altar and the inner buildings of the church afforded sanctuary. Archbishop Becket sought sanctuary at the altar but was nevertheless cut down. Later, however, sanctuary was extended to cover all the space between the church and its outer walls. Some churches had a special seat called a 'Fridstool' or chair of peace.

During the Middle Ages the period of sanctuary was generally forty days during which the felon was perfectly safe and the officers of the law could only seek by argument to induce him to go into banishment. The Rites of Durham (C16), author unknown, give a full account of the procedure by which a fugitive was admitted and the coroner summoned to hear his confession. If he agreed to

DEERHURST, GLOUCESTERSHIRE.
Saxon gable-headed doorway.

DEERHURST, GLOUCESTERSHIRE.
Saxon lintel over doorway to porticus.

banishment he was arrayed in special garments and escorted to a port. In smaller churches the procedure was simpler and only the validity of the felon's oath ensured his taking the journey overseas. It has been estimated that for several centuries there were a thousand persons in sanctuary during a given year and this is probably no exaggeration.

Taking sanctuary in a parish church required no structural provisions but controversy has ranged over the question as to whether the decorated closing rings on some church doors were connected with the right of sanctuary. One theory is that the fugitive who had hold of the ring could not be forced away without breaking sanctuary and the Constable of Arundel was made to go barefoot to the shrine of St Richard of Chichester in penance for having taken a thief who had hold of the door handle of Arundel church.

Against this it has been argued that the whole of the churchyard was included in the right of sanctuary and that the fugitive was already safe when he had reached the door. The truth may be mid-way and even those who were already in sanctuary may have clung to the door ring begging for admittance.

Some of these closing rings were elaborate and of unusual size and ornament like those at Durham Cathedral; Westcot Barton, Oxfordshire; Talaton, Devon and Fingringhoe, Essex. The privilege of sanctuary was abolished in the seventeenth century.

It is always a good idea to survey the exterior of a church as there may be a number of doorways to discover some not having doors but being filled in with rubble or brick. There will usually be a south doorway and a priest's doorway on the south side of the chancel near the sanctuary and probably a north or west doorway most likely now unused.

Saxon, C7–1066

STOW-IN-LINDSEY, LINCOLNSHIRE. Saxon doorway in north transept with irregular shaped voussoirs which are set along the radii of the arch. The left jamb has long and short arrangement of stones. All the stones are single stones right through the

Doorways differ according to their date. The early Saxon doorways were generally of a single order, high and narrow the door-head being either gable-headed composed of two stones forming the two sides of a triangle or semicircular with the head or lintel formed of, perhaps, one or two shaped stones. Where large stones were available they ran right through the width of the wall. The jambs, in the early part of the period, were square with very large impost blocks but later, were reduced in size and were sometimes roughly moulded. It is from the impost block that the arch springs.

The lintel was not considered to be a safe method of construction as it could be snapped by the weight bearing down from above. To relieve and discharge this weight an arch was often built over the lintel. This space, called the tympanum, later received decorative treatment, a good example of which may be seen at Kilpeck, Herefordshire. Sometimes a form of decoration was attempted on the impost block and the jambs may have a column or even a

BARNACK, NORTHAMPTONSHIRE.
First half C11 but could be earlier. Doorjambs are not rebated, the door shut flat across the inside. This was common in the late Saxon period. Round head composed of long voussoirs and plain slab imposts. Strips also go round the head but rest on their own independent square corbels projecting just above the imposts. The doorway has vertical strips on both sides resting, like the others, on square corbels near the ground. The stone seen above the keystone of the arch head is a corbel stone supporting a pilaster strip, part of which may just be seen.

HADSTOCK, ESSEX.
Saxon door c1020 constructed from four wide planks with joints of splayed rebates and frame formed of D- sectioned oak ledges the top ledge being bent to the shape of the door's head. The whole is fastened together with iron clench nails which pass through the ledges and lozenge-shaped elongated iron washers which were spread or wrapped over the ledges to prevent them from splitting when the points of the clenches were hammered over.

moulding around the arch. Some of the semi-circular heads were true arches composed of stones running through from front to back.

The doors were constructed of thick oak boards showing tool marks. These boards were placed vertically outside and horizontally inside and fastened together with long wrought iron nails driven right through and clenched on the inside. The door was also strengthened with iron straps.

It is rare to find a Saxon door but one may be found at Hadstock, Essex. This door was constructed in the eleventh century, prior to the Conquest, of four wide planks which must have been well seasoned at the time as the joints, which are rebated, have never opened. the boards are held together by ledges forming the interior frame of the door and are made of D-sectioned oak, the top ledge having been bent, either by steam or dry heat, to the semi-circular shape of the door head. There are also three horizontal ledges. All the ledges are fastened to the boards by means of iron washers and long iron clench nails. The washers are elongated so that they encircle the ledges and prevent splitting when the clench nails were knock through, the points of the clenches being bent over the washers.

It is thought that the church was built by Cnut as a 'thank you' for his victory over Edmund Ironside at the battle of Assendon in 1016 but there is also a school of thought that Hadstock is not the minister church of Cnut but that the honour belongs to Ashingdon, Essex.

Norman 1066–1189

When we look at some of the doors and doorways which were so beautifully decorated in the early centuries one is inclined to wonder why this was so. Christ told the people 'I am the door, by me if any man enter in he shall be saved', and so great care was lavished on the entrance to God's house.

The following poem from *The Village Church* by C. Lessingham Smith written in 1868 aptly describes an early Norman door:

> 'Ere through the Norman door we pass,
> Note well the structure plain and old,
> The time worn stone, the oaken mass with
> iron hinge of graceful mould.
> Outside it sleeps the world so cold!
> Inside, O what awakening love
> Reminds us oft of Him who told
> His faithful flock, "I am the door".'

Doorways were, as a rule, the most decorative feature of the small parish churches and practically every church had a north and south door usually near the west end of the nave.

BICESTER, OXFORDSHIRE.
C12 arch showing voussoirs forming facing on each side with centre filled with rubble plastered over.

The Normans continued with the semicircular head but now it was a true arch constructed of separate wedge-shaped stones known as 'voussoirs' which did not, however, run right through the wall as did the Saxon stones, but formed the faces on either side of the arch the centre being filled with rubble and plastered over. This form of arch was known as 'arcuated' where the opening is spanned, not by a lintel, as in the Saxon 'trabeated' style but by an arch of separate stones. this did not mean that the Normans did not construct doors with lintels and in many examples the actual door opening is square, the tympanum between the lintel resting on the impost blocks, and the arch being filled and frequently elaborately carved. The disadvantage of not running the voussoirs right through the wall was that elaborate centring or temporary support was required during construction.

These simple arches usually had plain square jambs with impost blocks chamfered on the lower edge. Occasionally the angle of the jamb was worked into a shaft having a capital and base. The capital was formed of a top member called the abacus from which the arch springs, the underneath being a cushion shaped stone the top part of which was square but round below. Connecting the top of the shaft was a half-round ring moulding called 'necking'. This form

Top left: LITTLE TOTHAM, ESSEX.
Early Norman north doorway showing voussoirs and plain square impost stones. Door has remains of original ironwork.

Above: AXMOUTH, DEVON.
Scalloped capital and necking.

Left: AXMOUTH, DEVON.
Volute capital, necking and hollow-chamfered abacus.

PAMPISFORD, CAMBRIDGESHIRE.
Norman south doorway with arcaded tympanum having ten small arches arranged radially around rim and filled with figures depicting the story of St John-the-Baptist. The arches are separated by tiny piers. The imposts are chamfered and the shaft capitals have primitive carving.

GREAT CANFIELD, ESSEX.
Norman cushion capital carved with two birds pecking a bearded face.

of capital was the most direct way of establishing an affinity between the square abacus and the circular shaft.

There were two variations of this capital one being similar in shape but cut with vertical flutes known as the scalloped capital. The other which came later in the period is called the volute capital and is carved with four leaves springing from the necking and bending over under the angles of the square part and ending in volutes. Sometimes the capitals had elaborate sculpture as may be seen at Stoke Dry, Leicestershire; Wakerley, Northants; and Liverton, Cleveland.

Good examples of Norman doorways are at Bishopsteignton, Devon; Windrush, Gloucestershire; Heckingham, Norfolk; Iffley, Oxfordshire; Tutbury, Staffordshire and some wonderful examples in Yorkshire at Adel, Alne, Berkin, Stillingfleet and Thorpe Salvin to name a few.

Perhaps one of the best examples of a Norman doorway is the most remarkable south doorway at Kilpeck church, Hereford and Worcester. It is beautifully sculptured representing on the two jambs of its arches, Eden, The temptation and fall of man, represented on the right-hand jamb as eating the forbidden fruit of the tree of knowledge of good and evil. On the left-hand capital are the lion and dragon contending, and on the left-hand jamb the Serpent is carved with head downwards as though the Power of Evil was defeated in the conflict. On the left-hand column are two figures believe to represent 'Church' and 'State', uniquely dressed in peaked caps, leather jerkins and trousers. The upper one holds a long weapon which may be a javelin or a sword and the lower one holds a palm branch.

KILPECK CHURCH, HEREFORD & WORCESTER
South doorway.

The tympanum has a formalised Tree of Life and is supported on a lintel cut with chevron. The abaci are carved with diaper pattern and support two moulded orders, the outer enriched with chevron ornament and a series of carvings which include a beak-head, dragon, head with heads and necks of two beasts protruding from the jaws and beak-head of muzzled bear.

The splayed label is unusually supported on the abaci and is enriched with carving terminating on each side in a large grotesque beast-head. The intervening surface of the label is filled with a series of nine medallions joined together by grotesque heads of monsters with open mouths.

The carving throughout this delightful Norman church is remarkable and well worth a visit.

The Normans soon overcame the use of elaborate centring by evolving the compound arch which was built up of concentric steps or recessed orders, a form devised to economise masonry.

Another important result was that it ensured easy fitting as small stones could be readily handled by one or two men. The method was to lay the innermost order of arch-stones or voussoirs on a narrow centring of timber and when it was complete and set-off another order overlapping on each side was laid on it, the process being repeated until the desired thickness of arch was built. To soften the effect of the sharp edges the orders were moulded with three-quarter rounds or bowtels as they are termed.

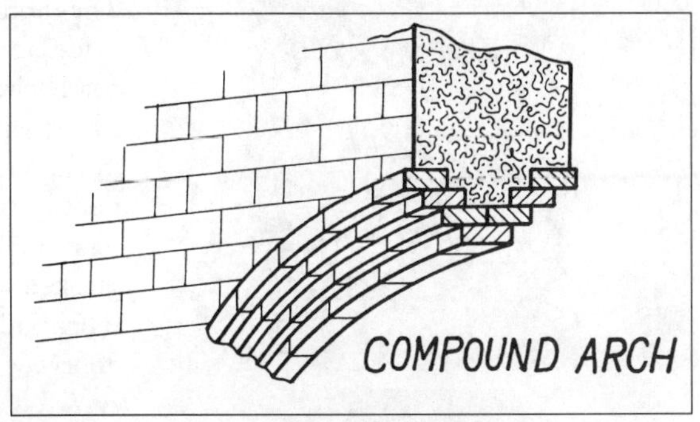

FIGURE 4.

These compound arches required jambs worked with a series of recesses and each of these angles might be worked into a shaft carved out of one piece of stone and not detached as they became in the thirteenth century although it is possible to find some detached shafts. The abacus or impost block was rarely omitted, its upper angle being square and the lower slightly hollow-chamfered. Between these two there was usually a V-shaped groove or quirk. The deeper the depth of the vertical face the earlier the period. Any mouldings were simple rounds and hollows.

Later in the period the mouldings became highly ornamental and usually in low relief. The favourite ornaments were chevron or zig-zag which was probably the most popular, the cable which looked like a rope, billet which was formed by cutting away portions of a round moulding, pellet-like round beads, lozenge, diamond and double-cone with the nail-head which was a later addition. Beakheads formed of grotesques may be found round the arch of the doorway

BUTTSBURY, ESSEX.
The north door is Anglo-Saxon and is made up of five boards and originally had nearly circular ledges fixed to its inner side by the same riveting method used at Hadstock. The planks also had similar rebated joints. Later, probably during the Norman transitional period the door was cross-planked and the dragon head type ironwork added. Re-shaped to fit later doorway.

BUTTSBUY, ESSEX.
Interior of north door.

and fine examples of these may be seen at Kilpeck, Hereford and Worcester, Elkstone, Gloucestershire, Adel and Fishlake, Yorkshire.

The doorways of this period are one of the chief glories of Norman churches and it is the detail of such doorways which makes them into works of art radiating exuberance and setting off the broad simplicity of surface and design of the whole church.

The Norman doors were formed of narrow boards arranged perpendicularly and nailed to wider horizontal boards on the inner side. Sometimes the hinges take the form of plain prolonged straps, as at Southchurch, Essex, but often the ends are turned into short scrolls like the ironwork to be seen at Navestock, Castle Hedingham; Margaret Roding and Wrabness, Essex and at Stillingfleet, Yorkshire, where the hinges were wrought with ships and dragons after the Viking form of decoration. Besides the two hinges there is often a central band which is similarly treated and so the whole door is covered with ironwork which added to its strength and produced rich effect.

Frequently the straps end in large crescent scrolls on each side which resemble a highly floriated letter 'C' which is believed to stand for St Clement the patron saint of smiths. These large scrolls sometimes cover the whole door, Essex has more extant Norman doors than any other county and may be seen at Willingale Spain, Eastwood, Waltham Abbey, Margaret Roding, Castle Hedingham and Little Totham, to name a few. At Buttsbury, Essex, the ends of the 'Cs' are treated in a similar manner to Stillingfleet and terminate in dragon heads. This ironwork is very interesting but would seem to have belonged to an earlier door. Other examples of fine ironwork may be seen at St Margaret's, Leicester, Edstaston, Salop, Compton, Berkshire and Merton, Surrey. Two doors which have exceptional ironwork are at Skipwith, Yorkshire and Hormead, Hertfordshire.

Early English, 1189–1280

The Early English period brought quite a number of differences to the Norman work, in the mouldings, capitals, shape of the shafts and especially the introduction of the pointed arch. This style of architecture known as Gothic was to usher in the splendid ecclesiastical buildings of the thirteenth and fourteenth centuries a style which covered the period when England was becoming more settled, when the distinction between Norman and Saxon was becoming less marked and when the complete autocracy of the sovereign had been destroyed by the nobles as a result of Magna Carta in 1215 and the Provisions of Oxford in 1237.

The great bulk of parish church building during this period was in additions and alterations to existing buildings and consisted, mainly, of lengthening chancels or rebuilding them on a larger scale, adding aisles and transeptal chapels although transepts went out of fashion later in the period when the Benedictines announced that such a plan was not suitable for a great church.

The Early English builders made their buildings as austere as possible as a symbol of the renunciation of the flesh and of worldly riches. This was encouraged by the Dominican and Franciscan friars who were now beginning to flock into the country.

The characteristic feature of the period was the form of the arch which was acutely pointed and known as the lancet arch like the windows of the period. This type of arch exerted less side thrust that the Norman semicircular arch and was much stronger enabling the height of all openings to be increased, e.g. windows, doorways, and archways, without detracting in any way from its ability to hold up the mass of masonry and timbering overhead.

During the Transitional period between the Norman and Early English periods arches tended to became slightly pointed and these may be found with scalloped capitals to the jambs.

The arch is now moulded with deeply cut rounds and hollows made easier by the increasing use of the chisel instead of the axe for stone carving. Previously carving, especially in Norman work, had been in very low relief clinging closely to the stone. In the Early English period considerable undercutting was achieved and it is fascinating to compare how the later thirteenth-century stone carver loved to bring his designs out in high relief and made the formal clinging patterns cut by his predecessors sprout from the stone. These beautiful mouldings were the delight of the Early English mason who concentrated on this form of decoration instead of ornament and because they were so deeply cut their projection was prominent in the ill-lit churches of this period. The one ornament which is characteristic of the period is the 'dog-tooth' and which originated from the old nailhead pattern by increased undercutting until it became a series of completely hollowed-out pyramids. This form of decoration may be found round the arches or between the orders.

In its fully developed Early English form the decoration of capitals became either a deeply undercut, very formalised, pattern of leaves known as 'stiff leaf' which stood out stiffly from the capital on long stalks, giving a strong feeling of supporting the weight of the arch above and sometimes having human heads carved amidst the foliage, or a deeply grooved pattern of concentric rings of mouldings.

The jambs followed the Norman pattern of recesses each with a shaft, perhaps one or two or even three orders of columns but whereas in the Norman period the columns were attached, that is carved out of the solid stone, now the shafts are generally detached from the jamb and became a characteristic feature of Early English work. This increased desire to have details free standing showed an increased interest in space. They were no longer, unlike the Normans, so interested in mass but wished to create a feeling of spaciousness by allowing the eye to travel past objects in the immediate foreground to see the possibilities of further spaces beyond.

Many of the smaller parish churches have the plainest of doorways with a one order arch chamfered on the intrados with a hood-mould over and a moulded impost block.

Some good examples of Early English doorways may be seen at, West Walton, Norfolk; Skelton (near York), Darrington, Yorkshire and Hedon, Humberside.

BINHAM PRIORY, NORFOLK.
West front. C13 recessed doorway with five orders of shafts grouped so that three stand in diagonal row and two are recessed in shallow hollows. Dog-tooth moulding around arch-head.

The doors of this period were still covered with ironwork retaining the crescent or anchor-pattern but in a more restrained form although the ironwork generally is more elaborate. There are, however, some splendid doors of this period and three of these are at Skipwith, North Yorkshire; Dore Abbey, Herefordshire and Eastwood, Essex. The construction is usually of three or four boards with either V-edges or rebated edges with three or four ledges on the inside surface or the portcullis type of rear-frame composed of crossed ledges.

One of the best carpentered doors is at High Roding, Essex, where the rear-frame is of the portcullis type with half joints the horizontal ledges having notch-lapped joints to the edge frame of the door. The edge frame and stiles have V-grooved edges which enable the whole frame to be assembled before the planks are slid into position. When the planks are in position the bottom rail was fitted on with stub tenons and pegged.

Decorated, 1280–1377

The doorways of this period were extremely plain with fewer orders and the mouldings were so deeply cut being generally continued round the arch and down the jambs to the floor without a break. Sometimes there are small shafts which are not free-standing but joined to the parent body, the jamb. The arch, although still pointed, is now more depressed.

The hood-mould, usually a scroll and small roll, continued but now terminates in finials or stops carved in floral or human masks such as heads of knight and lady or king and queen. Sometimes the hood-mould and arch are of ogee shape.

Enrichments are not often used in the mouldings but the ball flower, a globular flower with three incurved petals, may be found running round the arch and down the jambs. An example of this may be seen at Elmdon, Essex. A further enrichment which was popular was the square four-leaved flower sometimes connected by a running stem.

Later in the period the lower part of the doors had the joints of the panels covered by mullions and curvilinear tracery was applied up to the arch head. Other forms of tracery were also used like the fine door at Great Bardfield, Essex. As a result of this, ornamental door hinges began to die out although ironwork was still used in the form of long strap-hinges which were ornamented with cross-hatching or vertical lines and, in some cases, large leaf scrolls may be seen as at Dartmouth, Devon where the ironwork consists of leaf scrolls and two leopards.

Perpendicular, 1377–1547

The two-centred arch remained popular but was frequently much more depressed and of the four-centred type. The most characteristic feature was the framing of the arch in a rectangular hood-mould where the spandrel afforded a good opportunity for relief carving comprising tracery, heraldry, foliage, figure subjects or angels. A good example is at Hilborough, Norfolk. Sometimes the hood-mould is carried up in an ogee form and is ornamented with crockets and a finial, a good example of which may be seen at Witney, Oxfordshire in the doorway to the north-west chapel. Where ornamentation is to be found in the arch it consists of small leaves or flowers in square form and occurs in the wide shallow mouldings which were very popular.

Ironwork was much less used in this period and sometimes the front of a door was treated in the linenfold manner the rear usually being well jointed as at Salcott, Essex.

The early Perpendicular doors had good tracery and tabernacle work and fine examples are at Shalford and Prittlewell Essex; Send, Surrey, and Salle, Norfolk.

It would seem that the doors of this period vary from the utmost simplicity to elaborate decoration and panelling was now more important than strap hinges.

English architecture, at this time, showed a tendency to include lavish frivolities and this may be seen on some doors which would appear to place more emphasis on woodcarving than on door construction.

The larger and more cumbersome of the Perpendicular doors sometimes have small wicket doors within them as at Gedney, Lincolnshire and Thaxed, Essex.

English ironwork became practically extinct as an art except for small objects such as hinges and keyhole scutcheons.

In the seventeenth and eighteenth centuries doorways reverted to round arches. They are often large and usually have projecting key-stones and large voussoirs like the south door at Wimborne St Giles, Dorset. The doors are plain with little, if any, form of decoration but the principal panelled doors were frequently dated like Poynings, West Sussex, which is dated 1608.

Perhaps it is well to point out that when aisles were added to Norman churches in the thirteenth and fourteenth centuries the Norman doorway was frequently re-used in the new wall and so because one finds a Norman doorway it must not be pre-supposed that the wall is also Norman or that the doorway is in its original position.

13

Arches and Arcades

One of the charms of an average village church lies in the arcades, for a church without arcades loses those elusive vitas which are so pleasing to a visitor.

The arcade developed from the Roman Hall of Justice, the basilica, which was a rectangular building with a colonnade of piers at one end. These basilicas were used for purposes other than the administration of the law and, when Christian worship was permitted without the risk of persecution, the Christians adapted the basilica for worship. From this type of building the church gradually evolved its own structural requirements.

In the early Christian basilicas the aisles were separated from the nave by rows of pillars and the space from pillar to pillar was bridged over by a horizontal lintel or beam of stone which was a method borrowed from the Greeks by the Romans. This method is structurally bad where the openings are wide as long blocks of stone, supported only at the ends, are liable to fracture by weight resting upon them from above. This method of spanning an opening used by the Romans and frequently in the early Saxon period is known as 'trabeated'.

There were always difficulties in roofing over wide space with the need to have a steep pitch to throw off the rain and snow in the northern climes and this was an important structural reason to retain arcades when planning a church.

Aisles not only served as gangways but were required for liturgical reasons, for example, processions, and in later periods to provide space for additional altars and chapels.

From early times only the great churches in this country had aisles as may be seen in the remains of the seventh-century church at Brixworth, Northamptonshire, which, although built in basilican form did not have rows of pillars and the aisles were connected to the nave by the arches cut through the walls. Constructional skills developed and by the eleventh century there were churches like Great Paxton in Cambridgeshire which has fine arcades and show what good builders the Anglo-Saxons were.

In English medieval architecture arches are spanned, not by lintels, but by true anches formed of small wedge-shaped stones called 'voussoirs', a method known as 'arcuated'. The joints of voussoirs radiate from the centre at right angles to the curve of the arch. Each voussoir assists to key the arch, the central one forming the keystone or locking-stone in a round arch. Later when the pointed arch was adopted there is generally a central joint and not keystone.

An arch is usually supported on a pier or pillar which consists of four parts, the abacus, which had an earlier equivalent called and impost block from which the arch springs, the capital immediately below, the shaft and the base.

Saxon Period

The Saxons had three ways of bridging an opening:

1 By a lintel which was either horizontal or cut into the shape of an arch from a solid block of stone (trabeated style).
2 The semi-circular arch composed of regular voussoirs.
3 The triangular arch composed of two inclined stones, a style which is exclusively Saxon although probably borrowed from Irish sources, are used for door heads.

Where the semi-circular arch was used it sprang from massive impost blocks like those at Hovingham, Yorkshire, North Riding; Bradford-on-Avon, Wiltshire, or Hadstock, Essex and which are usually plain, occasionally decorated or moulded or have chamfered lower edge. Where there are capitals they may be crudely carved but interesting usually having interlaced carving, angles, birds, leaves, animals as at St Bene't, Cambridge, Cambridgeshire. Throughout the Anglo-Saxon period there was a gradual development from a single plain round shaft, impost block and base to a shaft between elaborately carved or moulded capitals and base. Despite the crude carving to be found there is also some very good work and there is no doubt that by the time of

BRADFORD-ON-AVON, WILTSHIRE.
Saxon chancel arch showing plain massive impost blocks and irregular voussoirs in semi-circular arch with stones running through from front to back. Much repaired.

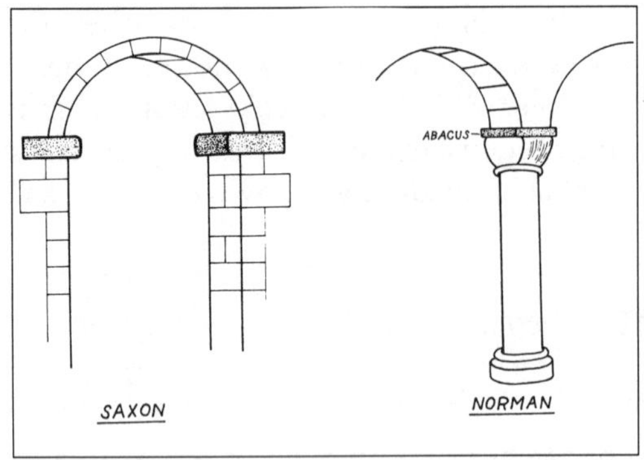

FIGURE 5.
Saxon and Norman arches.

the Conquest the work of the Anglo-Saxon sculptor was far in advance of any sculptural work produced in northern Europe.

This type of arch was most popular and was usually on the narrow side and built with quite large stones running through from the front to back.

The first masonry arcades were the result of cutting holes in the wall of the building to extend its accommodation by the addition of aisles. Later buildings were erected with aisles the main walls being supported from the beginning on an arcade rising from massive stone piers with bases made of roughly cut square blocks of stone left quite plain as, were the abaci. Occasionally, however, the Anglo-Saxons did show some initiative, for example at Hexham, Northumberland.

Norman Period

The first churches built in the Norman period following the Conquet were very solid looking and virtually devoid of sculptural decoration although they must have looked magnificent to the English who had in the main been used to buildings of timber. Most of them were built in the twelfth century although a few were built between 1080 and 1100.

Some eleventh-century churches had arcades as part of the original building like Great Paxton, Cambridgeshire, and the arcades of twelfth-century churches may also usually be found to be part of the original buildings and not added as many were in later periods when churches were enlarged.

The arches were often plain with square edges in the early part of the period but later they had semicircular rolls or were highly ornamented with chevron or zig-zag, pellet, billet, cable, diamond, double-cone, lozenge, nailhead and beak-head a decoration which includes the heads of birds, animals, dragons, and grotesques which were given long beaks or pointed chins which extended over a convex moulding to the roll below.

The semi-circular arch which has one centre situate half-way on the diameter was the main type used by the Normans before the middle of the twelfth century. There were variants to this type of arch where either less than a semi-circle was employed, called a 'segmental' arch and which was used where

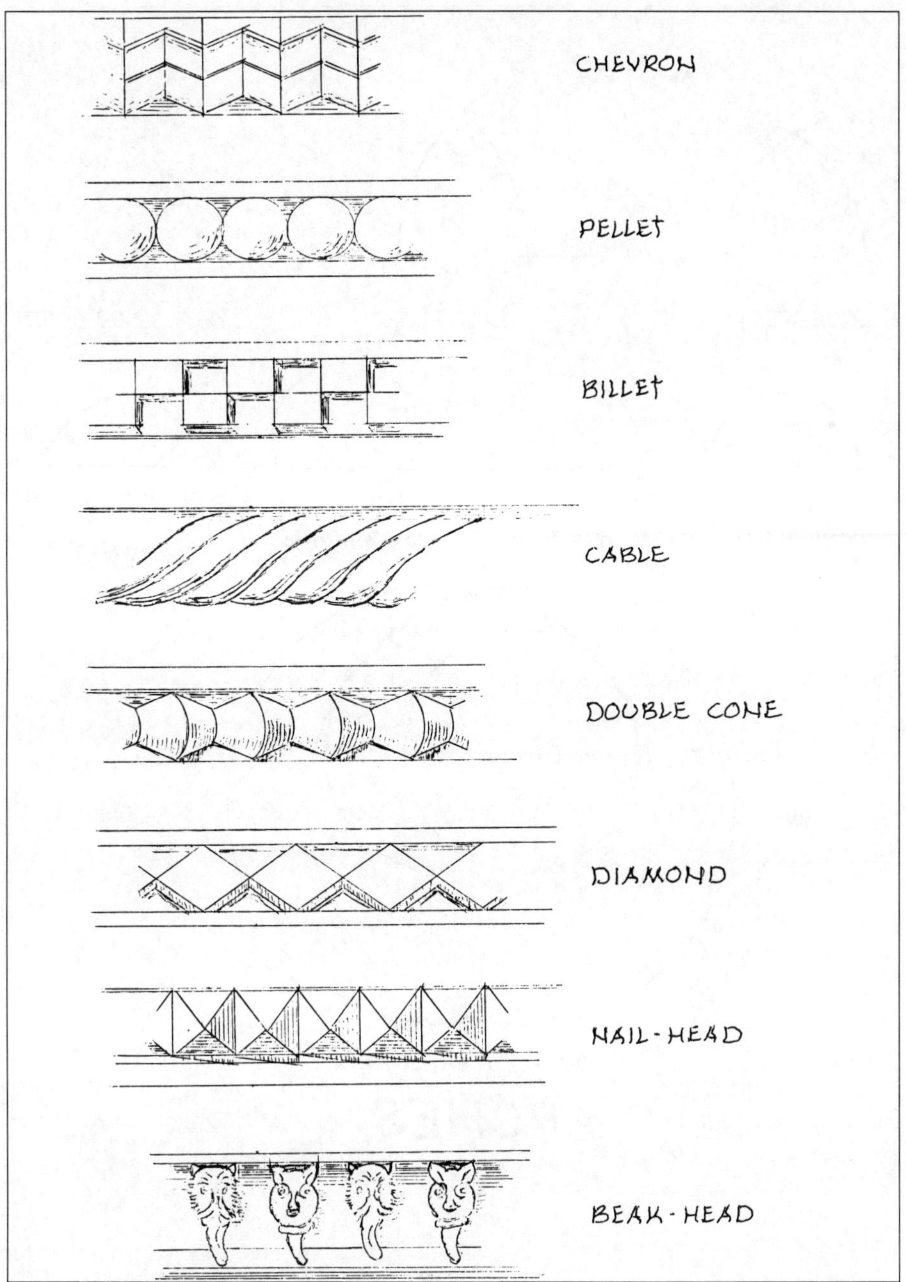

FIGURE 6.
Drawings of decorative mouldings of Norman period.

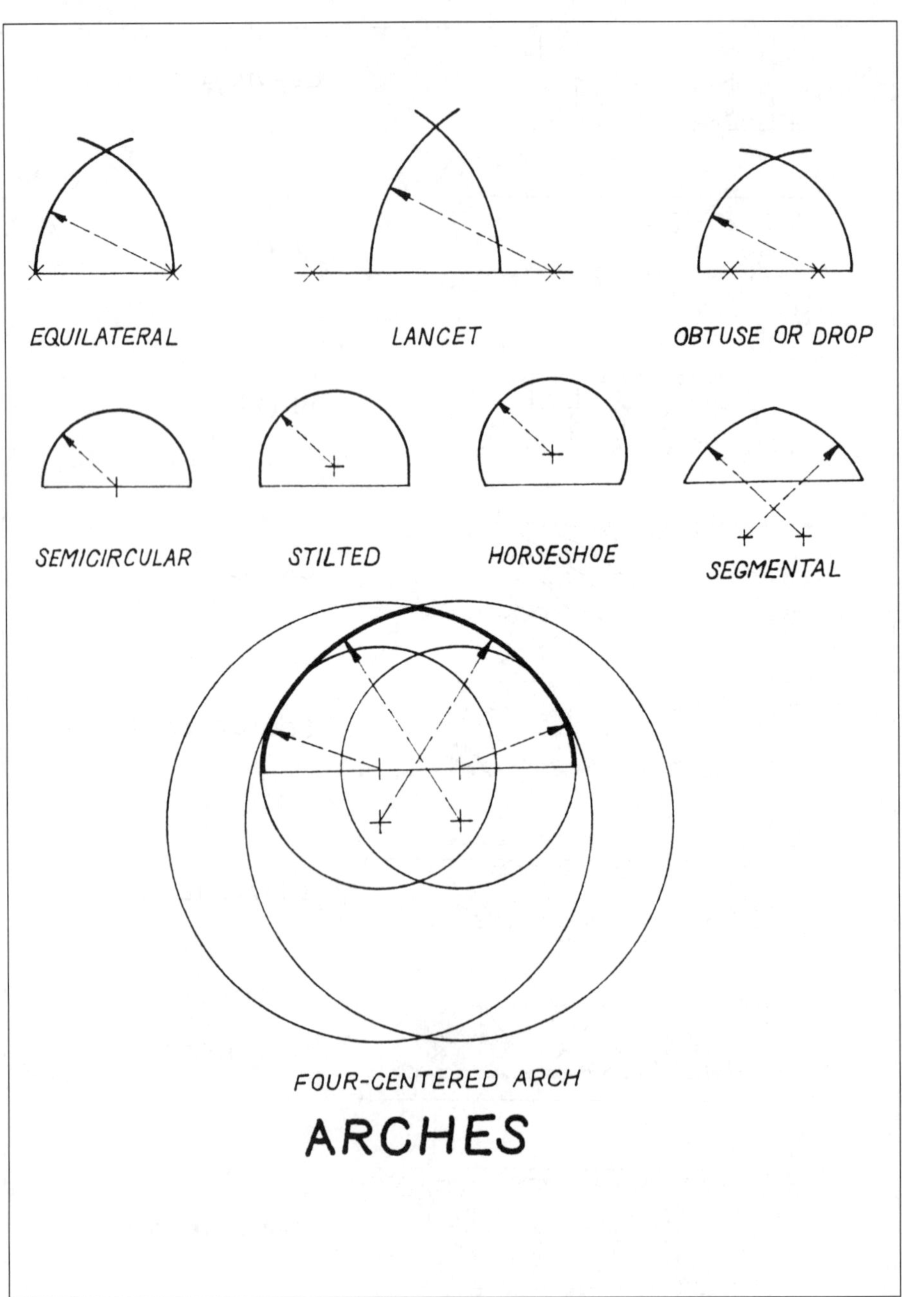

FIGURE 7.
Drawings of various types of arches.

height was limited or where more than a semi-circle was employed called a 'stilted' arch where the jambs continued for a way above the impost and which was employed when a taller arch was required. This type of arch was only used infrequently as indeed was a further type called 'horseshoe' because it was horseshoe shaped having the imposts slightly drawn in.

To construct an arch it is necessary to use elaborate timber centring on which to build and as the early Norman arch had very thick walls a large amount of timber was used. To economise in the use of timber centring in thick walls arches were later constructed in receding 'orders', known as the compound arch and consisted of two or more concentric rings using centring only for the first inner ring upon which others were built up using each ring as the support for the next ring.

These compound arches required jambs worked with a series of recesses where each of the angles is worked into a shaft, or a detached shaft might be inserted, to carry each arch ring, or certain rings, the remainder being allowed to run down the floor.

The impost block was rarely omitted and the upper angle is square with the lower angle having a hollow chamfer with a quirk or V-shaped groove between

FYFIELD, ESSEX.
Norman pier base, square with flattened roll moulding where pier joins base and spurs (damaged) at the corners.

the upper and lower angles. The depth of the vertical face and the chamfer are a good guide to dating and the deeper the vertical face the earlier the period. Where there were mouldings they were usually simple rounds and hollows.

The capital beneath the impost block began a variation on the cushion shape which consisted of a square upper section wit the lowers corners and edges rounded off. This plain cushion capital, imported into Britain from the area of the Rhine valley, developed in the early twelfth century with 'scallops' where the lower part of the cushion is cut with vertical flutes and was perhaps the most common decoration for the remainder of the Norman period.

Later the volute was used where four leaves spring from the neck and bend over under the angles of the square part and end in volutes. In later Norman work capitals had elaborate sculpture consisting of foliage, animals or groups of figures. The volute and leaf forms are clearly based on the Corinthian capitals of Greece and Rome and a reminder that the remains of classical antiquity continued to exert an influence throughout the Middle Ages.

BINHAM PRIORY, NORFOLK.
pier construction showing core and facing stones and mouldings.

The shafts or piers were usually massive and cylindrical but later octagonal and sometimes circular and octagonal piers were used alternatively down the arcade. Occasionally the shafts are decorated by channels or flutes cut in various forms, e.g. spiral, zig-zag or they may be square having small circular shafts at the angles or larger semi-circular half shafts on the faces.

The bases are usually low and square and where the shaft joins the base the join is covered by a flattened roll moulding the base being often ornamented with a spur or leaf ornament at each corner. This base helps to spread the supported weight of the pier which surmounted by a capital and abacus, provides a surface from which the arch springs and together act as an intermediate component between pier and arch. In the early Norman period the masonry was poor and to make the building secure great masses of material were used but later the masonry work improved considerably and workmen were fast discovering various ways of economising their material. Although Norman piers look solid they frequently only faced with stone the centre being filled with rubble and this may be clearly seen at Binham Priory, Norfolk.

Transitional Norman

Even when the pointed arch was introduced we find the semi-circular form of arch still being used and during the period *c1160–c*1200 there was a mixing of semi-circular and pointed arches. The Norman style was passing away but its passing was slow and gradual. The semi-circular arch was beginning to yield to the pointed arch and the solid and severe Norman architecture was given way to the beauty, brilliancy and lightness of the Gothic style. This transitional period was a short one lasting some forty years between *c*1160 and *c*1200.

Small ornamental arcades of intersecting round arches, which produced pointed arches, were popular and a good example may be seen at Much Wenlock Priory, Shropshire.

Good examples of this transistion are Boxgrove Priory and Burpham, Sussex; Canterbury Cathedral, Kent and Byland Abbey, Yorkshire.

Early English Period

The transitional ere of the last quarter of the twelfth century was one of much experiment in fining down the massive construction of the Normans and led in the thirteenth century to the golden age of Gothic architecture.

The introduction of the pointed arch with its diminished thrusts was fully recognised during the transitional period and in the thirteenth century became integrated into the structure and completely dominated the form and appearance of thirteenth-century Gothic art with vertical direction. The upright lines of buttresses, clustered shafts, window mullions, turrets and towers with the slanting lines of the pinnacles and spires added beauty and interest to the exterior.

Engineering skill had greatly increased and the buildings had come to understand the structural value of the pointed arch and the thrusts set up inside a structure based on arches. Stone cutting was much improved so that churches could be built much taller than previously and the whole structure much lighter. Piers were build of solid dressed stones all tightly fitting together and able to bear greatly increased weights.

The structural principle of the Early English church was that the walls were only built thick enough to withstand the sideways thrust or pushing of the arches at those points where they joined the walls. Between these points the walls may be as thin as practicable. This means that if the roof and vaulting thrusts come between the windows the wall at those points is made immensely thick and this increase in thickness took the form of buttresses.

There are three basic types of two-centred arches:

Equilateral

In this the springing point of one arc is used as an arc centre of the other and the radius is equal to the span of the arch.

Lancet

In this the centres are outside the area of the arch.

Obtuse or Drop

In this the arc centres are inside the arch.

The equilateral arch cannot, like the round arch, be varied except in size. The lancet produces steeply pointed arches which were very popular in the thirteenth century until about 1270 when the equilateral and obtuse arches were introduced. The obtuse produces a rather flatter arch which was used more in the latter part of the thirteenth century.

With the semi-circular arch thick walls were required to resist the thrust of the arch but with the obtuse arch the wall thickness could be reduced and with the acutely pointed arch still thinner walls could be obtained except that where

CHEDZOY, SOMERSET.
C13 north arcade. Chamfered equilateral arch with bell-shaped capitals.

KELVEDON, ESSEX.
Late C13 capitals. partly moulded, partly with stiff-leaf and crocket decoration.

the arch was very high stability was maintained by flying-buttresses and balanced by the weight of the pinnacles.

In order to lessen the hard edge of an arch order small rolls were introduced at the angle in the eleventh century and by the twelfth century it had become customary. After the early part of the Early English period a shallow hollow was introduced next to the roll which eventually joined up with the roll and together became known as the 'bowtell' which was the principal member of Gothic moulding.

Throughout the thirteenth century, in minor churches, the arcades were simple and consisted of two or three orders having the angles chamfered a feature which was also used in the reveals and mullions of windows.

Towards the latter part of the thirteenth century the straight chamfer may be found accompanied by the quarter-circle hollow chamfer. The straight and hollow chamfers were to continue throughout the remainder of the Gothic period with the hollow chamfer predominating.

The capitals are bell-shaped with a fillet or necking below and a roll moulding above. The abacus was almost always round but sometimes octagonal with a rounded edge and deeply undercut. Where the capitals had ornamental carving this took the form of conventional stiff-leaf foliage usually having long stalks.

BINHAM PRIORY, NORFOLK.
C13 west doorway having five orders of shafts unusually grouped together so that three stand in a diagonal row and the other two are recessed in shallow hollows. The capitals are of the crocket type with circular abaci and necking. The moulding is enlivened with some fine dog-tooth.

The leaves are shown in the act of unfolding and not fully open. The impression they give is that they are growing and that they will soon have opened into full foliage. This, no doubt, is what the carvers intended, to give us the promise of more life to come, a symbol of eternal life. Occasionally human heads, birds or animals are found carved amidst the foliage.

The Norman bases were poorly moulded but they gradually developed and in the mid-twelfth century they tended to project much less from the pillar above and began to follow their shapes. The roll mouldings became smaller and *c*1150 to 1260 a pair of roll mouldings incorporated a deep hollow between them, known as a 'water-hold' as it is capable of retaining water. This feature began to go out of fashion *c*1240 when the rolls were made larger and closer together with the water-hold space sometimes being filled with a smaller roll. The double or triple roll base became common for the remainder of the period.

The only enrichments which were characteristic of this period were the outward curved crocket used to terminate hood-moulds and the dog-tooth ornament which consisted of a series of small pyramids with their sides split upwards from the base almost to the point and slightly opened out forming four cornered stars which were placed diagonally. They were chiefly used in the hollows of arch mouldings.

From the straight chamfer was developed the 'wave' moulding which was obtained by altering the straight chamfer to a convex surface flanked by hollows. The wave moulding although more generally belonging to the fourteenth century occurred also in the fifteenth century when there was a tendency to deepen the hollows with a consequent reduction in the convex surface.

Decorated Period

The arch in this period was not so acutely pointed and when looking at arcades there is a recognisable widening of the arch. The mouldings became more numerous and broader but not so deeply cut and there were few hollows. The scroll moulding became popular together with the wave moulding especially during the first half of the fourteenth century. The ogee moulding made up of concave and convex curves was established in its own right in the first half of the century and it became one of the most characteristic mouldings of the Perpendicular Gothic of the fifteenth and sixteenth centuries.

The hollow chamfer introduced in the thirteenth century continued to be popular and in chancel arches and especially in doorways the moulding was continuous round the arch and down to the floor without interruption by capitals. It is in these hollows that the stylised flower decorations of the period may be found.

The abacus had now absorbed in the capital by the abolition of the undercut hollow, the upper edge, however, still remained rounded. Moulded capitals were usually composed of three parts; a top group of two rolls of small mouldings, the lower being of the same or slightly less projection, the bell and the necking. They are either octagonal or circular according to the shaft and were either wholly moulded or had beautiful life-like foliage, usually of oak, ivy, maple or vine leaves. The shafts in this period were usually octagonal but occasionally circular or on occasions four semi-circular half-shafts attached to a central square pier. In some rare cases there might be even eight or more half-shafts particularly in the latter part of the fourteenth century. The bases followed the capitals and were usually composed of a pair or triplet of rolls.

The popular ornaments of this period were the ballflower, a globular flower with three incurved petals and the square four-leaved flower together with the crocket both inward and outward curving. Some fine arcades with foliaged capitals may be seen at Patrington, East Yorkshire, Stoke-Gidding, Leics; Southwell Minster, Notts, Shotesbrooke, Berks; Tilty Abbey, Essex; Holbeach, Lincs; Snettisham, Norfolk and Winchelsea, Sussex.

Perpendicular Period

The fifteenth century was a great period of re-building which meant that many new arcades were constructed. As the arch, although still pointed, became more obtuse and tended to flatten so the pier capitals came closer to the crown of the arch thus visually enhancing the height of the piers.

As a means of spanning a space with the least rise in height the four-centred arch became common. This arch and its variations is to be frequently found in

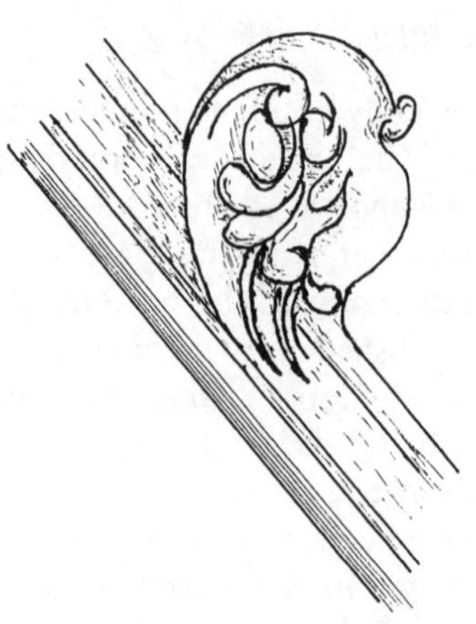

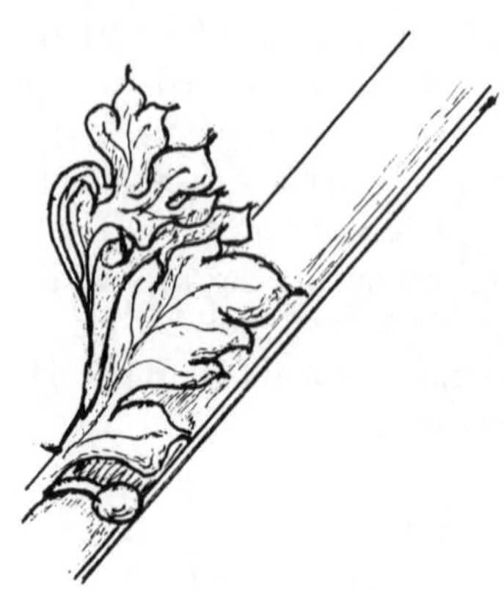

FIGURE 8.
Drawings of outward and inward curved crockets.

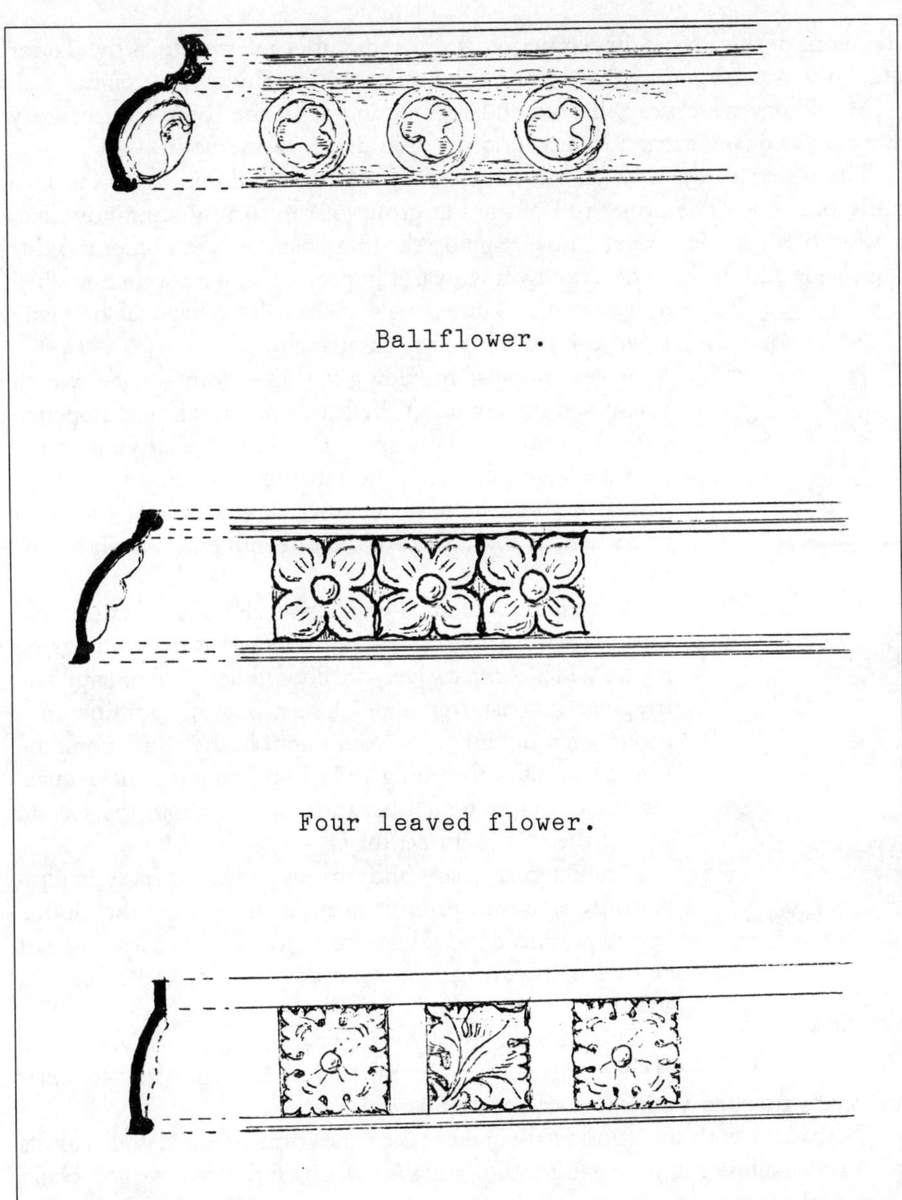

FIGURE 9.
Drawings of ballflower, four-leaved flower and square flower.

the work of the Perpendicular period and is sometimes referred to as the Tudor arch as it was commonly used during the reigns of the Tudor sovereigns.

Mouldings were very shallow and regular and as in the fourteenth century were occasionally carried right round the arch down to the floor.

The orders of the arch all but disappeared and the mouldings were cut into a diagonal line. The upper roll of the top group of capital moulding now had, instead of a rounded edge, an overlapping slanting chamfer, with other mouldings, wide and shallow, decreasing downwards in projection with sometimes bell and necking. The capitals are usually octagonal or many sided even if the pier is circular.

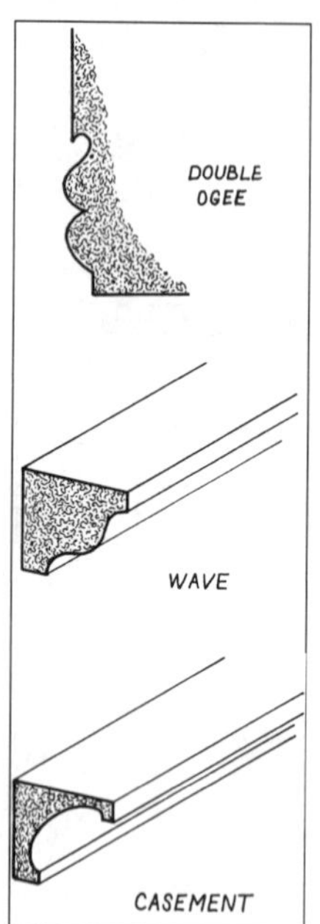

FIGURE 10.
Mouldings.

A very popular moulding was the 'double ogee' which resembled the curves of the leaves of a book when opened near the centre and consisted of a concave curve merging into a convex curve. Although this moulding was established in the fourteenth century it was one of the most characteristic mouldings of the fifteenth and sixteenth centuries.

A further moulding which was also characteristic and greatly used was the 'casement' which was the name given to the wide, comparatively shallow hollow, often large and irregular in character and taking a central position in a group of mouldings. It would appear that this moulding was the result of flattening and lengthening the three-quarter circle hollow which began to appear about the second half of the thirteenth century.

Mouldings are many and various and in the Early English period were given priority over decoration. As the Gothic period advanced mouldings came to take a less leading part and decorative ornaments and devices received increasing attention.

The piers are usually octagonal though some are square placed diagonally. Sometimes they had four semi-circular half-shafts attached with the battlemented capitals.

The bases were now considerably taller taken the form of a pedestal with its wide and shallow mouldings on top of a plain polygonal foot and which could be seen above the benches which had now become general in churches.

At the end of an arcade is a half-pier which carries one end of the arch and is bonded into the wall. This half-pier is termed a 'respond' and is sometimes specially decorated as in Stambourne church, Essex, where it is carved with the arms of the Mac William family who were one of the chief benefactors of the church.

Examples: Salle and Salthouse, Norfolk; High Laver and Great Bromley, Essex; Lavenham and Stoke-by-Nayland, Suffolk; Sidbury, Devon; Altarnum, Cornwall; Hillesden, Bucks; Ewelme, Oxon; Crewkerne, Somerset and Edington, Wilts.

Renaissance and Classical, 17th & 18th centuries

Following the Reformation the Gothic style was gradually replaced by a very difference style based upon classical traditions. The arch is once again semi-circular and high, the pillars following one of the classical orders. It was a slow process and down to the end of the reign of Charles I in 1649 and in a few places even later, masons continued in the ways of Perpendicular Gothic with a mixture of Classical. The restoration of Charles II in 1660 marked the attempt to revive the Classical architectural style although changes began to appear in the Elizabethan and Jacobean periods (1558–1625) in the design and decoration of monuments progressing to other fixtures and fittings. This style did not grow out of necessity or convenience like medieval Gothic but it was imported fashion. The Classical Age was so called because from 1660 until the middle of the eighteenth century a succession of architects, inspired by the recreation of the architecture of Imperial Rome, attempted to revive it both structurally and decoratively. The Classical period, so far as it applied to church architecture, comprised three periods:

(a) Wren: 1669–1721
(b) Baroque: 1700–1750 and
(c) Palladian: 1750–1830.

Stuart and Georgian Churches

Examples with name of architect:

London

St Stephen, Walbrook – C17 – Christopher Wren.
St Martin-in-the-Fields – C18 – James Gibbs.
St Clement, Eastcheap – C17 – Christopher Wren.
St Peter, Cornhill – C17 – Christopher Wren.
St George, Hanover Square – C18 – John James.
St John, Smith Square – C18 – Thomas Archer.
All Hallows, London Wall – C18 – George Dance the Younger

Outside London

Ingestre, Staffs. – C17 – Robert Hooke.
Willen, Bucks. – C17 – Robert Hooke.
Farley, Wilts. – C17 – Alexander Fort (probably).

Portland, Dorset	– C18 – Thomas Gilbert.
Euston, Suffolk	– C17 – William Samwell (probably).
Hardenhuish, Wilts.	– C18 – John Wood.
Blandford, Dorset	– C18 – John & Wm.Bastard.
Gayhurst, Bucks.	– C18 – Unrecorded.
Banbury, Oxon	– C18 – S. P. Cockerell.
All Saints, Oxford	– C18 – Henry Aldrich (probably).
Avington, Hants.	– C17 – Unrecorded.

The scornful description that churches of the Classical period were 'brick boxes' has been repeated so often that there is an opinion that all classical churches are very much alike. That this is not so is shown in the church architecture where there is a boldness and a readiness to experiment in variety. The ground plan of a Gothic church may differ little from that of a Classical church in that it may consist of a chancel, nave and aisles. The medieval church, however, started with a bay having other bays added to it until the building reached the required size but the Classical church was built as a whole from the beginning.

In the early stages of Protestantism new church building was not required, the Protestants taking over existing church buildings and adapting them to their own needs. As these old buildings fell into disrepair and the congregations grew, new facilities for worship were needed. There was much trial and error in finding the right shape of the church which allowed the preacher to use his normal speaking voice. There was now a shift from the altar to pulpit; no longer was the focus of worship on the re-enactment of Christ's death on the altar, it was now on the preaching of God's word from the pulpit.

The old churches which were well suited to create an air of mystery were not suitable acoustically for preaching, especially after the removal of choir screens and altars which had hitherto symbolised the separation of priest and people.

Some churches were built in many shapes, 'L' or 'T' forms, cross, round, oval, polygon and many others with the idea of concentrating on the principal liturgical centres of pulpit, communion table and font.

The Classical order consists of an entablature which is the horizontal superstructure supported by the columns and is made up of three principal pars, the architrave which is the lowest or weight-carrying member, the frieze and the cornice. The pillar has capital, shaft and base and there may be an abacus between the capital and the architrave together with an astragal, a small circular moulding between the bell and shaft.

The Roman Doric order is the simplest and is fairly plain. The shaft is tapered and may be fluted while the frieze above could contain vertically grooved blocks known as 'tryglyphs'. Sometimes there are small plain rectangular projecting blocks called 'dentils' in the bed-mould of the cornice.

The Ionic order shaft is more slender that the Doric and is usually fluted, the capital having two large volutes or spiral scrolls on the front face and two on the back.

The Corinthian order shaft is usually plain but the capital has a mass of spiky leaves consisting of laurel, olive or acanthus piled on top of each other and spreading outwards and downwards. There is also the Composite which is a mixture of Ionic and Corinthian having large volutes on its convex sided capital, the column being fluted or sometimes plain. The lower part of the capital has rows of acanthus leaves rather like the Corinthian. A further form is the Tuscan which was a mixture of Doric and Composite and consisted of plain mouldings at either end of the plain shaft.

The bases were composed of a variety of simple convex and concave mouldings resting on a large torus or convex moulding of semicircular profile, in turn resting on a large square plinth.

Classical ornamentation was vigorous and deeply cut and included, amongst others, luscious foliage and fruit as well as birds, cherubs, shells, etc. They were portrayed both stylised and naturalistic.

The seventeenth century produced some fine ceiled roofs with ribbed crossed vaults of plaster (Euston, Suffolk and Ingestre, Staffs.) and woodcarving, for example, the pulpit in Abbey Dore, Hereford and Worcester and screen and pulpit, Ingestre, Staffs.

In out-of-the-way villages local masons continued to build in the tradition of their grandfathers and many churches are scarcely indistinguishable from those built fifty to one hundred years before. On the other hand, there were many churches built in the modern style with round-headed windows having cherub-headed keystones, pedimented doorways, Classical columns, high semi-circular arches and fine western fronts, e.g. Minsterly, Shropshire.

In the eighteenth century Ionic columns, continued having garlanded capitals with the central space between the columns supporting lintels. The ceilings were frequently plastered (St Thomas, Stourbridge, Hereford and Worcester). Galleries were provided with the object of increasing the accommodation without enlarging churches to impossible dimensions. Although they were justified on utilitarian grounds they wee difficult to reconcile with a strictly Classical use of the orders and were always unpopular with architects. They were often, however, integral parts of Stuart or Georgian interior and later in the Nineteenth century many of them were removed.

Victorian

England had a religious revival in the early nineteenth century and from it came the formation of the Oxford Movement led by Oriel College. The Movement led the way in practical reforms in the Church of England, together with the Cambridge Camden Society who were later to be known as the Ecclesiological Society. The endeavours of the Oxford Movement and the Camden Society were to recapture the mystery, beauty and the magic of worship leading to an attempt to imitate perfect Gothic which they considered to be in the Decorated style. The interiors of the churches were also to be of that period and the altar was, once again, to be the focal point instead of the pulpit. The best architects of the period, men like Augustus Pugin, Sir George Gilbert Scott, Sir Charles Nicholson and Arthur Blomfield studied the construction of ancient building but the majority, regretfully, copied from books and other architects and so their productions are uniformly boring. Various component part were selected from past periods indiscriminately and because communication had become much easier architects could have knowledge of each other's work which brought uniformity. Although modern techniques were used there was no new style to fill the void and very often the result was a mish-mash of the various architectural periods. One good contribution emerged from the nineteenth century and that was the restoration of old buildings which had fallen into a bad state of disrepair. Although restoration of the buildings and the destruction of much of the contents was over zealous, it did, at lease, save many old churches from dilapidation and ruin.

14

Roofs and Roof Bosses

The basic requirement of a roof is that it should protect the interior of a building and throw off rain and snow as quickly as possible and in order to do so the sides of the roof are made to slope, but the pitch of the slope is largely determined by the materials used for covering. Even today many Suffolk and Norman churches have roofs which are still covered by thatch, and at the beginning of this century there were some three hundred, and so the pitch had to be steep to discourage rain water from lingering and soaking through.

With lead covering the opposite is true because if the slope is too steep the lead tends to slip and creep continuously downward by expansion and, owing to the weight, is unable to contract to its original position therefore needing constant attention. There are few old roofs that do not show insertions near the ridge to meet the gaps caused by contraction. Beautiful as these old lead roofs are, many poor parishes find it difficult to meet the heavy cost of re-casting the lead and frequently have to substitute slates.

EARL STONHAM, SUFFOLK.
C14 S.porch showing creeping lead roof.

The average life of a lead roof is only a little over one hundred years and for the greater part of that period constant repairs are necessary. When tiles or slates are used the problems are not so great and the pitch can be more or less a question of choice rather than necessity and so a certain amount of variety was allowable.

In the early Middle Ages a steeper pitch was often preferred in order to conform with the pointed arch whereas by the fifteenth century roofs were so greatly reduced in pitch that they were almost invisible when behind a parapet.

The general type of parish church had a timber roof, which was the cheapest and technically the most straightforward material to handle, usually covered with thatch, terra-cotta, stone, tiles or wooden shingles or lead sheeting.

The lead was normally melted on the site in a stone mortar and poured into moulds to make sheets. At High Easter in Essex some years ago, a stone mortar was found in the wall during repairs. It was originally a solid block of stone hollowed on two sides with pouring lips. On each side was a lug, the mortar being held in a frame, so that it could be tipped and the molten lead poured over the lips. To use it a fire was lit underneath, the hollowed top being filled with pieces of lead. When melted, the mortar was tipped on its stand and the molten lead poured into trays having sanded bases to make sheets. When found the mortar was in several pieces which is, no doubt, why it was discarded and used as part of the rubble content of the wall. The pieces of the mortar have been put together and a wooden stand made for it.

There are three main types of roof trusses:

1 Tie beam
2 Trussed rafter, e.g. having a king post or queen posts
3 Hammer beam.

The fundamental member met with in all roofs is the rafter which may be a principal or common rafter. The principal rafters of a roof are always much heavier and larger that the common rafters and normally correspond with the main bay divisions of the space below, e.g. the piers, buttresses or masonry between the windows. The principal rafters are huge pieces of timber averaging ten to twelve inches in depth and nearly as wide. The common rafters averaged six and a half inches by four inches and were invariably laid flat.

In general roofs fall into two classes, single frame and double frame. The single frame is one in which each pair of rafters is an independent unit of the roof, bearing independently its share of the stresses and duties of the roof. The simplest form is for each pair of rafters to be coupled with a collar but this form would be unsuitable for a large span.

The most common form is the single framed braced rafter type and a very large number of these exist.They are not the most satisfactory type of roof as their rigidity depends upon the joints being accurate and close-fitting, particularly the tenons, mortices and pins. Apart from the use for which they were designed they have little constructive strength and with the weakening of any one joint a greater strain is put on all the others and a progressive weakness develops in the whole structure. The bracing was composed of a collar beam situated between two rafters higher up the slope of the roof with curved braces

CHIPPING OGNAR, ESSEX.
Chancel roof of Norman church (*c*1080–*c*1100). The roof is composed of four different roof systems, the oldest being two couples of scissor braces in the centre of early C13. The braces may be seen extended through the collars to the opposite rafters and were dovetailed at their tops and notch-lapped at their lower ends.

from each rafter to the collar beam. An alterative was to extend the braces so that they became what is known as 'scissor beams'. This type of bracing was introduced into Essex during the first half of the thirteenth century. All these types have framing which forms complete trusses and are known as trussed rafter roofs.

The sockets used in the thirteenth century to hold the lower end of the brace to the rafter are called notch lap joints.

Later a secret notch lap joint which was cut to resist withdrawal was made so as to be invisible when the joint was assembled. The sole object of this technique being the deception of the viewer. This deception has been perpetuated today by cabinet makers in the jointing of cabinet work.

There were variants in the bracing and so, later, effort was made to strengthen the foot of the truss by providing a wall plate which is a timber laid longitudinally on top of the wall to receive the ends of the rafters so that they could be tenoned into the plate to counteract their tendency to move outwards. Provided the wall remained stable there was no fear of the wall plate shifting and the roof spreading

RIDGEWELL, ESSEX.
The arch braces to the collars are built in four timbers. The weakness of this construction necessitated repairs by the blacksmith lower down the brace(not shown). The lowering of the roof pitch caused the roof to begin to spread. See the pulling away of the collars from the principal rafters.

outwards. The short studs between the wall plate and the rafters are called ashlar pieces and provide extra support.

In later double-framed roofs, the rafters were not framed in the same way but were strengthened by the addition of purlins which were horizontal timbers beneath the rafters, parallel with the wall plate, to support the weight of the roofing material. These purlins were carried on extra strong rafters, part of the framed trusses, and are called principal rafters.

The various forms of roof were often, in the thirteenth century, combined by not having principal rafters but by forming the principal trusses of very strong tie-beams composed of horizontal timbers which stretched across and rested on top of the two side walls at regular intervals.

These tie beams tended to sag in the centre and so needed to be of great thickness and depth. Owing to their great length and weight they must have been difficult to transport especially over deep muddy and potholed medieval roads and weak narrow bridges. The beams of the roof of Abingdon Abbey, Berkshire, came from Wales and they were brought at great cost in wheeled carts each drawn by twelve oxen which took six or seven weeks gong to and from Shrewsbury.

On the centre of each beam stands a post, often fashioned into a column with capital and base, which supports a central horizontal called a collar beam purlin. The collar beam helps to support the collars which stiffen the rafters and any weight which is carried by the tie-beam is taken on the middle of it. The heavy tie-beam is tied into the wall plates which lie on top of walls and prevents the rafters from spreading and pusing out the walls. This central post, supporting the collar beam, is called a crown post but where it supports the ridge it is known as a king post. A further variety is a couple-close roof where a pair of rafters are

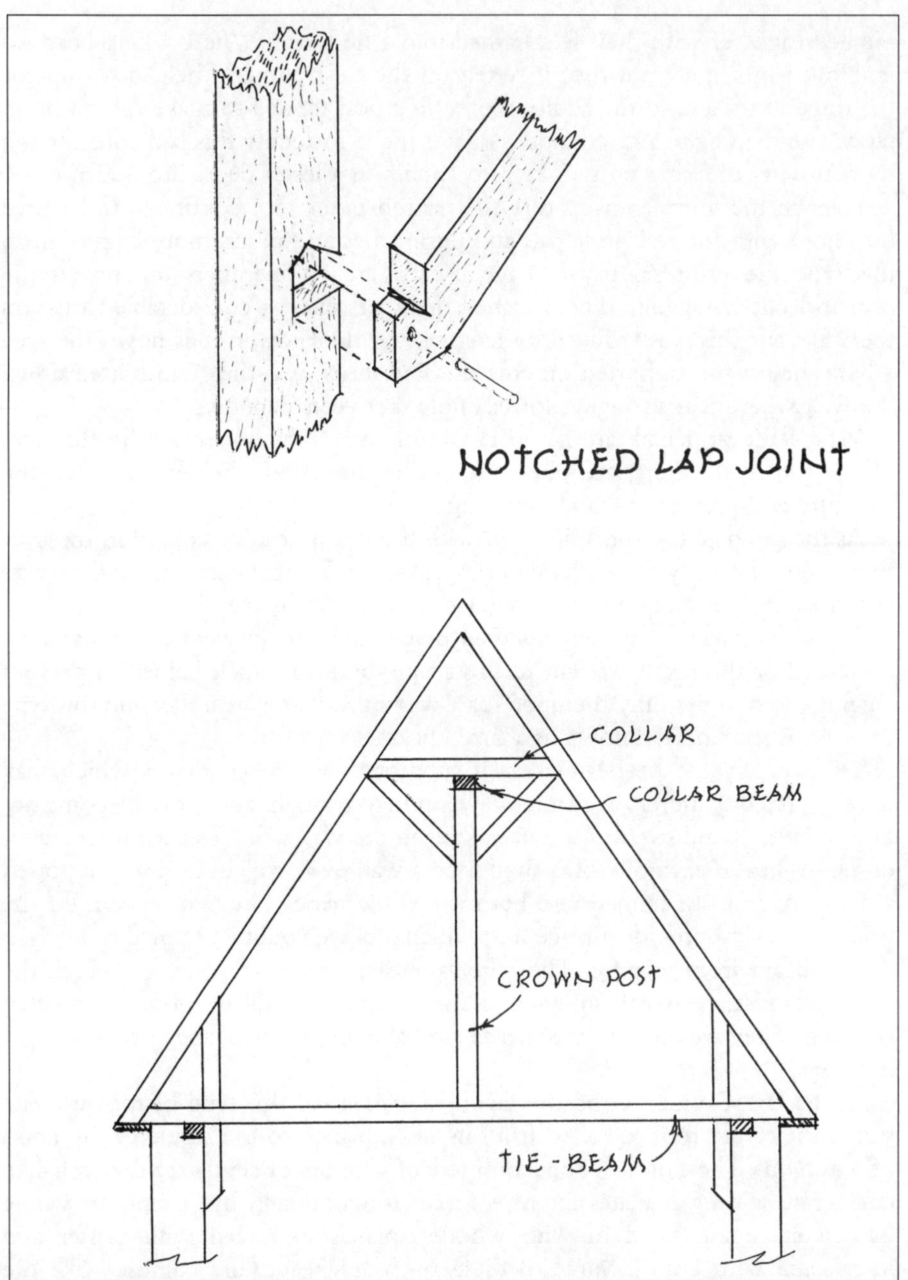

FIGURE 11.
Drawings showing notched lap joint and tie-beam and crown post roof.

pitched together with their feet framed into a tie beam. Where a king post was employed in a medieval roof it rested on the tie-beam and helped to support the ridge beam and so the addition of a king post tended to make the tie-beam sag worse than ever. An attempt was later made to rectify this bad construction by removing the king posts. This also applies in a lesser degree to queen posts.

Later in the fourteenth century the trussed-rafter roof continued to be used but those with formed principals and purlins became much more common. In this type the principal trusses have usually arched members to prevent the principal rafters sagging. These arched members exert a considerable thrust on the walls but this was reduced by lengthening their lower ends down the wall where they were supported on corbels. The thrust was thus transmitted down the wall where it is strongest, for example, between windows.

Where the principals are far apart wind braces, which spring from the sides of the principal rafters, are often used. The braces also helped to stiffen the structure and prevent it from collapsing.

As the pitch of the roofs dropped with the use of lead or copper in the later fourteenth and early fifteenth centuries beam roofs, which are almost flat, were constructed by placing beams at regular intervals across the church.

The beams needed to be cambered or pitched and so were either naturally cambered or the beam was cut to this shape, both of which helped to prevent sagging. Sometimes only the upper part was cut to form a camber and this type of beam is sometimes known as a firred beam.

Occasionally the tie-beam is itself supported on arched braces which may have traceried spandrels. A further development brought about by the construction of larger windows was to put corbels in the wall a few feet below the ends of the tie-beams each of which supported a wall post, which, in turn, supported a tie-beam and was framed into both it and the plate. The main reason for the wall post was to provide a place into which a brace could be framed to prevent the tie-beam from sagging. The corbels, either wood or stone, on which the wall posts rest are worth studying as they are usually full of interest and often amusing. They are often human heads, probably benefactors, angels or grotesque monsters.

In the late Gothic period the favourite variant of this type of roof was the wagon or cradle roof so called from its resemblance to the inside of the hood of a wagon. The construction consisted of a series of semi-circular arch-like rafters resting on wall plates and re-enforced longitudinally by purlins, the whole framework being filled in with wooden panels or ceiled with plaster and intersected with bosses. Some of these roofs are beautifully coloured like the one at St Mary, Bury St Edmunds, Suffolk while others have been stripped of their plaster and left exposed. The coloured bosses are most effective and are often carved with a variety of figures and subjects. The ceiling at Shepton Mallet,

Somerset, contains 350 panels and the designs are only duplicated once. In addition there are far more foliated bosses and it is believed that no one has yet discovered a repetition of a single design.

Towards the end of the fourteenth century the craft of the carpenter came into its own and the master carpenter was as important as the master mason. The fine constructions of Perpendicular church roofs increased the richness and delicacy of the churches of the time.

Flat roofs of the cambered-beam and firred-beam are common in the Midlands, and in Cheshire and Somerset they are treated with extreme richness while in Lancashire, Dorset, Shropshire, and Yorkshire the beams and purlins are richly moulded and frequently these are increased in number so that the roof surface consists of a large number of square, deeply moulded panels the intersections of which are decorated with carved bosses. Good examples of this type of roof may be seen at Astbury, Cheshire; Ruthin, Clwyd and Shepton Mallet, Somerset.

Kent, Sussex, Surrey and Hampshire continued with pitched roofs with their braced rafters, king posts and tie beams, flat roofs not being common.

In the far west of the country, Devon, Cornwall and Somerset the braced rafter roof was also retained but in a double form with principals and rafters but

HIGH EASTER, ESSEX.
Early C16 nave roof with flat pitch. Tie-beams on arched braces with richly carved tracery, wall posts and carved bosses.

Top left: BLISSLAND, CORNWALL.
Ceiled wagon roof.

Above: EARL STONHAM, SUFFOLK.
Late C15 single hammerbeam roof. Probably one of the richest in the country. The trusses alternate with pendant hammer-posts and hammer-posts carved in the form of prone angels. From middles of the arch-braces hang pendants and on their middles stand kingposts. All spandrels are carved and even the common rafters are moulded.

Left: AXBRIDGE, SOMERSET.
A remarkable example of a C17 plastered and coloured roof. It has thin ribs in lozenge, octagon and similar shapes with pendants at strategic junctions.

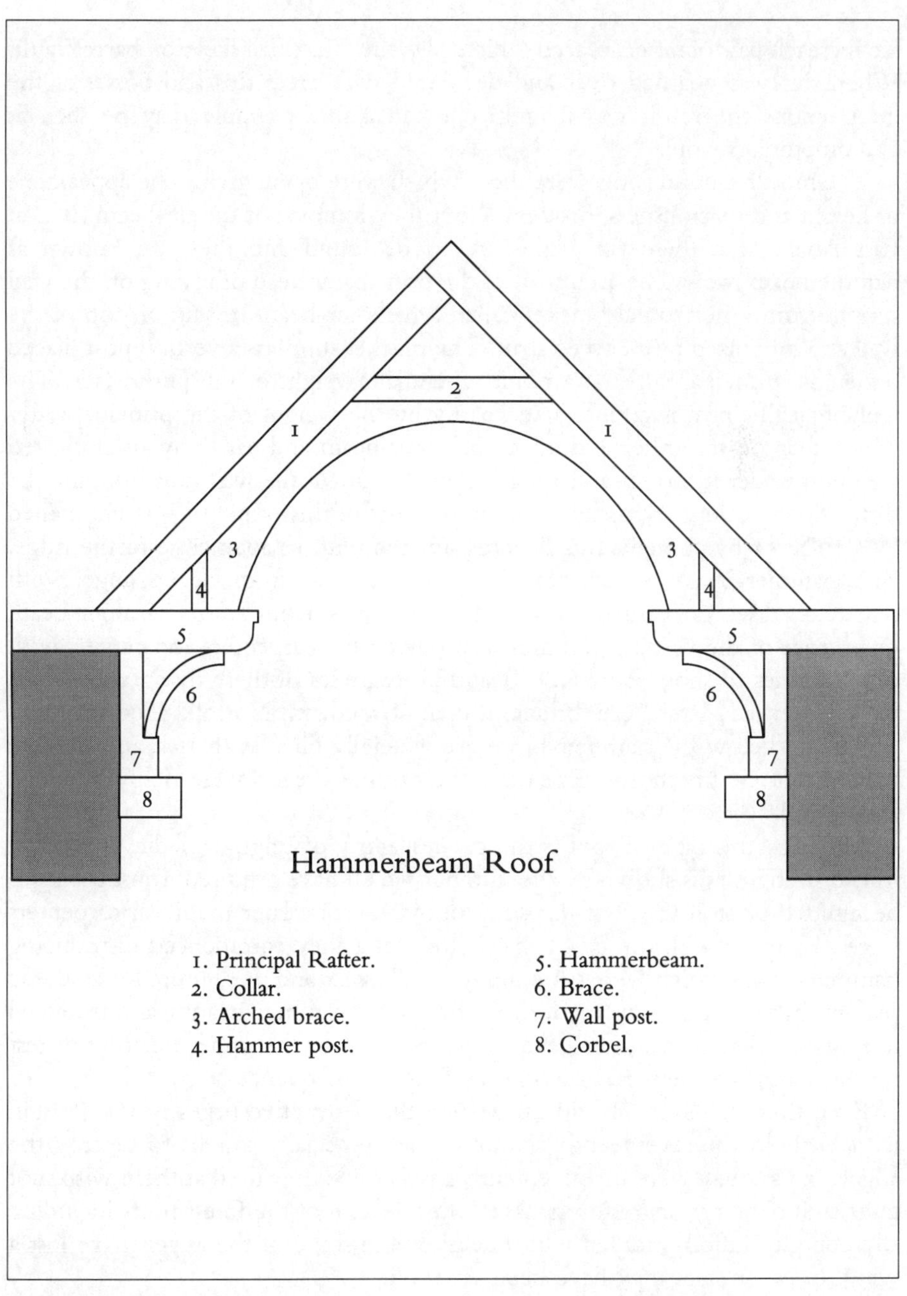

FIGURE 12.
Drawing of hammerbeam roof.

having each pair of rafters braced which gave the effect of a skeleton barrel vault. When this was boarded over and decorated with cross ribs and bosses at the intersections the result was magnificent and a fine example may be seen at Cullompton, Devon.

The most beautiful roofs were those which were open, giving the appearance of height and spaciousness, brought about they removal of the tie-beam. It is in East Anglia that these fine roofs are to be found and they are known as hammerbeam roofs. The arch strut of the principal instead of resting on the wall springs from a horizontal bracket called a hammer-beam resting on top of the wall and supported by a curved strut. The bracket supports a vertical post placed under the principal rafter at a point where the weight of the purlin falls. The weight of this post is counteracted partly by the weight of the principal rafter which rests on the other end of the hammer-beam and partly by an elongated wall post under it springing from a corbel way down the wall thus bringing the thrust down as low as possible. The upper part of this principal is strengthened by a collar or by curved struts forming an arch with its apex close to the ridge. The hammer-beam is sometimes carved into the form of an angel with outstretched wings, painted and gilded, or an angels stands on the hammer-beam or in front of the vertical post and so provided the carpenters and carvers with opportunities to show their skill, Beautiful examples of these flying angel roofs may be sent at March, Cambridgeshire and Swaffham, Norfolk. The spandrels above and below the hammer-beam are generally filled with rich and delicate tracery as at Gestingthorpe, Essex and the hammer-beams were richly moulded and carved.

Although this type of roof is the greatest glory of English medieval work it lacked strength as is shown by the number which have required iron tie-bars to be inserted to stop the roof thrusting outwards. The later medieval carpenters were so pleased with the effect that before long they commenced introducing hammer-beams which were structurally unnecessary and were more for aesthetic reasons than building construction. So the double hammer-beam was introduced having two tiers of hammer-beams on each side. As the upper tier cannot rest on the wall plate they are structurally of little consequence.

Even these lovely roofs did not escape the destructive urges of the Puritan iconoclasts in the seventeenth century. They especially sought to destroy the angels and as these were inconveniently inaccessible they fired at them with shot guns and in later years restorers have found several of the finest roofs including Blythburgh, Suffolk, riddled with buckshot and some of the angels have lost a wing. In other cases they have been sawn off.

By the seventeenth century fashionable ceilings were of moulded plasterwork consisting of arrangements of sunk or recessed and decorated ceiling panels of varying sizes known as coffered ceilings. The plasterwork was usually painted in white, gold or blue. Axbridge, Somerset, has a very fine plaster roof of the seventeenth century.

The timber used for roofs throughout the medieval period and afterwards was almost invariably oak although the single hammer-beam roof in Earl Stonham church, Suffolk has a glorious chestnut roof.

SOUTHWOLD, SUFFOLK.
Celure or Canopy of Honour above former rood. Single alternate hammerbeam roof with recumbent angels and arch-braced collars.

Celure

The eastern end of a nave roof may be more elaborately carved, panelled or coloured that the remainder of the roof. This was a canopy of honour called a 'rood celure' and was usually formed by panelling or by colouring and enriching the eastern bay of the nave roof. Such enrichment may also be found over the main altar and in both cases was used as protection for the rood and altar as well as being in honour of these two very sacred parts in the church. The protection was frequently necessary in churches where the roof, especially in the chancel which was the responsibility of the priest, was not in good repair.

Roof covering

Until the introduction of burnt clay, stone or slate, shingles or thatch was used.

In Anglo-Saxon times wooden shingles were used, particularly for churches. The carpenters were very clever in their use of timber and those parts of a tree which were unsuitable for beams were cut by hand so that the grain of the wood served to shed the water. The shingles were overlapped on the steeply pitched roofs so that the snow could not drift in between or rain penetrate. Shingles continued to be used into the fifteenth century but with the increased coset of timber they became uneconomic.

That was a very popular roofing material and has proved its worth for some thousands of years and churches in Norfolk and Suffolk may still be found with thatched roofs. Thatch is a durable covering being a good insulator and completely waterproof, but it needs a steeply pitched roof so that the rainwater may be shed quickly. Good examples are Hales and Potter Heigham, Norfolk and Bramfield, Fritton and Thornham Parva, Suffolk.

Thatched roofs for churches may be made from, reeds, rushes, barley, wheat or rye straw the best of which is the Norfolk reed which can last for a hundred years.

Apart from thatch and shingles another early form of roof covering was stone which was frequently used by the Romans to roof their houses. Stone slabs came from many quarries in the limestone belt which ran from Dorset to East Yorkshire but perhaps the best stone roofing slabs came from Horsham, Sussex and they are practically indestructible. Later with the reduction of the roof-pitch of church roofs sheet lead was an excellent material for keeping out the wet. The disadvantage of lead is its lack of rigidity; it will lie very well while flat, but if tilted too much the sheets sag and 'creep'. From the fourteenth century the tendency was to reduce the roof-pitch more and more until the roofs became almost flat.

Carpenters' Numerals

Looking up into the roofs of the medieval churches it can be seen that they are constructed of an enormous amount of oak timbers consisting of many pieces all of which must fit together accurately.

It was the normal practice for the carpenters to prepare the pieces in their yard and assemble them on the site. This meant that all the joints would also be made ready for assembly and would, therefore, require to be numbered and this was done with a system of Roman numerals, Arabic figures were unknown. The system was simple but effective the craftsmen using various combinations of I V and X which they were able to follow when it came to erecting the timbers and fitting the matching parts of the joists together. In their system the Roman IV became IIII and IX became VIIII. It seems probable that they adopted this system because XI upside down became IX which would be confusing. The number V was often cut upside down and by so doing it would be possible for IV to become VI if the timber was reversed and so they used IIII for IV. They also made one stroke serve for both ten and five when used together and two or more tens shared one crossing stroke thus saving time.

e.g. XV (15) XX (20) XXV (25)

Vaulting

BOXGROVE, SUSSEX.
Early C13 cross-ribbed or quadripartite vaulting. Painting on ceiling mid C16.

In the Middle Ages there was an ever present dread of fire which, owing to the vast amounts of timber was a threat to cathedrals, monasteries and churches. There were no adequate means of fire-fighting and the histories of many a cathedral and church give an account of devastating fires.

Canterbury Cathedral was devastated by fire in 1174 and the account of this catastrophe given by Gervall, a monk, tells of the anguish caused by the desolation of beautiful work, the result of labours over many years.

The problem was to safeguard the building against the risk and spread of fire and as a timber roof was the most inflammable part of the church an inner protection of stonework was devised and used when possible.

One of the ways of prevention in the eleventh and early twelfth centuries used by the Normans was a simple barrel vault in stone. The barrel vault was simply a long stone arch which was used where the walls were thick enough to resist the tremendous pressure exerted by this type of vaulting which was only suitable for comparatively small buildings and in this country was never used to any great extent. Where found in parish churches it was usually in the chancel and narrow aisles. However, at Copford, Essex, it is possible to see a Norman nave which originally had a barrel roof but which was removed in the thirteenth century. The springers are still to be seen, together with their colouring. Examples may be seen in the Dark Entry of the cloisters of Westminster Abbey, the chapel of St John in the Tower of London and the chancel of Kempley, Gloucestershire.

The masons soon learnt to produce a cross or groined vault by intersecting two barrel vaults at right angles dividing the vault into four panels formed by the crossing. A good example may be seen in Ely Cathedral, formerly an Abbey. The curves of the intersections form sharp edges, styled arrises or groins. Both the barrel and groin vaulting were copied from the Romans but unlike the Romans, who were able to erect groined vaults over buildings, with a span of eighty feet or more, the Romanesque builders constructed very few high groined vaults and as a rule they were only employed for low and narrow spans, e.g. the undercroft of Westminster Abbey and Lastingham, North Yorks. crypt.

The Romanesque arch created problems for the builders as the width of the archway is determined by the radius of the arch and so where a narrow transept met a wide nave the different widths of arch have to meet at the same height which means that the narrower transeptal arch has to begin from a higher springing point than the nave arch. The difficulty of building a stone vault over a wide space where the semi-circular arch is the only form of arch employed is because semi-circular arches are twice as wide as they are high. Because of this the wider the arch the higher the arch and the narrower the arch the lower the arch. A further reason is that in vaulting some arches will be wide and some narrow and so some arches will be high and some low and, therefore, it is difficult to vault wide spaces with arches of different heights. Supposing that a stone vault is to be built over a given space and the space is square. Four semi-circular arches will be built on the four equal sides of the square and being of the same width will all rise to the same height. Next it is necessary to built two semicircular arches on the diagonal lines across the square from corner to corner. A diagonal is longer than any side and so the arches on the diagonal lines will be wider and higher that the arches on the four sides of the square. The vault will, therefore, have four arches of equal height and two arches of greater height with very awkward results and that is precisely the trouble with which the builder of semi-circular arches was confronted. As soon as he altered the width of his arch he altered the height and so found that he could not have a satisfactory vault. This problem was resolved with the use of the pointed arch in the thirteenth century which enabled unequal widths of arch to reach the same height as the angle of the curve could be varied as required.

A further problem with the groined vault was that an exact model in wood had to be constructed and it was this which presented the difficulty as it required the use of planks which in the days before saws, were difficult to make. The only way was to cut down a tree and with an adze work away on each side of the trunk until this enormous amount of labour and waste of timber resulted in a plank. In addition to this, wooden vaults or centre supports were required. On the wooden centre, when it had been fixed in place, was laid a thick layer of mortar in which was packed pieces of undressed stone on edge. This was continued with smaller pieces of stone until the required arch form was reproduced. When the mortar had set the centre would be removed and reused to construct another vault. This centring was expensive and labour consuming even for a nave-aisle, chapel or crypt and so to construct on of these enormously heavy vaults over a lofty and broad nave would require enormously strong and extensive scaffolding and because of this the builders shrank from the task.

The solution to the expensive centring was to have two sets, one of stone which remained as an integral part of the vault and the other of timber which was supported by the stone centring. On the timber centring was built the web of the vault which was the filling in of the parts lying between stone ribs. This was probably effected by planks being laid across from rib to rib on which was built the web, the planks being re-used in other vaults of the same shape and dimensions. The stone centring was at first simply two transverse arches and two diagonal arches of stone which intersected producing eight ribs.

The four diagonal ribs divided the vault into four parts or cells and because they cross the vault and intersect at the centre the vault is termed an intersecting quadripartite ribbed vault or simply a cross-ribbed vault. An advantage into this type of vault was that as it was divided into four triangular cells they could be vaulted one at a time, the centring used for the first vault could be reused for each of the other vaults. In addition, if required, one or more of the cells may be taken out and replaced by a new one without pulling down all the other cells.

With a groined vault half of the whole weight was taken on the two transverse arches which, therefore, had to be broad and massive requiring very strong centres for their erection. In the cross-ribbed vault much of the weight falls on the diagonal arches and so the transverse arches could be built much less massively and with less centring, e.g. Beverley Minster Choir, Humberside. Where there are a series of cross-ribbed vaults, as at Beverely Minster, three ribs spring from the capital of each vaulting shaft so that lateral thrusts of the vault are forced down vertically and more effectively distributed. In some early eleventh-century vaults one of the diagonal arches was built complete and then the second arch was built in two halves butting against either side of the complete arch at the point of intersection. Later the two arches were provided with one common block at the apex which was shaped with four shoulders to receive the four ribs built up to it and when later the block shoulders were greatly lengthened the block was of considerable weight. This block, which gradually grew larger, was common to four or more ribs and is termed a keystone or, more gradually, a boss and, being large and heavy, it weighted the ribs at their apex and prevented them from rising. The weight of the boss was still further increased in later vaulting by prolonging it downward when it was termed a pendant.

An additional arch was later added between the main transverse arches and supported on a minor pier which divided the vault into six unequal parts making a sexpartite vault.

The groined vault was invariably built in rubble but when diagonal ribs were introduced the cells continued to be constructed of rubble as dressed stone, i.e.

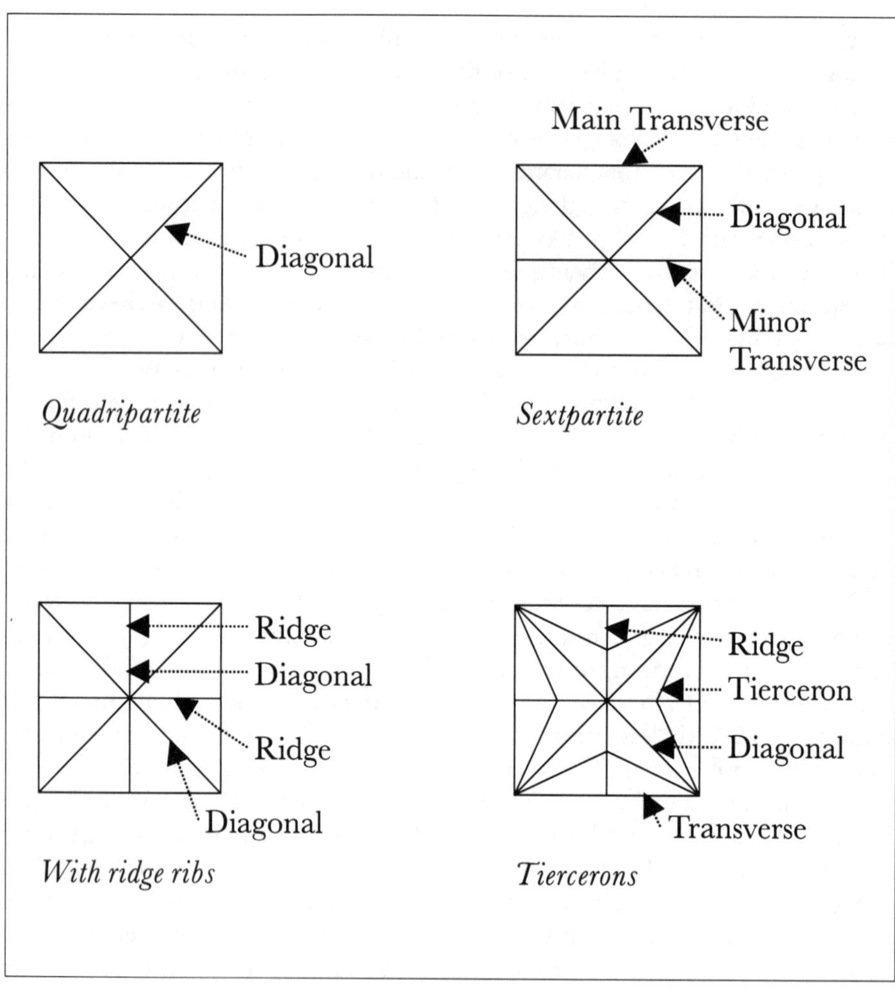

FIGURE 13.
Examples of transverse and ridge ribs.

ashlar would have been too expensive. The rubble web would be at least a foot thick and its great weight required extra thick walls, piers and arches to support it. To lighten a rubble vault light stone, e.g. chalk was used as it was not only light but easy to work. The best material was a deposit called tufa which came from Kent or Worcestershire and which has a rough surface giving a good hold for mortar. A large part of the vaults of Worcester Cathedral are built of tufa. Where the vaults were built of rubble they were rough and unsightly and so the rubble was covered with a smooth coat of plaster which was decorated with painted scroll work and other designs, e.g. Boxgrove Priory, Sussex.

When two half cells of a quadripartite vault was filled in with coursed ashlar a ragged joint was left where the upper courses met at the ridge and this was made even worse where they were filled with coursed rubble. To cover this joint and hide it from view a new rib, a ridge rib, was inserted. Each vaulting bay has two ridges, one running lengthwise and the other crosswise and so two ridge ribs were required.

With the introduction of the ridge ribs further diagonal and transverse ribs were introduced called 'tiercerons' which sprang from the same capitals as the diagonal and transverse ribs. They resemble the diagonal ribs as they run obliquely but they differ in that they do not rise to the central boss but to some point on one of the ridge ribs. The addition of tiercerons greatly facilitated the process of filling-in the cells especially where rubble was uses as they cut by at least half the distance to be spanned by centring. They never lost their popularity till the last days of Gothic architecture.

Until the fourteenth century all the ribs of vaults had some important constructional object but in the last years of the thirteenth century ribs were introduced which were merely decorative. These ribs, called 'liernes' or tie-ribs, do not rise to the central boss neither do they spring from the capital of a vaulting shaft but pass from any point on any one rib to any point on any adjoining rib as may be necessary to produce attractive patterns. This style of vaulting rarely found its way into parish churches except in porches and under towers but examples can be seen in Thaxted, Essex, Malmesbury, Wiltshire and Elkstone, Gloucestershire.

The use of the lierne rib revolutionised vault construction. With the addition of ridge ribs and tiercerons followed by liernes the vault became nearly all rib and so the difficulties of web construction with its need for wooden centring almost disappeared. Now every part of a small vault in a cloister, aisle or porch could be filled in by simply dropping down a flat slab which rested on the rebated ribs thus forming a rib and vault panel.

Some builders went further by cutting down the surface of a stone slab on either side leaving a rib projecting in the centre. Gloucester Cathedral cloister and Henry VII's Chapel, Westminster Abbey, are examples.

One more artistic and constructional triumph came in the fifteenth century. It was one of those things which was bound to come in the development of the English vault though it never came to France, Spain or other great Gothic areas. The English mason was always looking for short cuts and to get the maximum result with the minimum of labour. To save himself trouble he had persisted in retaining a web of rubble but later he substituted ashlar blocks all of the same width to fill the webs; to save himself trouble with the ragged joint at the ridge he added a ridge rib and to save trouble in centring he added tiercerons. To make web construction even easier he spread a network of liernes over the whole

LICHFIELD CATHEDERAL, STAFFORDSHIRE.
C13 tierceron vaulting.

TEWKESBURY ABBEY, GLOUCESTERSHIRE.
C14 lierne vaulting.

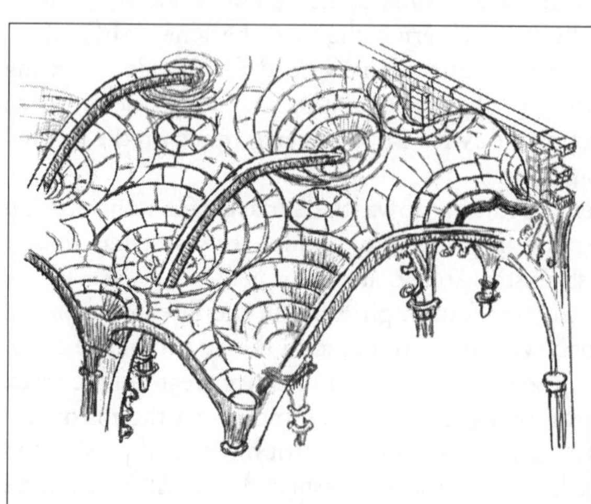

FIGURE 14.
Fan vaulting with pendants as seen from above.

cell so that the web construction only consisted of dropping in thin panels between the ribs and later cut panel and rib out of the same slab. The more he reduced and simplified the construction of the web the more intricate and complex he made the construction of the rib.

It was in the sophistication of rib construction that the final triumph was to be made, a new form known as fan-vaulting. In this form numerous ribs spread out at equal angles and with the same curve producing, when view from below, a fan-like appearance where the bundle of ribs form an inverted cone or part of a cone having concave sides. The vault ribs formed panels patterned to represent window tracery and were close together that the rib and panel could be cut from one piece of stone. The ribs acted as stiffeners for the shell and could be freely arranged. Toward the end of the fifteenth century fan vaulting achieved some remarkable developments when the central bosses or vaults were elongated into pendants. A very fine example is the vault of Henry VII's Chapel in Westminster Abbey.

CIRENCESTER, GLOUCESTERSHIRE.
Early C16 fan vaulting.

It will have been seen that the four celled vault had two arches intersecting at its apex. In some eleventh century work one of these diagonal arches or ribs was built complete and then the second arch was built in two halves butting against either side of the first arch at the point of intersection. The next step was to have a common block at the apex of the two arches the block being shaped with four projections to receive the four ribs built up to it. This block or keystone of the vault was even in Norman times occasionally carved with some device and when Gothic architecture was developed it soon became the rule to carve all roof bosses. Several small Norman churches have elaborate carvings on the keystones, e.g. Elkstone, Gloucestershire, where a strap-pattern in the centre is surrounded by four human heads looking outwards; Iffley, Oxfordshire, where there is a coiled dragon in the centre surrounded by small heads looking inwards; and Kilpeck, Hereford & Worcester, where there are four grotesque heads but it is difficult to tell whether they are animal or human.

The importance of roof bosses has only been appreciated comparatively recently and because of their position have remained undisturbed during the periods of iconoclasm and have the ravages of nineteenth-century restoration. The reason for their perseveration is because they are usually so high up that the detail cannot be seen with the naked eye and binoculars or a long-focus lens are required to reveal their beauty. Because they could not be seen from the ground and because all the details are there it would seem to prove that this glorious work was executed for the glory of God and not of man.

Deep and elaborate carving belongs very much to English craftsmen as the French, as a rule, carve the roof bosses with shallow figures on a plaque. There are exceptions and bosses are found carved in the English in some French churches and in the French style in some English churches. It was probably William of Sens who worked on Canterbury Cathedral who set the fashion for the English style. The pilgrims who made their way to Canterbury would have seen the elaborately carved roof bosses in the choir which was being built in the years following the devastating fire in 1174 and would have carried back their ideas to the buildings which were springing up in various parts of the country. It was not the designs which they took back with them, although this was probably done in some instances, but the general idea of carving the keystone with elaborate carving which, it is believed, came from Canterbury.

Vaulting ribs were built up on centring until they nearly met, then the keystone was lowered into place to keep the ribs firm. The keystone was usually carved so that the mouldings of the vaulting ribs appeared to be continued on the boss projections. This would not have been possible if the boss was carved before being lowered into place as it would have been almost impossible to carve the moulding so exactly that the real vaulting ribs fitted precisely with their continuation on the boss itself. On examination it is usually found that the

LINCOLN CATHEDERAL, LINCOLNSHIRE.
C13 Boss carved in workshop.

rib and boss mouldings are exact and so this must mean that the boss, or perhaps part of it, was carved after it had been dropped into place.

Although this was the usual procedure we find in St Hugh's Choir in Lincoln Cathedral quite a large number of bosses where the fit between the projections and the vaulting rib mouldings is very poor and in some cases looks as though their was no attempt at making a fit at all. It would seem, therefore, that many of the Lincoln bosses were carved in the workshop before they were put into place. St Hugh's Choir was built in the twelfth century when the carving of bosses was in its early stages but by the time the Angel Choir in Lincoln Cathedral was built in the second half of the thirteenth century the art had reached it apogee and craftsmen had learnt the technique of carving *in situ* and which became the general practice. It is interesting that one of the bosses in the south-west transept is only partially finished, the general lines of the design being marked out but only two thirds being finished which goes to prove that the best work was carried out *in situ*.

At first the boss was no larger than the voussoirs of the ribs but it very soon grew larger and more important. The advantage of making it large and heavy was that it weighted the ribs at their apex and prevented them from rising. They would, indeed, have looked heavy without their ornamental carving but with the carving they, without doubt, improve the look of a vaulted roof despite the fact that details of the carving cannot be seen by people in the church below. It was characteristic of the medieval craftsman to carve his design with as much care as if it was to be seen close to, even to the extent of figures holding books in their hands on the pages of which are lines and dots representing writing which cannot possibly be seen from the floor below without artificial aid. These bosses may be found in the transepts at Norwich Cathedral.

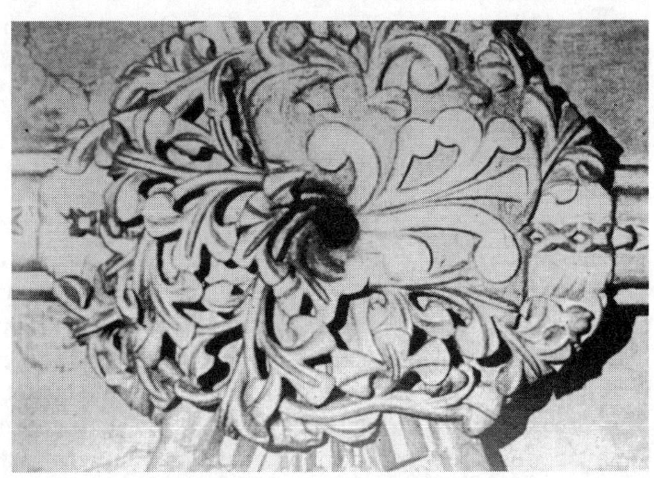

LINCOLN CATHEDERAL, LINCOLNSHIRE.
C13 Boss carved in situ but unfinished.

The weight and size of the boss was later in the fifteenth century still further increased

HOLY TRINITY, STRATFORD-ON-AVON, WARWICKSHIRE.
C15 Boss in north porch.

in purely English fashion by prolonging it downward when it was termed a pendant. In late vaulting the pendants often reached large dimensions like those in Henry VII's Chapel, Westminster and Oxford Cathedral.

The early bosses were mostly foliated which varied from simple, stylised, to naturalistic which abounded in the fourteenth century and was very fine work. Heraldic bosses arrived early in the fourteenth century and in the fifteenth century became more and more common. In later work sculptural representations of the life of Christ were common, e.g. Nativity, Maji in Adoration, Triumphant Entry into Jerusalem, Last Supper, Annunciation and Crucifixion. The life of Virgin Mary, Saints and Angels, men and women, heads, birds and beasts, everyday events and grotesques are also to be found. The Green Man too was not neglected. This pre-Christian symbol of fertility probably connected with the success of the harvest is depicted as a face or head with leafy stems growing out of the mouth or sometimes out of the eyes, ears, nose or forehead. The Green Man was frequently carved from Norman times to the end of the Gothic period and many examples may be found, e.g. Warmington, Northants; Patrington, Yorks; Hereford Cathedral; Worcester Cathedral; Tewkesbury Abbey, Gloucestershire; Ely Cathedral; Norwich Cathedral; Sampford Courtenay, Devon and Pershore, Hereford & Worcester.

The number of bosses increased in importance and volume during the late fourteenth century both in stone and timber roofs. In Exeter Cathedral which was rebuilt between 1301 and 1335 there are more than five hundred carved bosses and in the vast late fourteenth-century church of St Mary Redcliffe, Bristol, there are over eleven hundred bosses. Such was the dedication for carving and ornamentation that the masons working way above the clerestory carved hundreds of tiny figures on bosses; foliage, masks of men and monsters, satyrs and beasts as well as woodland leaves and flowers. Also to be found are the Lamb of God, St George wrestling with the dragon, a peasant with tooth-ache and two lovers kissing. All these were obviously carved with care of creation for its own sake as once the scaffolding had been removed no one would be able to see them.

When the might of the medieval Church was broken and iconoclasts swept through every place of worship with axe and hammer, smashing and defacing the sculptural masterpieces which appeared to them to be idols, the invisible host of carved roof-bosses remained untouched and unknown for almost four hundred years until binoculars and the telephoto lens of the modern camera revealed the glory of the English medieval craftsmanship.

15

Sepulchral Monuments

The desire to commemorate the dead in a worthy fashion is among the deepest instincts of humanity and it is not surprising, therefore, that it brought forth the finest art attainable. It may be debatable as to whether that art is good or bad and depends upon the age and taste of the beholder.

Monuments, effigies and chantry chapels of the medieval period reveal many insights into the lives and thoughts of those who were largely responsible for laying the foundation of the England we know today. What makes them important is their completeness of design which has not been merged into what has gone before or remodelled into what came after as were the greater buildings which have been handed down to us. The effigies and memorials also form a complete sequence of the clothes worn by the aristocracy, and sometimes merchants, showing the evolution of defensive armour produced by the gradual developments of new methods of warfare as well as the changing fashions of the ladies' costumes and head-dresses.

These monuments also offer a wonderful field of the study of heraldry and in particular the art of the sculptor, the modeller, metal worker and smith as well as revealing the various materials which have been used, such as Purbeck marble and other marbles, stone, wood, alabaster, gesso and enamels. Alabaster was our English marble which came principally from Derbyshire and Nottinghamshire, especially from Chellaston in Derbyshire with Nottingham as an important centre for its manufacture. The most costly material was bronze which will only be found in Westminster Abbey, Canterbury Cathedral and St Mary's church, Warwick.

In addition to all this the histories and tragedies of the families represented by their monuments presents and wealth of information which enables us to realise the life, aspirations, religious emotions and artistic impulses of the people who living during some of the most interesting and disturbing periods in English history.

It is not possible to judge the quality of the sculptors's art as the early effigies were covered with modelled gesso and paint which has disappeared leaving only the base figure for us to examine. The effigies on tombs we now see retain little evidence of their former decoration. In Puritan times they were whitewashed and later suffered far worse indignity at the hands of the so-called 'restorers' who when not destroying them scrubbed and re-worked the surfaces of many of the effigies removing not only the whitewash but the coloured decoration as well to the detriment of their value and loss of beauty. This desecration is not so apparent where the tombs are constructed of alabaster as the beauty of the material helps to compensate for the absence of its original colour and gilt.

In the thirteenth and fourteenth centuries the stone and wooden effigies were coated with gesso which was a mixture of size and whiting forming a very smooth plaster. Timber was often used for an effigy as it was very suitable for conveying over rough cart tracks and was much lighter than stone and less liable to fracture. The block of oak was hewn out of the solid trunk, the underside being hollowed out and sometimes filled with charcoal to prevent decay by damp. The block was carefully modelled and the cracks covered by canvas and glue over which was spread the gesso. Details such as ringed mail were impressed by stamps while the gesso was in a soft state. When the gesso was dry the effigy was coloured and gilded, which was a fine art and very costly. Good examples of this work may be seen at Hildersham, Cambridgeshire and Goudhurst, Kent.

In the early twelfth and thirteenth centuries stone coffins were in general use for the eminent and wealthy some of whom were buried in the floor of the church with the lid forming part of the pavement as at Knapton, Norfolk, while others were allowed to remain above ground and were carved with quatrefoils. Those we now see may not be in their original positions. The privilege was also reserved for the bodies of founders or benefactors. Their tombs were generally recessed under low arches in the north wall of the chancel.

When the church became full the stone coffins were interred in the churchyard on the south side as near to the church as possible and were sunk to the level of the earth as at Greensted, Essex.

The favourite ornament on the early covers was a cross and circle without lettering, the profession or occupation of the deceased being shown by symbols on one or both sides of the cross such as a sword or shield for a man-at-

MASHAM, N. YORKSHIRE
C14 coffin lid with shears symbol.

WATERPERRY, OXFORDSHIRE.
C14 canopy.

arms; a bow, arrow, axe or horn for a forester; a pastoral staff and chalice for an ecclesiastic; sheers, gloves, fish, pincers or carpenter's square for various tradesmen. Later these symbols were incised with a figure representing the deceased to be followed later still by a carved semi-effigial figure which developed into a complete effigy.

Prior to 1275 the slab coffin covers were narrower at the bottom than at the top but later they were made the same width. When tombs were placed away from the walls without canopies, the coffins were enclosed in chests constructed of thin stone slabs and so lost their coffin-like appearance.

During the second half of the thirteenth century canopies appeared over tombs which were usually low. The tomb was enclosed on both sides by walls each containing arches filled with open tracery resting upon shafts having capitals and bases. Above the arches would be moulded gables.

SALISBURY CATHEDERAL, WILTSHIRE.
C14 tomb chest with effigy.

In the case of highly important personages the effigies were on top of a table tomb sometimes beneath a canopy. Most of these effigies were of stone but some were of timber, usually life size, and showing a person in the prime of life. They are usually shown in armour with heraldic shields, often cross-legged and having a life-like appearance as if about to rise. The head of the effigy, when in armour, usually rests on a helm and the feet on a lion symbolising bravery. Sometimes the feet of a female rest on a dog indicating fidelity.

From the second half of the fourteenth century to the seventeenth century effigies of knights, where entitled, will show whether they were Knights of the Garter. This Order was inaugurated on St George's Day 1348 at Windsor Castle. The origin of the Garter is not certain but the story favoured by historians is the emblem, the blue garter, had its origin in an incident at a ball at Calais, when the Countess of Salisbury, Joan the Fair Maid of Kent, later to become the wife of the Black Prince, lost her garter whilst dancing, and Edward III returned it with the words *Honi Soit Qui Mal y pense.*

The wearing of livery collars was also general at this time. The two most frequently found are the SS collar which formed the distinctive badge of the House of Lancaster and the Yorkist collar of the Suns and Roses. The SS collar was worn by person of every degree from royalty to esquire as well as by ladies and civilians. Henry IV introduced it before his accession and it is supposed to symbolise the word 'Soverayne'. The SS of the collar were usually made of gold or silver sewn on a ribbon of silk or velvet joined by a buckled locket but sometimes was wholly made of metal finely worked. Two very fine examples may be seen on the effigy of Sir John Savage, Macclesfield, Cheshire (1470) and Lady Benedicte Vernon, Tong, Shropshire. The Yorkist collar of the Sun and Roses was similarly made and worn and good examples are to be seen on the effigies of Sir Robert Harcourt (1471) at Stanton Harcourt, Oxfordshire and Sir Ralph Fitzherbert (1483) Norbury, Derbyshire.

On fifteenth century tombs where they are effigies of husband and wife they are sometimes shown hand in hand instead of, as usual, their hands in prayer.

There is a romantic glamour about the crusader which seems to inspire picturesque but inaccurate theories. There is

NORBURY, DERBYSHIRE.
Bedesman with rosary.

a supposition that all round churches were built by Templars and that all cross-legged effigies represented men who went to the Crusades while the straight-legged ones stayed at home. This fashion, which is particularly English, did not become popular until the mid thirteenth century when the Crusading period was almost over and yet a large majority of the knightly effigies made in the next century were shown with crossed-legs should not be accepted as evidence of this without further evidence from records or heraldry. There are many effigies and brass engravings, however, where it can be proved that the cross-legged figures commemorated never set foot in the Holy Land. Perhaps a better reason was that the Church regarded cross-legs as a symbol of an interruption of the normal flow of life and so it probably meant that they died at an early age.

Following Henry VIII's death there was a wave of iconoclasm in which many objects were ripped out of parish churches and sold or broken up. These extremists, in their frenzy, pulled down crosses in the churchyard, prised up brasses from the floor and desecrated family tombs and monuments. At Inkpen, Berkshire, the stone figure of a Crusader, Sir Roger de Ingpen, was thrown out into the farmyard adjoining the church were it was used as a whetstone for three hundred and fifty years.

By the beginning of the thirteenth century tombs were being decorated with small figures of apostles and saints in roundels and quatrefoils which may be seen on the tomb of Bishop Henry Marshall in Exeter Cathedral. The next step was to place figures round the tomb under arches as may be seen on the base of the shrine of St Cantilupe in Hereford Cathedral.

Near the end of the thirteenth century, c.1290, the first genuine adoption of the weeper motif appeared when the tomb was decorated with a series of little figures placed under canopies and representing the relatives of the decreased including the deceased's children who are usually shown with the boys on one side of the panel and the girls on the other. Frequently the children are seen holding a skull which indicates they died some time before the deceased. The ravages of infant mortality were often indicated by the dead babes wrapped in their chrisom clothes. The weeper motif continued through the fourteenth century especially on alabaster tombs which became very popular. From Chellaston, Derbyshire, in 1391 were introduced angel-weepers holding shields in front of them with both hands and which may be seen on the tomb of Sir Thomas Arderne and his wife Matilda at Elford, Staffordshire, who are shown holding hands. These angel-weepers became very popular taking the place of the relative weepers which were not used again until the close of the fifteenth century. A fine tomb showing both relative and angel weepers is that of Sir Ralph Fitzherbert (1473) and his wife Elizabeth at Norbury, Derbyshire.

A further variation was the use of bedesmen, 'prayermen'. They are usually standing, as at Elford, but sometimes seated, as at Stanton Harcourt, and generally hold a rosary or prayer book. These figures may also be found on the feet of the effigy or carefully seated upon the animal on which the feet rest as on the tomb of Sir Nicholas Fitzherbet at Norbury, Derbyshire and on the tomb of John Lord Bouchier (1400) and wife at Halstead, Essex, where there are two bedesmen between them at their feet.

LITTLE EATON, ESSEX.
C17 children weepers.

With the return of weepers in the fifteeneth century the vogue continued well into the seventeenth century and many may be seen carved on the sides of the heavy structural monument of the Elizabethan and Stuart periods.

Prior to the Reformation effigies wee shown in a reverent attitude with hands folded in prayer but during the Reformation upheaval a variety of irreverent attitudes were adopted, the most popular being that of lolling on an elbow, an attitude strangely out of place in a church of today but perhaps not so when we reflect on the way many people behaved in church in those days. Originating in the reign of Elizabeth, but becoming popular during the seventeenth century, was the attitude of kneeling which was, of course, quite unobjectionable. Children were shown kneeling, which was

GREAT WALTHAM, ESSEX.
C17 standing wall monument. Effigies on shelves stifly reclining on elbows.

FELSTED, ESSEX.
Rich chapel. Tomb of Lord Chancellor Richard Rich, died 1568 and his son Robert second Lord Rich died 1581 and his brother Richard, which was probably erected *c*1620 by the third Lord Rich. Lord Chancellor Rich is shown reclining on his elbow looking at his son kneeling by the side facing a prayer desk. In a hollowed cave behind the prayer desk lies a shrouded skull, a memorial of brother Richard.

supposed to denote submission to their parents. Sometimes all attitudes may be found on the same monument.

HATFIELD BROAD OAK, ESSEX.
C17 ledger stone.

In the fifteenth and early sixteenth centuries the figures round the sides of the tombs were set in niches under canopies or cusped or ogee arches. Unfortunately many of these figures are either missing from their niches or are badly damaged.

Tombs of the seventeenth century are perhaps the most interesting and show an uneven progression from Jacobean to Classical style which prevailed until the late eighteenth century. It involved accurate portraits, figures and canopies and heraldry became even more important. The tombs of the first quarter of the century, generally termed Jacobean, are of great interest and beauty. They are usually of immense size, lavishly coloured and adorned with innumerable shields charged with coats of arms. The crests at the heads and the animals at their feet are usually works of art in themselves.

Embellishments, which seem meaningless to us today, were typical; the strapwork and crestings, skull, skeletons, bones, hour-glasses, scythes and coffins all reminders of death. Figures representing the Virtues – Faith Hope, Charity, Fortitude, Justice, Prudence and Temperance and other figures including cherub heads.

It was in this century that following the decline in brass making, massive incised stones or floor-slabs were used as memorials. They were usually made of bluish-grey hard stone with the memorial carving at the head of the slab and the inscription below. Black marble and alabaster were also used. They were normally works of art and were executed in low relief so that they would not be an impediment to the feet of people walking over them but not always, as in some cases the heraldry has been very deeply carved and is easily noticed when walking down an aisle. Was this done with the object of drawing the attention of the passer-by to the memorial stone in the hope that the person would say a prayer for the sould of the deceased? The heraldry and the beautiful lettering on these floor-slabs is well worth studying.

The eighteenth century brought monuments which cannot fail to be noticed because they often dominate and even dwarf the church. The sculpture is as magnificent as reverence is lacking. Black and white marble superseded alabaster at the end of the seventeenth century and colour ceased. Figures often stand in a posture which does not produce humility but rather self-glorification. The attire was often classical costume with wigs but sometimes the figures were dressed in a Roman toga which, although essentially eighteenth century, may be found in the last part of the seventeenth century. A fine example is the monument to Sir William Maynard at Little Easton, Essex.

Prelates show the least change in pose and by the first half of the fifteenth century have their hands joined in prayer. The inevitability of death and the contrast between wordly pomp and future corruption was a constant theme of preaching and between the fifteenth and seventeenth centuries it was expressed by the gruesome fashion of portraying the deceased dignitary as a corpse or skeleton. Sometimes a snail, mouse, frog or snake are shown crawling over the body as at Tewkesbury Abbey, Gloucestershire, on the tomb known as the Wakeman Cenotaph named after the last Abbot, John Wakeman. Also the

WARWICK, ST MARY, WARWICKSHIRE.
Beauchamp chapel. Tomb of Richard Beauchamp, Earl of Warwick, died 1439, showing barrel form of hearse of copper gilt.

chapel of Bishop Richard Fleming (*c*1430), Lincoln Cathedral. During this period the deceased was laid above in his robes of office while underneath lay the cadaver. Later in the period the representation of the dead body was shown in a winding sheet (Canon William Parkhouse (1540), Exeter Cathedral and John Beresford and his wife Agnes in Fenny Bentley, Derbyshire), where they both lie in shrouds tied up above their heads, at the ankles and below their feet so that no part of them may be seen. Their twenty-one children are also shown shrouded round the tomb. Although John Beresford was not a cleric the effigies are a very good example of the prevailing fashion.

Metal Grates and Hearses

At the close of the thirteenth century the smith was occasionally called upon to supply enclosures to protect effigies and tombs from accident or wilful damage but by the fourteenth century it was general to enclose tombs by grates. Characteristic of the English grates was the practical design which was adopted during the latter half of the fourteenth century., The construction took the form of a top and bottom rail having connecting bars or standards which were spaced close enough to prevent a person climbing over and were spiked to hold candles which were provided on the abit of the deceased when prayers were said for his soul and the souls of his family. The corner standards are often stronger in order to give adequate strength as well as additional decoration. A very fine example protects the top part of Queen Eleanor's tomb (1292) in Westminster Abbey, the ends of the standards being finished with trefoiled spikes which were very probably used as prickets. Another good example enclosing the table tomb and effigy is that of Sir John Swinford (1371) at Spratton, Northamptonshire

TEWKESBURY ABBEY, GLOUCESTERSHIRE.
Wakeman Cenotaph. C16 cadaver with snake, frog etc.

In the fourteenth century wrought iron hearses were erected over tombs of persons of distinction for their protection with prickets for candles. The word 'hearse' in Middle English meant 'a moveable frame' over a tomb as protection, to hold candles and to take a

KIRKDALE, N. YORKSHIRE.
C19 Cartouche tablet.

black pall or cloth cover during Requiem or other funeral services. One of these medieval palls survives at Arundel, Sussex. Many of these hearses were made of wood and were part of the church furnishing but have now disappeared, only a few metal ones remaining.

On the tomb of Sir John Marmion (1387) at West Tanfield, North Yorkshire, is a fine example. It is lightly constructed with corner standards each having a spur at the foot and surmounted by prickets composed of four leaves over a twisted ring with a spike in the centre. The side and top bars are battlemented, the top bar holding three more prickets. Another example in barrel form, is over the tomb of Richard Beauchamp, Earl of Warwick (1439) in St Mary's church, Warwick. The tomb was made in 1455 some sixteen years after his death and a timber hearse was made as a pattern followed by the barrel hearse to be seen today protecting the effigy. It is made of copper gilt and the tomb has standards of brass at the corners.

Cartouche Tablets

The word cartouche comes from the Latin word *carta* meaning 'leaf of paper' or 'papyrus'.

Cartouche tablets are a type of wall monument which became common in the seventeenth and eighteenth centuries. They are usually of marble and resemble a scrolled or ornate form enclosing an inscription in the centre with a coat of arms or crest over.

Wall Tablets

A memorial wall tablet is usually composed of a rectangular lettered panel surrounded by a carved frame or flanked by columns or pilasters.

CRESSING, ESSEX.
Early C17 wall monument. Kneeling figures. In the predella are kneeling daughter and baby in a cradle.

16

Armour, Civilian and Clerical Costume

The effigies to be seen on table tombs provide an excellent opportunity to study the changes in armour between the twelfth and seventeenth centuries.

In the twelfth and first half of the thirteenth centuries the head was encased in a flat-topped cylindrical helm and the body in a shirt of mail reaching to the knees and which also covered the arms and hands. The legs and feet are also covered in mail and the shield is long and kite-shaped. The sword is long and hung from a narrow belt. This form of armour lasted until *c*1250. (Knight, Temple Church, London).

The helm continued to be flat-topped until *c*1280 but now had a moveable visor. After 1280 it became conical. The hood of mail covered the head and neck coming partly over the shirt of mail. During the early part of the thirteenth century the shoulders were protected by leather pads called ailettes. The ailettes became necessary as the conical helm caused the sword to glance off the helm but these are rarely carved on effigies but are shown on brasses. (Sir Gerard de L'Isle (died *c*1287) Stowe Nine Churches, Northants.)

The shirt of mail continued with the arms and hands being covered. The legs encased in mail with the knees and elbows covered with plates or cops made of steel and leather. These cops helped to prevent the drag of the mail upon the joints allowing freedom of movement.

The surcoat is shortened and the shield smaller containing the arms of the deceased. The sword-belt holds the scabbard in two places with a small guiding strap in between, the sword hanging diagonally across from right to left. A very good example is the effigy of Madoc ap Llewelyn ap Griffin (*c.*1331), Gresford, Clwyd. In the period between 1320–1350 hardly two effigies are alike. The long surcoat had been found dangerous, becoming entangled with the legs of the wearer when unhorsed and so it was shortened to the knees at the back and to the thighs in front, the sides being well split up. It was also tightened over the body and heralded the coming of the jupons.

The head was now protected by a basinet of steel either round-topped, conical or ridged. Attached to the basinet by staples, was hung the camaille constructed of banded mail protecting the neck and top of the shoulders.

In addition to mail the body was now further protected by plates of steel which cover the front parts of the legs and feet and back of the upper arms, the knees, elbows and shoulders have circular cops. Gauntlets took the place of the mittens and a series of small plates cover the feet over the mail. Under the shirt of mail was a padded garment covering the body from the neck to the knees and upper part of the arms, the lower edge of which is usually shown.

The sword is fastened to the belt in various ways but usually by two swivels fastened to the scabbard and was kept in place by attachment to the waist belt. (Sir John D'Abernoun (1327) Stoke D'Abernon, Surrey).

During the last half of the fourteenth century and first quarter of the fifteenth century the head is protected by a conical helmet. The camaille is composed of banded of linked mail and is attached to the helm by means of lacing.

Over the armour is worn a jupon, a tight fitting garment upon which were emblazoned the arms of the wearer. At first the jupon was full skirted but was later cut short and finished with an ornamental border. A shirt of mail was still worn but the effigies do not show what armour was worn beneath the jupon although a breastplate was certainly worn. The arms are protected by pieces of plate, the shoulders with flexible laminated plates and the elbows with decorated cops. The hands are encased in steel gauntlets.

Round the hips, horizontally, is a rich belt composed or ornamental squares with clasps of various designs. The sword is worn on the left side and at first a second belt was used to which the sword was attached but later it was fastened to the ornamental belt suspended from a single point. One the right side appears a dagger hung from the belt by a chain.

Over the thighs are breeches composed of padded material on which are fastened steel plates, the knees with cops of steel and leather and the legs in plate. Near the end of the period the edges of the plate are often ornamented with a border. The feet are covered by pointed shoes composed of overlapping pieces of flexible plate, the joints between them and the shin guards being protected by mail as were the inner parts of the knee joints, shoulders and elbows. The spurs are fastened

LITTLE DUNLOW, ESSEX.
Armour showing plates and tuilles.

BLACKMORE, ESSEX.
Armour showing taces.

with ornamental buckled straps. (Hilton, *c*1400, Swine, Humberside).

During the fifteenth century up to 1435 there was a gradual disappearance of the camaile, jupon, mail shirt and the horizontal sword belt. In their place appeared the knight in a complete suit of plate armour. The bascinet becomes flatter and in place of the camaille is introduced the plate beaver and gorget. By this addition the full armour of plate enclosing the wearer from top to toe was completed. The body is protected by breast and back plates which are finished at the waist by a short skirt of taces which were supported on a lining of leather or some other strong material. In the early part of the period there was an apron of mail which shows beneath the plates but this gradually disappeared and was followed by plates called taces which were fastened to the lower edge of the skirt. The elbows had enveloping reinforcements, the shoulders had extra protection in the form of large laminated pauldrons and roundels which guarded the armpits but sometimes these were replaced by oblong plates called palettes. Gauntlets were now given mittens instead of separate fingers. The toes of the sollerets were extended to excessive length and during the period a pair of pointed plates, known as tassets, hung by straps to cover the top of the thighs.

In the early part of the fifteenth century the hip-belt was worn over the taces but though usually, not always, the sword was hung at the left side by a narrow belt passing diagonally from the right hip and the dagger was fastened to the taces on the right side. Some good examples are Ralph Green (1418) and wife, Lowick, Northants and Sir Ralph Fitzherbert (1473) and wife, Norbury, Derbyshire.

This armour of this period showns no major change but there were some adjustments. The laminated pauldrons were replaced by large single plates shaped to the shoulder and often deeply ridged to obstruct sword cuts. The elbow cops grew larger and larger, especially when the shield was finally dispensed with after 1450. Effigies were usually shown bareheaded with the head resting on a tilting helm.

About the middle of the fifteenth century the sallet became popular taking the place of the bascinet. The sallet was similar to a wide-brimmed army 'tin-hat' having a projecting brim at the back to guard the neck with a visor in front but these were not seen on effigies as heads were usually bare-headed although examples may be seen on brasses as on the brass of R. Staunton, Castle Donington, Leicestershire.

The skirt of taces grew shorter but there was an increase in the size of the tuilles which were pointed plates hung over the thighs in the form of guards.

In the second half of the century the sword was worn in front of the body instead of at the left side, and the tabard begins to show itself as a short sleeved surcoat reaching to the middle of the thighs, charged with the wearer's arms. (Edward Stifford, 1499, Lowick, Northants).

The extravagances of the previous period vanished. The arm defences were smaller in size and were turned up at the neck as pike guards. The elbow and knee cops with the reinforcing plates were also smaller. The greaves or leg defences although practically unchanged were made with great skill to fit the subtle lines of shin, calf and ankle and the pointed sollerets were replaced by clumsy square-toed sabbatons.

The mail shirt now reaches almost to the knees and was sometimes slit up for convenience in riding. It was partly covered by the short skirt of taces from which hung two tuilles of varying size. The tabard now frequently appears.

During the latter half of the sixteenth century and the first quarter of the seventeenth century comprising the Elizabethan and Jacobean periods was seen the last stages in the use of armour for defence purposes. It gradually became superfluous, passing into disuse as firearms developed.

The tuilles were replaced by very small tassets consisting of rows of hinged plates lined with leather for defending the front of the thigh.

It was not long before armour was altered to conform to the then fashion of long doublet and puffed trunk hose and so the mail skirt and skirt of taces disappeared but the tassets were longer and larger and buckled to the projecting edge of the pointed breastplate which had become more rounded. Under the tassets, protecting the thighs down to the knees, were plates called cuisses. Pauldrons, made of several plates lined with leather, were also very large and almost met in front (Sir Gabriel Poyntz, (1607) and wife, North Ockendon, Essex). This tomb chest has an unusual feature, a tester unsupported by columns. As the period progressed the short round breastplate developed a central ridge and then a larger waist until it resembled an Elizabethan doublet.

At the beginning of the seventeenth century the breastplate became short again and rather flat. The short laminated tassets which had overhung the cuisses were extended from the waist to the knees displacing the cuisses. Under the tassets were worn puffed breeches and instead of plate leg defences jack-boots were worn (Lord Norris, 1601, two weeper sons, Westminster Abbey).

Civil Costume – Male

In medieval times most European countries passed 'sumptuary laws' against the private extravagances, especially in food and clothing. Some of the extravagances in the clothing fashions are depicted on brasses and tomb monuments, e.g. long sleeves, long pointed shoes, fur-trimmed robes and hats, especially woman's clothing. The contrast with the peasants' clothing, however, is not seen as the clothing portrayed on effigies in parish churches is usually that of merchants, the well-to-do or the aristocracy.

Exact grading of fabric, colour, fur-trimming, ornaments and jewels were laid down for every rank and income level. The middle class might be forbidden to own a carriage or wear ermine and peasants to wear any colour other than brown or black. According to a law of 1363 a merchant worth £1000 was entitled to the same dress and meals as a knight worth £500 and a merchant worth £200 the same as a knight worth £100.

The manor courts were expected to do what they could to suppress finery being worn by the lower classes. They were required to

> 'enquire whether any have used in any of their garments, velvet, satin, damask, taffeta, sarcent, chamlet or any fur or gold or silver otherwise than as the statutes made in the 14th year of Henry VIII and 1st and 2nd years of Philip and Mary do allow, you should present offenders.'

Expenditure of money by commoners did not suit the nobles because, among other reasons, they saw it benefitting the merchant class rather than themselves. The clergy considered that this expenditure drained money from the Church and so condemned it on the moral ground that extravagance and luxury were wicked and harmful to virtue. Generally the sumptuary laws were favoured as a means of curbing extravagance and encouraging thrift in the belief that if people could be made to save money, the King could obtain it when required.

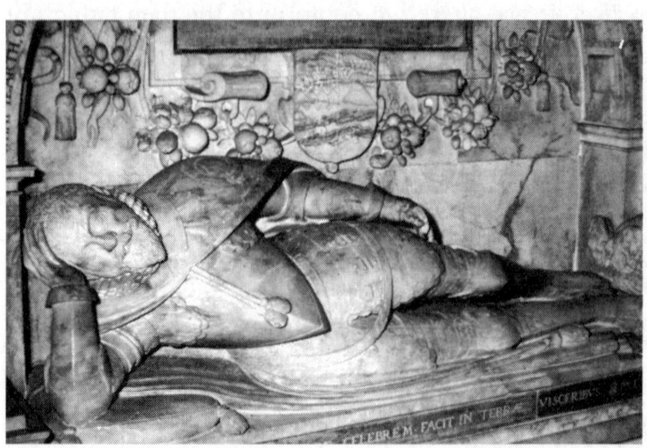

THEYDON MOUNT, ESSEX.
Armour showing pointed breast-plate.

The sumptuary laws proved unenforceable, the prerogative of adornment, like the drinking of liquor in a later century in America, defied prohibition.

Prior to the fourteenth century effigies are shown in armour and the earliest civilian fashion is the long cote-hardie a form of tunic reaching almost to the ankles and slit up in front. The sleeves reach to the elbows where they extend into hanging lappets. The forearms are covered by the tight fitting sleeves of the under tunic which have a row of buttons from wrist to elbow on each sleeve. Over the shoulders is worn the close fitting tippet or cape with a hood attached. The legs are in tight-fitting hose and the feet in long pointed shoes, either laced up at the sides or fastened with a strap across the instep. Hair is worn long with a forked beard but towards the end of the century the hair is worn shorter and the tippet usually omitted. A baudric, which was an ornamental sword belt, is sometimes worn. (Civilian, (1370), Shottesbrook, Berkshire.)

In the fifteenth century the tunic was extended to the ankles and buttoned close to the chin with full sleeves gathered at the wrist and secured with a narrow belt from which hung a short sword (Nicholas Canteys, (1431), Margate, Kent). A mantle, fastened by two or three buttons on the right shoulder, was worn at the beginning of the century but later fell into disuse. The hair was again worn long and the legs and feet were covered as before.

By the middle of the century the tunic was shortened, the sleeves being less full, and the shoes continued to have pointed toes. The hair was worn short.

After 1470 the tunic gave way to a long gown worn to the ankles, lined and edged with fur and open in front. The sleeves were wide, and round the waist was a girdle from which hung a rosary or purse (William Staunton, (1450), Elford Staffordshire).

By the end of the fifteenth century the gown acquired a broad collar and cuffs of fur with the fronts turned back to show the fur lining. Sometimes a belt was worn but it was quite usual for the gown to hang loose.

The next change was about 1525 when the gown was shown unbelted with long hanging false sleeves. Under the gown was worn the skirted doublet. The toes of the shoes were square like the sabbatons of contemporary military armour. The hair was generally worn long. This costume persisted until the early years of the reign of Elizabeth when the skirted doublet became shorter and was worn with trunk hose later replaced by stuffed breeches. The hair was cut short again and pointed beards occur. Ruffs came into fashion together with little frills at the wrists.

The long gown was usually confined to men of mature years whilst the young men and boys wore a short full cloak. Shoes were small and round toed.

At the time of Charles I ruffs and frills were replaced by collars and cuffs, the breeches were smaller and jackboots frequently worn. Both the long gown with false sleeves and the short cloak again appear.

BERDEN, ESSEX.
Costume – long gown.

During the Commonwealth period (1649–1660) hats had broad brims and boots had wide tops. The love locks and long hair of Charles' reign vanished and the hair was straight and cropped. Ruffs of plain linen were worn at the wrists and the plain white linen or cambric collars were of various sizes. The coats were often sleeveless or had coloured sleeves sewn into the coat under the shoulder wings. Puritans wore a longer version often completely buttoned with the shirt slit at intervals and plain, narrower sleeves. The embroidered sword-belt and sword formed part of the accessories. The long wide breeches reached to just below the knee.

In the years 1660 to 1689, with the return of the monarchy, dress became gay and colourful. The short jacket remained fashionable with elbow length sleeves ending in a cuff. Sometimes the sleeve had a slit in the front. The jacket was secured by a top button only so that the white shirt, which ended at the wrist in deep ruffs showed through. The jacket and petticoat breeches resembling knee length skirts, were both decorated by satin and velvet bows and loops. Lace edged neckwear and garter sashes with silk stockings were also worn, Shoes returned to fashion and were usually made of black leather.

Although men continued to wear their own hair, curled and waved to shoulder level, the periwig became very popular forming an enormous mass of curls and ringlets over the head on to the shoulders and reaching well down the back. The periwig changed its form during the period when it developed a centre parting on the forehead where it rose higher and, in the reign of James II, it formed two high masses of curls on either side of the parting.

During James's reign the broad brimmed hat remained. Silk breeches, fastened at the knee by a buckle or buttons, were worn under a silk coat with pockets situated low down and trimmed with gold braid or buttons.

In the eighteenth century the coat was more waisted with a fuller and wider skirt, rather longer than before and slit up at the back. Pockets were now low on the hips. The shirt was of silk, cambric or linen with a full puff at the wrist terminating in lace ruffles and the cravat was very long and full, having lace or fringed ends. Later in the century, a silk embroidered waistcoat was worn with velvet breeches. The full wig, stockings and buckled black shoes still continued.

As wall monuments had become popular the bust took the place of the full effigy. The cost of a wall monument was far less than a table tomb and effigy as well as taking less room in the church.

Civil Costume – Female

The earliest female costume shown on effigies was composed on an underdress consisting of a kirtle which was a long loose gown having tight sleeves with rows of buttons set closely together underneath. Over this was worn a gown which was either sleeveless or with close sleeves reaching to the elbow which was known as a cote-hardie. A wimple, which was a material scarf, completely concealed the throat and a *couvrechef* or veil covered the head, falling to the shoulders. Over all this was worn a mantle. The hair was worn in a narrow fillet across the forehead. (Sprotbrough, South Yorks, *c*1310, and Lady Maud Harcourt *c*1370 Stanton Harcourt, Oxon).

In the second half of the fourteenth century there was a good deal of variety in fashion. The plain button kirtle fitting closely to the waist was frequently worn simply with the mantle, fastened by a short cord across the breast. The cote-hardie was either buttoned or laced from the neck with tight sleeves which had long strips hanging from the elbows known as liripipes. The neck line was low and square and the dress fitted tightly to the body. The shoes were pointed. Another popular costume was the sideless cote-hardie with the sides of the garment cut away as far as the hips leaving only a narrow piece in front of the body and two strips over the shoulders. It was usually edged with fur. A further variety was the long plain cote-hardie gathered into a round

TROTTON, SUSSEX.
Earliest brass of a female effigy, *c*1310, Costume showing long loose cote-hardie revealing close-fitting buttoned sleeves of kirtle. Hair bound by narrow fillet across forehead.

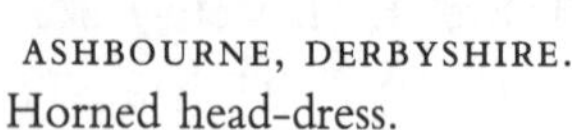

ASHBOURNE, DERBYSHIRE.
Horned head-dress.

ALBURY, HERTFORDSHIRE.
Butterfly head-dress.

neck-band and buttoned all the way down the front. (Hilton, *c*1370, Swine Priory, Humberside.)

The head-dresses during this period were of great variety and were very ostentatious falling into three main classes: (1) Braided (2) Veiled and (3) Nebuly or Reticulated. In the first the hair was plaited at the sides of the face and fastened by a jewelled fillet (Joan of Carlisle – tomb of Edward III, 1377, Westminster Abbey). In the second the head-dress consisted of two kerchiefs, one bound tightly round the head enclosing the forehead and the sides of the face and the other falling loosely over it (Catherine Norwich wife of Sir Wm. De la Pole, 1367, Holy Trinity, Hull, Humberside). The third type consisted of the hair plaited and gathered tightly in a net to frame the face. A tress of hair usually fell on each shoulder with its end rolled up and netted into a ball. (Maud Harcourt, (1370), Stanton Harcourt, Oxon.)

A further head-dress was the Crispine with the hair gathered into cauls which were jewelled nets on each side of the face with a gold, silver or coloured net known as the crespine. Later in the period, *c*1345, its character changed and instead of covering the whole head or being shaped into cauls it was fashioned into two cylinders one on each side of the face, which were fastened to the metal fillet. The cylinders were open at the top so that the coiled plaits could be inserted. These cylindrical cauls were made of gold, silver or other metal mesh and had a solid band at top and bottom which was sometimes studded with jewels. A small light veil was often attached to the back of the head-dress. (Queen Philippa, (1369), wife of Edward III, Westminster Abbey.)

During the first half of the fifteenth century there was no striking change in fashion and the kirtle, mantle and sideless cote-hardie continued to be worn.

About 1460 a new style of gown came into fashion consisting of a long full robe worn over the kirtle. It was cut low at he neck and bordered with fur. It had either long tight sleeves with cuffs to the wrists and sometimes turned back to show a fur lining or, alternatively, wide fur-lined sleeves. It was close-fitting to the waist and fastened with a girdle. Generally the nets of hair curved upwards to make horned head-dresses, much disliked by the clergy, and later there was a variation called the mitred head-dress where the horns became more pronounced (Lady Elizabeth Fitzherbert, (1483) Norbury, Derbyshire).

The mitred head-dress gave way to a brief fashion of the butterfly where the nets of hair of the previous style were moved to the back of the head and the hair dragged back from the forehead. On the nets was erected a large framework of wire covered by a light gauze veil. This style was not shown on effigies as it was difficult to portray but may be seen on brasses.

At the end of the century the butterfly gave way to the pedimental where the face was framed by stiff embroidered bands which met at a sharp angle in the middle of the forehead and hung down to the shoulders on each side. The hair was drawn into a sort of cap at the back of the head and occasionally covered with a veil. (Sir Wm. Smythe (1525), and two wives, Elford, Staffs and Henry VII, 1518, and Queen Elizabeth of York, Westminster Abbey).

About 1525 the gown was slightly changed and the sleeves became very wide reaching to just below the elbows where they were finished with a deep band of fur. Beneath the gown there were full sleeves gathered at the wrists. The neck had a square opening which was filled in by the partlet, a piece of pleated linen fitting the neck. The hanging bands of the pedimental head-dress were doubled up and pinned in front. A rich girdle was worn with a long end hanging almost to the ground either in front or at the side. Sometimes a long chain hung from the girdle and supported an ornament or perfume box.

During the reign of Edward VI the fashion began to change and the pedimental head-dress gave way to the Paris cap or French hood sometimes called the Mary Queen of Scots head-dress. It consisted of a close-fitting metal framework with a curved border, resembling a horseshoe although sometimes pointed, coming over the ears with a velvet hood hanging down

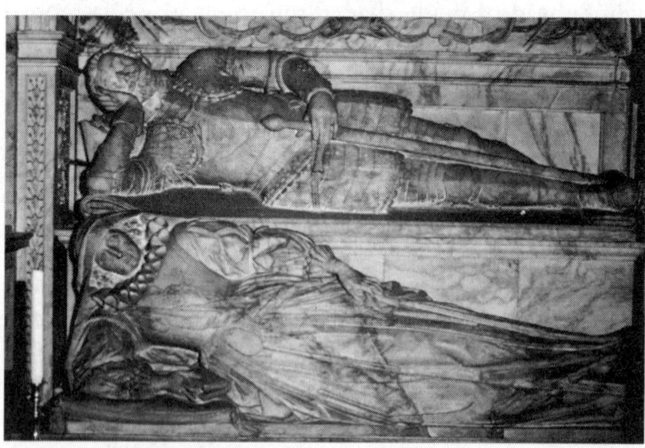

THEYDON MOUNT, ESSEX.
Costume showing Paris cap or hood and ruffs

behind. It was set back on the head and showed more hair on the forehead. (Lady Culpepyr, 1537, Goudhurst, Kent.) Substantially, the gown was the same as before except that from the waist downward it was open in front to show the petticoat. The partlet was finished with a small frill which later developed into the Elizabethan ruff. The sleeves of the dress were short and puffed and the striped sleeves of the under-dress were edged at the writs with a small frill.

This fashion developed into the familiar Elizabethan dress about 1570 when the petticoat became elaborately embroidered and more exposed. The carving of these embroidered petticoats, like the armour, was frequently beautifully executed and deserves close attention. The over-gown was fastened at the waist by a small sash and the sleeves disappeared. The characteristic ruff came into fashion and the dress was distended at the hips by a weird contraption called a farthingale which was sometimes wheel-shaped and was a framework made of whalebone. The Paris cap was still worn (Sir Cope d'Oyley (1636) and wife, Hambleden, Bucks.)

In the reign of James I a high lace collar was worn rising high at the back of the neck. The head-dress was composed of a high coiffure dressed up in front over a wire framework and was decorated with jewels. Later the hair-style became more natural and was lower, without the framework.

During the late seventeenth and early eighteenth centuries a gown was worn with the skirt looped up at the sides to show the petticoat worn over a hoop. The neck line was worn low with lace neck and sleeve frills and the bodice was vandyked, that is split down the front and laced. The sleeves finished at the elbows with sleeve puffs and the hair was worn in a series of elaborate curls over the forehead, later to be covered by a wig. (Sir Robert Clayton, 1707 and Lady Clayton, Bletchingly, Surrey.)

After this period wall monuments became general in parish churches and a bust effigy was more usual. Whether a bust or whole figure is shown it is usually clothed in a rather shapeless drapery.

Widows wore a dress which, for almost three centuries, remained unchanged. In the fourteenth century it consisted of a kirtle, mantle and veil head-dress with a plaited barbe or gorget of finely pleated linen fitting closely to the chin. In the fifteenth century the kirtle was covered by a long tight-sleeved dress and mantle. The veil head-dress and the barbe were as before. This costume survived into the sixteenth century but the habit of indicating widowed state by a long veil steadily increased.

Clerical Vestments

The vestments of the clergy were continuous and show little change. They comprised the amice, alb, stole, maniple and chasuble. The amice, which was originally a hood, was a scarf consisting of a rectangular piece of linen with an ornamental edging fixed to the longest side which was turned down to form a collar. The ornamental border was called an 'apparel' and the amice was the 'helmet of salvation'. The alb was a long, loose-fitting linen garment, reaching to the feet, with long sleeves. It was usually white but was sometimes coloured and denoted 'purity'. Round the neck was worn a stole, a long embroidered strip a few inches wide crossed on the breast and held by the girdle of the alb. It was worn beneath the chasuble and the ends were fringed and visible below the chasuble. The symbolism represented 'cross and grace'. The maniple, like the stole, was a strip of embroidered silk about three feet in length which hung over the left arm. It was originally a towel and purse combined.

Covering the other vestments was a large circular or oval garment called a chasuble which had a central head opening and hung down so as to cover the upper arms. It was made of very rich material, velvet or cloth of gold with orphreys which were strips embroidered in coloured silks, gold threads and pearls. With higher dignitaries, for example, a bishop, a broad orphrey ran down the centre of the front and back. (Bishop Harman, 1555, Sutton Coldfield, West Midlands.)

Archbishops wore a pall or pallium which was a strip of white wool embroidered with crosses and placed over the shoulders forming a double 'Y' with the arms meeting round the neck.

The mitre in its early form was low and had plain edges. Later it grew in size with crockets added to the horns. Later still it became more rounded in outline. This type of head-dress was worn by the bishops and some abbots and was the symbol of authority and of the apostolic commission (Acts 2:3).

CLERICAL VESTMENTS.

The ordinary parish priest is shown wearing a cassock which is a button-through gown. There are various colours according to rank or order. Over the cassock is worn a white linen surplice having long flowing sleeves. Over the surplice was the amice. Sometimes the priest is shown wearing only the cassock and sometimes may be shown in full vestments, wearing a cope, a large semicircular cloak made of rich material, fastened at the throat by a large jewelled broach called a morse.

After the Reformation the clergy were generally shown as wearing the ordinary civil dress of the period, the doublet and hose and gown with false sleeves or the Geneva preaching gown.

Bishops wore the rochet, a sort of alb of white linen with sleeves which became of enormous size. Over this was worn the chimere, a sleeveless gown of silk, usually black but occasionally scarlet. It was open in front and worn with a long stole-like scarf with the ends hanging down in front.

Effigies of clerics may be seen at:

Worcester Cathedral *c.*1240 Bishop.
Welwick, Humberside *c.*1310 Priest.
Dorchester, Oxon. *c.*1300–30 Abbot.
Canterbury Cathedral 1444, Henry Chichele Archbishop.
St Mary Redcliffe, Bristol 1474, Wm. Canynge, Priest.
Gloucester Cathedral 1535, Wm. Parker, Abbot.
Sutton Coldfield, Warwickshire 1555, Bishop Harman.
Holy Trinity, Guildford, Surrey, 1633, Archibishop Abbot.

Between us and the men and woman whose monuments appear in our parish churches and cathedrals many centuries have passed and it is, therefore, appropriate to quote the eloquent words of Mr J. A. Froude, the nineteenth-century historian.

PILTON, SOMERSET.
C14 Easter Sepulchre.

'And now it is all gone, like an unsubstantial pageant faded; and between us and the old English there lies a gulf of mystery which the prose of the historian will never adequately bridge. They cannot come to us and our imagination can but feebly penetrate to them. Only among the aisles of the cathedrals, only as we gaze upon their silent figures sleeping on their tombs, some faint conceptions float before us of what these men were when they were alive; and perhaps in the sound of church bells, that peculiar creation of medieval age, which falls upon the ear like the echo of a vanished world.'

17

Easter Sepulchres

An Easter Sepulchre is a name given to a recess in the north wall of the sanctuary or to a recessed tomb with a canopy over. On Good Friday in the medieval period it was customary to place the Host and Crucifix in the sepulchre where they were watched day and night until they were removed to the High Altar on Easter morning. This procedure was carried out with great ceremony and signified the burial of Christ and His resurrection from the tomb (Ashbourne, Derby, C15; Hathersage, Derby, C15; Pilton, Somerset, C14).

Originally, an Easter Sepulchre was a moveable piece of furniture consisting of a timber framework four to five feet long, three feet in height and two feet deep, which was draped with hangings or palls and sometimes faced with carved panels depicting the closing scenes in the life of Christ, the burial and the Resurrection. (Ripon Cathedral, N. Yorks, C15—Rare.)

In the records of St Stephen's church, Coleman Street, London, is a specification of the sepulchre: 'Item. One sepulchre over gilded with a frame to be set on with four posts and crests thereto'. It goes on to include, 'great angels to be set on the sepulchre. Stained cloths with the Apostles and Prophets beaten with gold with the Creed . . . '

People left instructions in their wills to the effect that their tombs should be used as receptacles for the sepulchre. Thomas Windsor or Stanwell, Surrey, who died in 1486, by his will instructed that, 'his body should be buried on the north side of the chancel and a plain tomb of marble of competent height be erected to the intent that it may bear the blessed body of Our Lord and the Sepulchre at the time of Easter to stand upon the same'.

Numbers of canopied tombs which were built in the north walls of chancels in parish churches were used for this purpose. (Ightam, Kent, C14; Blackeney, Norfolk, C13; Much Marcle, Hereford and Worcester C14.)

Later, however, stone sepulchres were specially built to enshrine the Blessed Sacrament, the finest examples dating from the fourteenth century, and were similar in design to the wall tombs they superseded. They generally consisted of three stages, a basement on the front of which were panels or niches containing figures of sleeping soldiers carved in relief, an arched recess in which the Sacrament was deposited and a canopy adorned with sculpture representing the risen Christ. (Pilton, Somerset – C14.)

The use of the Sepulchre continued up to and a little beyond the Reformation. In 1538 Bishop Langland preaching before Henry VIII finished by exhorting his congregation

> 'as of old custom hath here this day been used, everyone of you, or ye depart with most entire devotion kneeling before Our Saviour Lord God who lyeth in yonder Sepulchre in honour of Him, of His passion and death and of His five wounds to say five paternosters, five aves and one credo that it may please His merciful goodness to make us partners of the Merits of His most glorious passion, blood and death.'

In that same year the light was kept burning before the Sepulchre during Easter was expressly excluded from the list of superstitious lights. The Sepulchre was watched day and night and in the wardens' accounts of All Hallows-on-the-Wall, London, for 1531 is an item; 'for brede and dryncke for them that wachyth the Sepulchre, 1d.' Sepulchres were finally disused in the reign of Elizabeth and in the second half of the sixteenth century many more were burnt or sold. Some were given to the poor for firewood and others made into cupboards, shelves, hencoops and other items.

Requests to maintain lights in the form of candles on prickets in front of the Sepulchre were very numerous and those who could afford it left enough to pay in perpetuity for a taper weighing five pounds which was known as the giant Paschall Candle. In 1528 Richard Nethersole left the church of Wymynswold, Kent, a cow the profit from which would maintain a taper of four pounds of wax and in 1516 Thomas Hunty of Cransley, Northants. bequeathed '10 ewe sheep to the preparing and furnishing of the Sepulchre and that the increase of them may be to the supportacion of the same.'

18

Brasses

The use of engraved latten plates as memorials appears to have been introduced from the Low Countries during the later thirteenth century as an improvement on the incised slab of stone used previously. They became extremely popular covering a wide field extending from the small and simple to the large and ornate memorials. It is thought that a least 150,000 brasses were laid down of which number about 4,000 of all descriptions remain, the others having been destroyed during religious and civil upheavals, metal thieves, neglect and vandalism as well as by so-called church restorers. Nevertheless the number of brasses in our churches is ten times more than the brasses remaining on the Continent due to our geographcal situation. The Continent has had to suffer plunder and destruction by invading armies and in France during the Revolution of 1789 sacrilege and destruction was very great. In their excess of zeal the Reformers in the reign of Edward VI committed much destruction as evidenced by Weaver who said, 'the foulest most inhumane action was the violation of funeral monuments; tombs hakt and hewn a-pieces . . . for greediness of the brass'. The brass or latten was sold and many churchwardens' accounts for the period show the sales and the sums received.

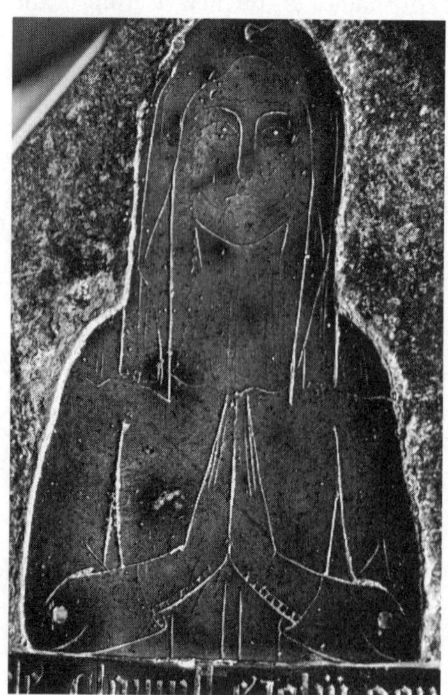

WEST HANNINGFIELD, ESSEX.
Early British brass of a woman - 1361

The earliest known surviving brass is in Verden, Germany, dated 1231 and probably the finest brass of Flemish workmanship is at Ripsted, Denmark, dated 1319. The earliest English brass, however, is of a male *c*1277, Sir John D'Abernoun at Stoke D'Abernon, Surrey and of a female *c*1310 Margaret de Camays at Trotton, Sussex.

To appreciate English brasses it is necessary to consider the incised slab which was probably the forerunner to the brass memorial plate and which exerted a great influence on the art of the first engravers of brasses at Verden and Ripsted and who later brought their craft to England. The brass did not, however, supersede the stone slab as there is ample evidence that the incised stone was being carved up to the beginning of the seventeenth century.

The incised slab is derived from the stone lid which covered the coffin and which was at first carved with long slender crosses, with or without a simple Lombardic incription. Sometimes a symbol such as a sword or chalice indicating the occupation of the deceased was incised on the slab. Later in the twelfth century a 'portrait' of the deceased was incised and was further enhanced by carving the figure of the deceased in semi-relief which eventually led to the carving in full relief.

This type of memorial was not very popular in Britain due to the expense of importing Tourai stone and Italian marble. For every thousand slabs that survive on the Continent it is said that there are only a hundred remaining in Britain whereas for every hundred brasses remaining abroad there are one thousand examples to be seen in Britain.

The craft of brass engraving was able to develop independently of competition and influence from abroad. Brass plate was more durable, more easily worked than stone and gave more opportunity for detailed engraving. Much experiment, however, was carried out with incised slabs and there is sufficient evidence to show that during the thirteenth century many types of inlay were attempted in order to make them more attractive, including marble, alabaster and hard compositions. These experiments were brought about by a growing demand by influential persons to be buried in the church and to have a monument there. Originally, tombs in the chancel were reserved for priests or church founders but burial in a holy place was nevertheless much desired and there were many requests coupled with gifts which often proved irrestistable. There was, however, no room for large numbers of raised effigies and the only practical representation was a flat one on the gravestone.

Brasses were usually laid as commemorative memorials either by the person named, during his lifetime, or by his executors after his death. The functions of the memorial brass were to establish the identify of the deceased in the family line by an inscription which showed who was buried on the spot: to record the role of the deceased, knight, priest or merchant as it was important to record the correct succession as priest followed priest in the church and knight followed knight as lord of the manor; care being taken to show the proper vestments and insignia, e.g. shields of arms relating to the deceased's status. Perhaps the most important function was to attract the prayers of passers-by for the peace of the soul of the dead man.

People of the period strongly believed that those who had lived a Christian life must first pass through a period of purgatory or spiritual purification, before entering the future life which awaited them. During this intermediate period the dead were not able to help themselves and so they needed to be helped by the prayers and devotions made on their behalf by living Christians especially on the anniversary of their 'obits' and so the date of death was always shown. An exception may be seen at North Ockendon, Essex on the brass of Wm.Poyntz (?1504) and Elizabeth his wife (1502) where the date of William's obit has been left blank. The insertion of the date would have been left for the descendants to fill in, which they failed to do. It was always the deceased's desire to be placed as close as possible to an altar in which holy relics had been set and where prayers were regularly said. Brasses are, therefore, commonly found near altars, the earliest member of the family lying nearest to the altar while others had their brasses placed on top of raised tombs in the chancel. A good example of a table tomb brass is at Wymington, Beds. John Curteys (1391) and wife.

Most medieval inscriptions conclude with a prayer that God should have mercy on the soul of the deceased or in asking for prayers on their behalf and people were concerned that such inscriptions should not be omitted. It can be understood, therefore, why many people had their brasses prepared in their lifetime with the date being left blank.

During the sixteenth century there was a marked change in the teaching of the English Church regarding the earlier beliefs of the value of prayers on behalf of the dead and instead, attention was drawn to the worldly achievements of the deceased. Inscriptions tended to record the deceased's good deeds to prove that he or she deserved to be remembered. Usually they refer to the virtues of the person concerned and right through to the eighteenth century it became the accepted practice to praise or commend the departed.

Brasses are representations in two dimensions of the three-dimension sepulchral effigies on top of medieval tombs. The dead are shown like a funeral effigy with hands in prayer and peculiarly with eyes open which are also found on most funeral monuments. As with effigies, the deceased is often shown with his head resting on a helm and his feet on a beast. Sometimes the legs are crossed like the effigies of knights of the later thirteenth and early fourteenth centuries. The idea of family representations instead of the single figure occurred during the fourteenth century both on brasses and effigies on tombs and even children are introduced. Occasionally they are shown in swaddling clothes (Those.Greville, 1492, Stanford Rivers, Essex, Anne Consant, 1606, St Leonard, Deal, Kent). This continued into the seventeenth century and a fine example may be seen on the tomb of J. Torksay, 1614, Barwell, Leicestershire.

Although brasses aim to commemorate the person they depict they were not attempts at portraiture as the task of actually drawing the design for a brass was

LITTLE HORKESLEY, ESSEX.
Canopies over knight effigies showing armour of C14 and C15.

YOXFORD, SUFFOLK.
Shrouded effigy of Tomesine Tendring and her 7 children.

usually entrusted to the engraver. It is not unusual therefore, to find that a characteristic 'face' developed which was used on all the brasses coming from his workshop. There are, however, examples of brasses which have been 'personalised' for example the beard of Sir Wm.Tendring, 1408 at Stoke-by-Nayland, Suffolk, is an attempt at capturing a feature which contrasted with the current fashion. Wm.Palmer, 1520, at Ingoldmells, Linconshire, who was a cripple, is shown with his 'stylt' or crutch, and Alice Giffard, wife of Sir John Cassey, 1400, Deerhurst, Glouchestershire who has her pet dog named 'Terri' at her feet.

Many important tombs had stone canopies rising over them and these features were also used on brasses and were sometimes very elaborate.

Another feature which occurred frequently was the marginal inscription with the symbols of the four Evangelists – the eagle (St John), the winged lion (St Mark), the winged ox (St Luke) and the winged man (St Matthew) at the corners who were associated with protection (Wymington, Beds. – 1391).

From about the first quarter of the fifteenth century emphasis upon the material side of death frequently appears in the design of funeral monuments. It is possible that this was one of the results of the bubonic plague epidemic which raged in

LAMBOURNE END, ESSEX.
Merchant's mark.

1349, commonly known as the Black Death, and which devastated the world. Whether this was the reason or not the figure of death became prominent in art from that time onward. Shroud brasses began to make their appearance, the viewers being shocked into piety by the representation of death and so being made aware of their certain end and the need to pray for the dead as they would wish people to pray for them when their time came. These brasses took the form of the deceased wrapped in a burial shroud or as a skeleton. Deceased children were also shown wrapped in a shroud (Yoxford, Suffolk, 1485; Watlington, Oxon, 1501 and Wiveton, Norfolk, *c*1540). Occasionally a shroud Brass may be shown depicting worms attacking the corpse. At Oddington, Oxfordshire, the worms are actually the size of eels.

The late seventeenth and eighteenth centuries furnish many examples of emblems of mortality such as skulls, hour glasses. Time with his scythe and angels blowing trumpets reminding the view of the Day of Judgement.

Brasses are valued not only as records of particular person or their individual peculiarities but as records of the classes of people represented which, apart from military effigies, were mostly of the middle classes, the traders and merchants. These merchants often had the mark, which they used on their goods for purposes of identification, put on a shield and a good many of these are to

CLOVELLY, DEVON.
C15 Bishop's crozier.

be found on brasses and are known as merchants' marks. By the end of the sixteenth century merchants' marks had almost disappeared. Some of the merchants had treated their marks as a form of heraldry, but in England the practice was not recognised by the heralds and, in fact, authority was obtained by the Carlisle Herald to confiscate or obliterate all merchants' marks displayed in an heraldic form. (Robt.Barfot, 1546, Lambourne End, Essex and Sylvester, 1577, Burford, Oxon).

The use of these marks gradually died away as many great families became extinct during the civil wars of the late fifteenth century giving rise to the new bourgeois class which bought from the Tudors landed estates following the dissolution of the monasteries. These families gradually acquired armorial bearings and so gave up using their merchants' marks.

There were also many brasses commemorating the aristocracy, the landed gentry and the titled. These people were the defenders of the faith whose ancestors had fought at the Crusades as well as amongst themselves and who owned estates covering very large areas. They were always shown in armour, unless they were ecclesiastics, and so a clean picture of the evolution in armour, costume, particularly female, and vestments from the thirteenth century to the seventeenth century may be seen.

The evolution of defensive armour was determined by two inter-relating factors (1) the development of new weapons by the aggressor which had to be countered with improved armour worn by the opponents if they were not to die on the battlefield and (2) the need for agility in attack and retreat which restricted the armour of armour that could be carried. This conflict arising out of the need for mobility against the instinct of self-preservation, is clearly depicted on the brasses of medieval warriors. With the introduction of hand guns and cannon the effective range between armies increased and the need for a head-to-toe elaborate covering of armour diminished.

For details of the evolution of defensive armour please see page 166.

Examples of Armour of Various Periods

13th Century	1277 Sir J.D'Aubernoun, Stoke d'Abernon, Surrey
	1289 Sir Roger de Trumpington, Trumpington, Cambridgeshire
14th Century	1323 Sir Wm.Fitzralph, Pebmarsh, Essex
	1325 Sir J.de Creke, Westley, Waterless, Cambridgeshire
	1360 W.de Aldeburgh, Aldborough, Humberside
	1380 Sir J. de la Pole, Chrishall, Essex
	1390 Sir A.Luttrell, Irnham, Lincolnshire
15th Century	1400 Sir G.Felbrigg, Playford Suffolk
	c.1400 Lord Willoughby D'Eresley, Spilsby, Lincolnshire
	1406 Earl of Warwick, St Mary, Warwick

1415 J.Peryent, Digswell, Hertfordshire
1416 Sir S.Felbrygge, Felbrigg, Norfolk
1445 T.de St Quintin, Harpham, Humberside
1458 T.Shernborne, Shernborne, Norfolk
1460 Anonymous, Adderbury, Oxfordshire
1470 R.St Leger, Ulcombe, Kent
16th Century 1507 Viscount Beaumont, Wivenhoe, Essex
1547 Sir R.Verney, Aldbury, Hertfordshire
1549 John, Lord Marney, Little Horkesley, Essex
1558 Sir H. Sacheverell, Morly, Derbyshire
1577 F.Clopton, Long Melford, Suffolk
1629 Sir E.Filmer, East Sutton, Kent

Brass Making

Brasses were engraved on sheets of latten which is an alloy of copper similar to modern brass but with a different compostion. Usually it was a mixture of 75% copper, 19% zinc, 2% tin and 4% lead, but the composition varied. As calamine ore (zinc carbonate) was necessary to provide the zinc oxide ingredient and as this ore was not mined in England until the reign of Queen Elizabeth the latten sheets were imported during the medieval period from the Continent, principally from Flanders and Cologne. The sheets from Cologne were called 'Cullen' plates.

The method used, now called a cementation process, was to grind up calamine ore (zinc carbonate) and mix it with charcoal and small pieces of copper. These were placed in a crucible and heated sufficiently to distil out the zinc but not enough to melt the copper. The zinc being volatile permeated the pieces of copper and formed brass. With increased heat the latten was melted and poured into moulds of shallow stone matrices to a depth of about an eighth of and inch but was often uneven in texture and subject to air bubbles. The metal was then left to cool. Where a large rectangular brass was required, as at St Albans, Herts, and Chigwell, Essex, it was necessary to use a number of small rectangular pieces each having a maximum dimension of about three feet by two feet.

In Elizabeth's reign a special company was established to make latten plates which were hammered much thinner than the earlier cast latten. This method involved water-powered hammers which were used to beat the metal into small sheets. Although sufficient quantities of sheet metal, required to meet the demand, could be produced by this method, the quality obtained was not all that could be desired. The machine-hammers of the fourteenth to the eighteenth century (when the process of rolling metals was introduced) could not be expected to turn out sheets of very accurate width and thickness and this is proved by the uneven sizes of many early brasses.

Engravers did not necessarily cast their own plates and their location was determined by the market for their work. The engraving centres thus tended to appear where there were thriving centres of trade, e.g. Antwerp and Bruges in the Low Countries, East Anglia and London.

Before engraving, the design was drawn out, then copied on to the metal with paint or a pointed instrument. The lines were then engraved with graving tools which were sharp metal chisels held in the fingers and struck with a specially shaped hammer. A further hand tool which was very sharp and controlled by the hand was called a burin. When all the lines had been engraved they were blackened with bitumen or some other colouring of natural pigment and the surface was finally polished. In some cases the surfaces were gilt and in others enamelled trays of copper were set in the brass (Lord Bouchier, 1483, Little Easton, Essex: Sir John de Say (1473), Broxbourne, Herts). Once the brass was ready it was set into the appropriate gravestone into which an exact recess or indent had been cut. This recess is known as the matrix.

Prior to *c*1340 brasses were fixed in the matrix by means of bitumen but after this date English masons became more competent and began fixing brasses with brass rivets to set securely in hollows which were prepared in the matrix and filled with lead. The channels down which the lead was poured can frequently be seen in the matrices of lost brasses. By this means small figures could be secured as well as large unriveted figures which had relied mainly on their weight to hold them in place (Sir Wm.Fitzralph (*c*1323), Pebmarsh, Essex, Sir R. de Trumpington (1289), Trumpington, Cambridgeshire).

The finished memorial was then dispatched by water or road to its destination and it would appear from surviving contracts that it was the maker's business to lay it in its intended place.

It would seem from the various tasks involved that the maker required the skills of the mason, metal worker and painter as well as having the facilities to sell and deliver his finished work. The demand for brasses in churches throughout the country in the fifteenth century led to the establishment of provincial centres outside London the most notable of these being York, Norwich, Coventry and Cambridge.

Inscriptions and Lettering

The inscriptions on brasses varied from century to century presenting a survey of the different types of lettering, positioning on the brass and the sentiments expressed.

The early inscriptions were placed round the edge of the slab in which the brass was set and each letter was cut separately out of the brass and set into its own matrix. Unfortunately many of these have been lost. This, however, was not

NAVESTOCK, ESSEX.
Brass inscription.

satisfactory and the letters were cut on a narrow strip of brass to form a border (Sir Wm.Fitzralph, *c*1323, Pebmarsh, Essex).

Later brasses had a small rectangular plate below the figures known as foot inscriptions. There were also scrolls which were mostly short prayers or occasionally verses of scripture.

In the thirteenth and fourteenth centuries the language used was Norman French which survived until *c*1420 but Latin was used during the period for ecclesiastics, with a few exceptions, through later centuries. Throughout the fifteenth century Latin was used, but in some cases French, Latin and English may be found used in one inscription. In the sixteenth century English took the place of Latin except for inscriptions to ecclesiastics which remained in Latin in all periods.

The earliest type of lettering which was used was Lombardic where the letters are not joined together but are entirely separate and beautifully formed, giving the appearance of being engraved in capitals. Unfortunately, being small pieces of isolated brass, it was easy for them to be prized up and stolen by church thieves. At the beginning of the fourteenth century Lombaric gave way to early Black-letter which was replaced in the fifteenth century by straight Black-letter and in the sixteenth century by Tudor Black-letter. Black-letter had letters which were angular and compressed and were composed of thick black lines all of which makes it difficult to read. This lettering varies from decade to decade, declining during the Tudor period. From the beginning of the seventeenth century roman capitals were generally used, though not entirely, and were followed in the eighteenth century by copperplate which was easy to read. Roman numerals were used until the sixteenth century but Arabic numerals began to make their appearance *c*1450.

The sentiments expressed in the fourteenth century were simple, for example, the inscription to Sir John D'Aubernoun, Stoke d'Abernon, Surrey, reads:

> SIRE; JOHN: DAUBERNOUN: CHIVALER, GIST: ICY: DEV: DE: SA: ALME: EYT: MERCY:

The Latin inscriptions of the fifteenth century are more difficult to decipher due to the many contractions which are used. They usually begin with 'HIC JACET' or 'ICI GIST' – 'Here lies' followed by the name of the deceased and wife then 'QUI MORUST' or 'QUI OBIT' – 'Who died on' followed by the date. The inscriptions usually end with 'CUJUS ANIME PROPICIETER DEUS, AMEN': 'MAY GOD HAVE MERCY ON HIS SOUL, AMEN'.

After the Reformation the petitions at the beginning and end of an inscription were often erased. Sixteenth-century inscriptions lost the dignified restraint of epitaphs found on earlier tombs. Later in the seventeenth and early eighteenth centuries this dignified restraint further degenerated into the debasement of the flattering and moralising laudations that we see displayed on many brasses of this period. The brass of Nicholas (1609) and Dorothy Wadham (1618) in Ilminster church, Somerset is interesting. Nicholas and Dorothy were founders of Wadham College, Oxford and the inscription contains a reference to the fouding of the college:

> He still shines with a great light that glitters in the east.Do you not see? Look at the towers set on the other side of Isis where he built habitations for the Muses and lofty temples to God. There you behold the rays of Wadham's countenance.

The other interesting feature is that the inscription at the foot of the brass is set upside down, i.e. facing west whereas the figures are in the traditional eastward-facing position. Although the possible reason for this is that the brass is awkwardly placed in the corner of the transept, brasses placed in an aisle of a church sometimes had the inscription facing west to catch the eye of a passer-by and so perhaps encourage him to stop to read it and pray for the soul of the deceased.

Palimpsests

The word 'palimpsests' comes from the Greek 'palin' -again and 'psestos' – scraped or rubbed, and is not really correct when used to describe re-used brasses. The original use was to describe manuscripts on papyri or leather where the ink had been cleaned off so that they could be re-used. There are a few brasses where the upper side has been re-engraved merely by adapting an effigy of a later date. Most brasses which are termed palimpsest are those which have been turned over and engraved on the reverse side perhaps also being cut to a new shape.

There are two main classes of palimpsest brasses, (1) brasses which are engraved on the reverse side and, (2) appropriated and converted brasses. The most numerous are in the first class as, very often, spoiled plates from continental workshops would be exported to England and English spoilt plates would be re-used.

The main reason for the existence of so many palimpsest brasses were the dissolution of the monasteries in the sixteenth century and the looting of the

Netherland churches in 1566. The brasses from the monasteries were either melted down or sold to the brass-workers to be used as fresh plates. Sometimes the original plates were cut up and new brasses engraved on their backs while other plates were merely reversed and a new engraving made.

Anti-Catholic feeling developed in England in the late sixteenth and seventeenth centuries which led to the destruction and mutilation of many brasses. Any 'Popish' sentiments in inscriptions, representations of the Trinity, crosses and saints were removed.

Sometimes fragments were joined to other fragments so that a partial reconstruction could be made. Occasionally the heraldry or inscriptions on a brass enable it to be traced to its church of origin whether in England or Flanders.

The great majority of palimpsest brasses cannot be seen as the earlier side is nearly always hidden, riveted and bedded with bitumen in the matrix. There is evidence that many English brasses made between 1520 and 1580 are palimpsest.These brasses, because they are engraved on thick and solid pieces of metal instead of on flimsy sheet, half filled-in rivet holes and maybe several pieces of joined metal suggest that they are palimpsest.When a brass becomes loose and before it is re-fixed it is possible for the earlier side to be cleaned and examined and for a rubbing to be made for the purposes of record.

Appropriated and converted palimpsests form a much smaller class. The 'appropriated' brass is one to which a new inscription and shield of arms have been added and used as a memorial for a later owner. (Bromham, Beds, originally to Those. Widville, (1435) and two wives. Appropriated in 1535 to Sir John Dyve, wife and mother). The 'converted' brass is an appropriated brass which has been re-worked, in part, to suit a later owner. There are very few of this type but examples may be found (Dunham, Bucks. priest in vestments, 1440). Re-used in 1545 by altering the shape of the toes of the shoes and adding some shading and a new inscription.

An unusual example of a converted palimpsest brass is at Waterperry, Oxon. where partial re-engraving has been done on the original except the marginal inscriptions. It was discovered fro this inscription that the original brass dated 1440 was in memory of Simon Kemp who was buried in the Priory church of the Holy Trinity, Leadenhall Street, London, which was handed over to the King in 1532.

The building was granted to Lord Audley who, wishing to clear the site for re-building, sold the materials to defray the cost of demolition and removal. Among the materials was Simon Kemp's brass which was bought by a London workshop and re-engraved for Walter Curson and his wife in 1540 and who were buried in Austin Friars, Oxford. When the Priory was dissolved it was transferred to Waterperry. The adaptation is peculiar. The male figure has been given a new non-palimpsest head and shoulders but the rest has been re-engraved so as to transform a fifteenth-century armour clad figure into one in Tudor sixteenth-century armour with mail shirt and broad-toed sabbatons instead of the pointed sollerets. The female figure has been cut into two below the waist and the upper half then turned over and re-engraved but the lower half has been left unaltered as part of the original figure, the result displaying a rather hybrid costume.

Examples of Palimpsest Brasses:

Buckinghamshire (Denham). The whole plate on reverse shows a 15C figure with inscription and shield. Obverse, Priest in mass vestments.

(Hedgerley). The Resurrection and parts of inscriptions c1530. Obverse, Margaret Bulstrode, 1540.

Cheshire (Chester, Holy Trinity) Inscription of 1545. Obverse, portion of large armoured figure, *c*1520, showing Order of the Garter.

Derbyshire. (Norbury). Sir Anthony FitzHerbert and wife, 1538, with portion of a large female figure and Lombardic inscription on reverse, *c*1325.

Essex (Upminster). Part of an Abbot, 15C. Obverse to a civilian *c*1530. (Part of the Abbot may be found in Baylord church, Herts. used to complete a brass of 1545).

Hertfordshire (Great Berkhamstead). Part to Thom. Humfre and wife Joan Bayntum in shrouds with children and St Michael weighing souls *c*1500. Observse, inscription to John Waterhouse, 1558.

Kent (St John, Margate) Part of the border of Flemish brass containing scenes from the Life of Man, 15C. Obverse, inscription to Thoas.Flutt, 1582.

Lincolnshire (Laughton). Brass of 1400 appropriated and used without re-engraving. Memorial to two men who died in 1546 and 1549 respectively, a new inscription being added.

London (Isleworth). – Saint under canopy, Flemish 14C. Obverse, inscription to Wm.Chase, 1544.

Norfolk.(Halvergate). Half effigy Bro.Wm.Jernemy. Obverse, Alice Swane, 1540.

Oxfordshire (Shipton-under-Wychwood). Plate 1548 showing a woman in a shroud with English verse inscription. Obverse, Black-letter inscription *c*1494 confirming a grant to a guild or fraternity in return for dirges and masses.

Suffolk (Hadleigh). Portion of large Flemish civilian brass, 1500, with elaborate background. Obverse, inscription to martyred Taillour, 1555 Engraved in 1560.

Warwickshire (Haseley) – Part civilian 15C and portions of Flemish canopy work. Obverse, Clement Throkmorton, 1573.

19

Fonts and Font Covers

At the beginning of the history of the Church when, as we read in the Book of Acts of the Apostles, the people, on hearing the Good News about Jesus Christ, asked 'What shall we do?' and the answer was 'Repent and be baptised every one of you in the name of Jesus Christ for the remission of sins'. (Acts 2:37,38). As we find in the New Testament, baptism was a recognised part of the Christian life. The rite of baptism was full of rich meaning and symbolism which used water for religious purification in the washing away of original sin, being born again of water and the Spirit and initiation into Christian life; the divine family of God.

The Baptismal Service

Before considering the actual font it is necessary to look at the form of the medieval baptismal service and some of the changes which have been made.

Most baptisms took place in church and the service was long and elaborate, being in two parts, one taking place outside the church door usually in the porch and the other at the font. In the fourteenth century the naked infant was plunged into the water in the font, the bowl of which was large enough for this purpose, its forehead being anointed which the sacred chrism (oil) and bound round with a white cloth called the 'chrisom', as a symbol of the cleansing of its sins, which the mother returned when she came to be churched. If the child died within a month the chrisom was used as a shroud. The child's sponsors made the Christian renunciation and promises on its behalf and were thereafter related by 'spiritual affinity' both to it and to each other. To have 'lifted up the same child from the font', which meant that the child was born before the marriage, was a canonical impediment to marriage though a dispensation could be obtained.

The service was long and elaborate and full of symbolism such as the exorcism of the evil spirit, the unction or anointing with spittle (saliva) and anointing with oil. Often the north door of the church was left open during the baptism so that when the evil spirit was exorcised it would be free to leave the church. This door was called the 'Devil's door'.

At the end of the Middle Ages, about 1500, the baptismal service was still set out in the service books in three parts, the making of a catechumen (preparation for baptism), the blessing of the font and the baptism. Although virtually confined to children it still bore traces of its direct descent from the primitive rite for the baptism of adults. The first part is held at the door of the church and consisted chiefly of exorcism. The priest first signed the child three times with the sign of the Cross, recited appropriate prayers and then commanded the Devil to depart from it, hence the Devil's door. This was followed by further signings and the Gospel of Jesus' welcome to the children in St Matthew (Chapter 19:13–15) was read. After a charge in English to the godparents they joined with the priest in repeating the Lord's Prayer, Hail Mary and Apostles' Creed. After the final signing the child was taken into the church.

The blessing of the font consisted of a litany, a collect and a lengthy Preface exactly similar in form to that of the Mass after which the priest poured holy oil into the water. The baptism began with the godparents' renunciation of Satan, his works and 'pomps' after which the priest anointed the child with the 'oil of salvation'. The godparents made their profession of faith and the child was immediately baptised by the threefold immersion. It was then anointed with oil (chrism), clothed in a white robe (chrisom) and given a lighted candle. The parents were then charged by the priest in his own words, to preserve the child from fire, water and all other dangers and the godparents to teach the child the Lord's Prayer, Hail Mary and the Apostles' Creed, to return the chrisom and to bring the child to confirmation as soon as the bishop came within seven miles of the church.

Luther reduced the length of the baptismal service in 1526 by curtailing the lengthy exorcism to a single solemn appeal on oath. During the next few years various other forms followed but during the Edwardian Reformation when the Protestants gained ascendancy in the Council, Cranmer issued a Book of Homilies together with Injunctions which conflicted with the King's Book of 1543. As a compromise he issued the first Book of Common Prayer in 1549 (Edward VI) which was largely a condensation and simplification in English of the former Latin service books. This book, however, proved to be ineffective but nevertheless marked a stage in the doctrinal reformation.

This first Book of Common Prayer retained the two parts of the baptismal service (1) exorcism at the church door and (2) baptism at the font. The service was still of considerable length which included several 'dark and dumb ceremonies' with attendant prayers. Of these ceremonies the placing of salt in the mouth, which was carried out with the words, 'Receive the salt of wisdom', signing of the hand, anointing of the breast and the giving of a candle were discarded and with them a number of prayers. Signing of the forehead, exorcism of the Devil, anointing of the head and the giving of a white robe were retained. The two final Gospels were omitted and there were some minor changes. Cranmer, in his treatment of the baptismal service, kept the essential and preserved the structure, but at the same time reducing the number of ceremonies and prayers, filling up the gaps with exhortations from material obtained from the pre-Reformation Latin service and early Lutheran sources.

In the second Book of Common Prayer of Edward VI in 1552 Cranmer vigorously remodelled the baptismal service so that it became definitely Protestant. Instead of the church service being in two parts, one at the church door and the other at the font, the whole service took place at the font. The superstitious ceremonies of exorcism, giving the chrisom (robe) and unction were removed together with the blessing of the font and the godparents' repetition of the Creed and the Lord's Prayer. The prayers which had been used at the blessing of the font were now incorporated into the service and the questions were addressed to the godparents instead of the child, the godparents offering, not their own faith, but a promise of the child's future faith. The signing of the Cross was kept and the service was made to illustrate the purpose of baptism.

Cranmer gradually refined and clarified the service of baptism, parts of which had been suggested by continental Reformers but had been clumsily and lengthily worded. Without significant alteration the 1552 baptismal service passed into the 1662 Book of Common Prayer which is the one used today and which is substantially the 1552 Book of Common Prayer service with minor ceremonial additions. It was the parent's obligation to have their infants baptised publicly on a Sunday or Holy Day and the clergys' duty to make a solemn appeal to their congregations not to defer christening longer than the first or second Sunday after birth unless for an acceptable reason. The font and no other receptacle should be used and the child should be signed with the Cross by the minister. In the Church Courts there were many cases brought against incumbents and parents for neglecting to have children baptised within the period. In 1584 a case was brought against one Edmund Binder, incumbent of Blackmore, Essex, who was in grave trouble because two children died unchristened by his negligence because he would not christen them before the following Sunday and they died in the meantime. As a result he was suspended.

The Font

A font is a receptacle to hold water and derives its name from the Latin *fons* meaning 'a spring of water' and is frequently the oldest thing in the church. Even it a church has been rebuilt it may never have been necessary to renew this particular feature and so a medieval font may be found in church which has lost all trace of its medieval foundation.

Most fonts are made of stone, a few of wood and some of lead. Usually they are lined with lead unless made of impervious stone such as granite or Purbeck marble. Although there is a sufficient number of dateable fonts available to allow a historical sequence of their shapes to be determined it is not always easy to date fonts.

In the early days of Christianity partial immersion in rivers was usual and on a capital in Adel church, Yorkshire, as well as on the font in Castle Frome, Herefordshire, the water is shown rising around the waist of the catechumen. Almost side by side with the practice of partial immersion there was another usage where the water flowed from above and descended on the catechumen's head and over his whole body whilst standing in a vessel or shallow bath to catch the water. There was also the act of affusion and in the fresco in the gallery of the sacraments in the cemetery of S.Callistus in Rome (*c*200) the catechumen is shown as a nude boy standing in water with water being poured on his head by the baptizer. Further ritual grew up comprising the triple immersion of the head in the name of the Trinity, the Father, Son and Holy Ghost. This was effected either by passing the head into the falling water or someone pouring water over the head three times. Whichever method was used, it was not necessary to stand in a great depth of water.

In the separate baptistries of the ancient churches in France and Italy are found tanks where a number of adult person could be baptised at the same time, e.g. Pisa, Florence and Ravenna in Italy and at St Jean, Poitiers, in France. These tanks are about six or seven feet across and from three to four feet deep. The catechumen stood in two feet of water and either immersed his head three times or water was poured over his head three times.

Baptism was the rite of initiation into the Church and the uninitiated were not to enter the holy precincts until they had been admitted through baptism (Acts 12:37,38) and so the baptistry erected for the celebration of the rite was isolated from the church as baptism was the door to all the other Sacraments and no one could participate in them until that person had first been baptised. This ceremony continued right through the Middle Ages and even when baptism was administered at a font inside a church part of the ceremony took place in the church porch.

The size of the baptistries and the tanks was necessitated by the fact that the bishops were the only ones allowed to baptise and, in theory, if not always in practice, baptism and confirmation were administered together. Bishops being busy people, and travelling being difficult, found it necessary to restrict baptism to two or three times in the church year, usually Easter and Pentecost and there would, therefore, be a very large number of catechumens.

When the village church obtained baptismal privilege it became usual to baptise within the church and the use of separate baptistries came to an end. The Council of Auxerre speaks of baptisms taking place by permission in villages as early as AD 578. In AD 747 Cuthbert, Archbishop of Canterbury, ordered all priests to baptise regularly and so baptism inside the church became legalised. Pope Leo IV, in the ninth century, recommended that every church should have a font. It was not, of course, possible to have a font of the size that had previously been used, as room could not be spared and, in any case, by the ninth century the greater part of western Europe was nominally Christian and so adult baptism became less common. The main reason for the change was the increasing use of infant baptism which, although not legally recognised, had been in use, to a degree, from the earliest days of Christianity.

In England a canon of the time of King Edgar, AD 960 ordered that the baptism of an infant be not delayed longer than thirty-seven days. From the eleventh century onwards infants were baptised within a few days of their birth and often on the same day.

Baptism of adults had now become the exception rather than the rule and so with the growth of infant baptism the large tanks became unnecessary and would have been out of place at the west end of all but the largest churches. When an adult was to be baptised it would have been by affusion.

The later Middle Ages brought about a complete transformation of the architectural setting of baptism in so far as detached baptistries were rarely built and the font came to be placed within the church itself. The large tanks, however, continued to be used particularly in Italy, France and Germany. The font was now much reduced in size and new forms evolved.

There are four principal methods of baptising (1) Submersion, where the candidate goes completely below the surface of the water (2) Immersion, where the head is dipped with or without the candidate standing in the water (3) Affusion, when the water is poured over the head and (4) Aspersion, when the water is sprinkled on the head. Immersion is now rarely used and normally denotes submersion.

From an examination of the dimensions of the early Christian fonts it is evident that the great majority of them were not capable of being used for submersion of adults. If baptismal practice was uniform it must have been either by immersion or affusion. It was the practice for the catechumen to stand upright in shallow water but when the baptism of infants became the norm it was not possible for a baby to do this so partial submersion was substituted for the older form of semi-immersion. The immersion of infants came into common use although probably not total submersion due to the fears about the immersion of the child's head. In the thirteenth century St Thomas Aquinas said that immersion was the more common form and that to be on the safe side it would be better for immersion to be practised not affusion.

The fifteenth-century font at Gresham, Norfolk, shows the baptism of a baby by immersion and it is known that Richard Beauchamp, Earl of Warwick, was baptised in 1381 by immersion as were Prince Arthur, eldest son of Henry VII,

King Edward VI and Queen Elizabeth I. The present Book of Common Prayer of 1662 in the rubric for the Publick Baptism of Infants allows for the baby to be immersed. With the growth of infant baptism the need for the large baptismal tank ceased to exist.

Saxon

No fonts prior to the Anglo-Saxon period are to be found in parish churches in the British Isles. There are many remnants of Saxon churches and so it is reasonable to find some fonts of this period. Perhaps the finest is at Deerhurst Gloucestershire, *circa* ninth century, which is carved with the Celtic trumpet spiral bordered by the vine scroll, a motif from Northumbria. The base pillar on which it rests is not part of the font, it is in fact, part of a carved cross. This was often the case where the village cross was destroyed. This font was found in a farmyard at Deerhurst and the pillar nearby.

Another unusual Saxon font is at St Martin's church, Canterbury. The base is reputed to consist of a medieval mill-stone which is unusual in itself, but one would expect to find the bowl of stone carved out of a solid block whereas, in fact, the bottom part consists of two sets of carved stone bricks. The carving on these bricks is matched by the carving on the rim which suggests that the rim originally formed the top of the lower part. This being feasible it would have made a small bath suitable for the baptismal of the Saxon king, Athelstan, and his thegns. The further tier of carved bricks in the form of intersecting arcading which suggests Norman work, was to heighten the font which would have been required after the era of adult baptism, for the baptism of infants.

DEERHURST, GLOUCESTERSHIRE.
C9. Celtic trumpet scroll.

One reason for so few pre-Conquest fonts is that, although by the seventh century every priest could baptise and every parish would have had some kind of baptismal vessel, perhaps only a stone basin or even a wooden tub, these would have had a limited life and also would have been later considered as unworthy. A further reason is that following the Conquest most of the Anglo-Saxon churches were replaced in the twelfth century by a Norman church and, as a rule, a Norman font would replace the Anglo-Saxon font.

Most fonts of this period were tub-shaped, often crudely carved and sometimes rudely hewn in shape, although there are some finely carved pre-Conquest fonts to be found in the country. A number have a band or cable ornament copied from the remains of Roman monuments, of which there must have been many at that time, while others have interlacing and spiral ornament, heads and figures.

Norman

During the eleventh and twelfth centuries the tub font remained popular and consisted of an unmounted bowl resting on the ground and which was mounted at a later date.

Norman fonts, like their buildings, were solidly formed and so have withstood the intervening centuries. These fonts, when the practice of infant baptism became usual, had to be raised and so bases were provided to raise them up and

MUCH MARCLE, HEREFORD & WORCESTER.
Tub-shaped banded font.

FYFIELD, ESSEX.
C12 – Blank arcading on two sides with fleur-de-lys on two sides.

a good example may be seen at Mitcheldean, Gloucestershire, the bowl of the font being beautifully carved with the figures of the twelve Apostles. Another example is at Much Marcle, Herefordshire, where there is a plain tub font which has three flat bands representing the ropes which would have been used to bind together the staves of a wooden tub font.

MICHELDEAN, GLOUCESTERSHIRE.
C12 – Apostles. Added base.

Norman fonts appear to have escaped mutilation by the iconoclasts unlike those of later periods with their delicate carvings, traceries and figures. The later Norman font bowls were mainly square and made of Purbeck marble with either zig-zag decoration or simple arcading consisting of series of round-headed arches on the faces of the bowl later developing into intersecting arcading. This type of font was 'factory made' at Purbeck in Dorset and is easy to recognise. There are many examples in the various counties, for example White Roding and Fyfield in Essex where zig-zag and arcading may be seen and at Locking, Somerset, where the bowl has four primitive men in armour, one at each corner, stretching out their arms to join hands.

There are, however variations in decoration to be found and at Burnham Deepdale, Norfolk, is a fine font of the Norman period on which three of the four bowl faces are carved with the Labours of the Month.

Face 1	January, Man with drinking horn
	February, Man warming his feet
	March, Digging
	April, Pruning
Face 2	May, Beating the Bounds — Rogationtide
	June, Weeding
	July, Scything corn
	August, Binding a sheaf
Face 3	September, Threshing
	October, Grinding corn

November, Slaughtering
December, Feasting

In many cases fonts were covered with elaborate though somewhat grotesque figure sculpture, e.g. emblematical creatures such as Agnus Dei, or Lamb of God, shown as a lamb holding a bannered cross in its uplifted foot, symbols of the Evangelists; Matthew, Mark, Luke and John shown respectively as a winged man, winged lion, winged ox and an eagle, figures of the Saints, scriptural scenes and so on. There is also a widely distributed class where ornament consists of human heads, generally four in number.

Early English

Some fine fonts may be found in the overlapping period of the Norman and Early English periods like the one at Bodmin, Cornwall. It is polypod having five supports with a square bowl richly ornamented. The cup-shaped lower part of the bowl is supported on a circular shaft with four detached shafts at the angles and human head capitals projecting from the rim of the bowl. At Springfield, Essex is a beautiful thirteenth-century font decorated with stiff-leaf scrolls and large rosettes and is considered to be the best font of this period in Essex. Many fonts of this period are termed 'Purbeck fonts'. They usually have square or octagonal bowls with broad flat surfaces normally resting on a central shaft with four or more shafts with one at each angle. These fonts were extremely popular and to cope with the demand there was a factory at Purbeck producing ready-made shafts, moulded and floriated capitals and bases.

The change from the figure sculpture, either grotesque creatures or scenes from the Scriptures or lives of the Saints, which had been characteristic of a large class of Norman fonts were out of fashion and the ornamentation was taken almost exclusively from architectural design. This elaborate ornamentation faded beore the dazzling shine of the polished Purbeck 'marble' stone.

The fonts made of freestone are less in number but are most interesting because of the great variety of design and bowl shapes which are sometimes circular, square, octagonal or hexagonal. The supports also vary, the early fonts of the period usually had detached shafts at the corners which rise to the top of the rim while the later fonts have engaged shafts at the corners supporting the base of the bowl.

Apart from the architectural ornamentation of the period, for example, the roll moulding, the fashion of covering the surface of the font bowl with ornament was seldom adopted. Where it is to be found it frequently takes the form of conventional foliage known as stiff-leaf which is characteristic of the style of the period. Good examples are to be seen at Springfield and Fryerning, Essex.

SPRINGFIELD, ESSEX.
C13 font.

ROYDON, ESSEX.
C13 having masks in the four diagonals.

The designs of freestone fonts in this century are very fine so that Francis Bond's description of the period is very appropriate when he wrote that it was the 'the golden age of font design in the comparatively few examples executed in freestone.'

Decorated

Fonts of the Decorated style, *c*1280 to *c*1377, are few in number due probably to the ample numbers which were provided in the Norman and Early English periods. Their design was perfected, and to a large degree standardised, but there is no doubt that the fourteenth century may, perhaps, be called 'the brilliant age of lavish font ornament'. Purbeck marble has gone out of fashion and much of it had by this time lost much of its polish and had begun to decay and so the masons resorted to freestone.

At Roydon, Essex, is a font of the transitional period Early English/Decorated, *c*1300. The bowl is octagonal with four masks, probably workmen, in the four diagonals. The bowl is supported by a large central stem and corner supports with roll moulding at top and bottom of each. The rim of the bowl has been replaced. A further example may be seen at Michelmersh, Hampshire.

The fashion was to do away with the shafts whether detached or engaged and to have polygonal bowls, usually octagonal. These bowls were mounted on polygonal pedestals and are known as monopod fonts. The simplicity of the thirteenth century had become unfashionable and in its stead rich detail was lavished on the bowls and pedestals. Perhaps some of the best at to be found in the eastern counties of Suffolk and Norfolk.

Now that the majority of bowls had eight faces it was necessary to find the best way of filling them. In the previous century arcading had provided the answer but now people were tired of it and required something different. Where money was scarce and ornamentation could not be afforded the faces were left blank. In most cases, however, the faces were beautifully ornamented. Some fine examples may be seen at Lostwithiel, Cornwall, where the faces of the bowl are carved with sacred and secular subjects which include, a bishop's head, a grotesque, a hunting scene, the Crucifixion and a dog biting a rabbit. At Ware, Hertfordshire, there is a delicately finished and exquisite figure sculpture on the octagonal bowl. Each face is recessed with a crocketed arch containing a figure or subject. The figures depict St Christopher carrying the infant Christ, St George slaying the dragon, St Catherine with sword and wheel, St James dressed as a pilgrim, St John the Baptist, St Margaret of Antioch, the Blessed Virgin and the Archangel Gabriel. Not content with all this the carvers included a row of demi-angels. They bear alternatively emblems of our Lord's Passion and musical instruments.

During this period the window tracery underwent great change and was of many patterns. Examples of these patterns were used to fill the faces of the bowl and pedestal together with the niche on each of the faces of the pedestal which held a figure. Unfortunately these are now almost always missing. Farringdon, Berkshire, is a good example of window tracery.

There were two types of niche which were favoured and which appeared late in the thirteenth century. One type was a straight-sided pediment, richly crocketed and cusped with a foliated finial. The other type, which was the most popular, was the new form of arch called the ogee, a form of 'S' shaped double curve which was greatly used until about the middle of the century when its popularity declined although it continued to be used in Gothic architecture. A very fine example of a font having ogee canopies on each face of the bowl may be seen at Rayne, Essex.

The early niches were shallow and did not contain figures but they quickly became deeper and contained figures of saints or scriptural scenes. Often at the corners of the base of the bowl were heads or masks, angels or foliated ornaments as at Finchingield, Essex. Where foliated ornament appeared it was more realistic than in the previous century and not so deeply carved. Later in the period the pedestal tended also to be richly decorated sometimes with niches with or without figures or window tracery forms. Examples may be seen at Willingale Spain, Essex and Faringdon, Berkshire.

This century had been called the 'Decorated' period when geometrical designs were used particularly in window tracery and circular or squared quatrefoil panels may be found round the octagonal bowls, as at Willingale Spain. Later the cusped lancet window form and shields were also favourite ornaments and these are to be seen together on the octagonal bowl at Great Saling, Essex and at Broadhembury, Devon.

FINCHINGFIELD, ESSEX.
C14. (c1375).

Figure sculpture which was common on Norman fonts but was rarely used in the thirteenth century, reappears and is much more lifelike than the grotesque figures of the Normans.

The splendid architecture of the Decorated period was reaching its apogee when it was suddenly halted by the terrible pestilence which we know as the Black Death and which came to this country in 1348. The pestilence swept through the country and by 1349 had become so widespread that the consequent mortality paralysed the country. It is estimated that about half the population perished although there is some doubt concerning this.

Building operations practically came to a stop due to the scarcity of masons and in 1350 when the great rebuilding of Gloucester Cathedral was completed the surviving masons and other were organised and sent out into various parts of the country. It is very probable that this accounts for the standardisation of architecture for about the last quarter of the century when the new Perpendicular style quickly found its way into parish churches.

Perpendicular

This period tended to become the setting for the work of craftsmen in glass, sculpture and wood carving and so we find that their skill is directed especially to church furnishings and ornaments. Many of our finest churches were built in this period by the great wool and cloth merchants.

Gothic architecture was a thing of continual movement but in the perpendicular period, which lasted some one hundred and seventy years of thereabouts, it began to show signs of deterioration. In the best work there must be progress. Once the movement ceases then development fails and in the Perpendicular period it slowed down and began to come to rest and so with the ceasing of movement deterioration set in. In the Early English and Decorated periods there was a feeling about the architecture and furnishings, the carving was more vigorous in the Early English period and more natural in the Decorated period but in the Perpendicular period everything showed that skill and dexterity were the things after which the craftsmen were striving. One sign of this was the repetition of forms of ornament but despite this the period had many deserving qualities particularly their timber and vaulted roofs which were gloried in by the carpenters, wood carvers and masons. Screens, canopy work, stalls and misericord, pulpits and fonts, as well as parts of the fabric, were clothed with miniature buttresses, pinnacles, vaults and battlements.

With so much attention being given to the furnishings of the church, the font was very much included and the number of Perpendicular fonts far exceeds those of any period since the Norman.

The octagonal bowl was now usually employed and many of them had plain uncarved faces which were either meant to be later carved or painted. Perhaps this was not carried out for various reasons, for example, lack of money or the benefactor died. Some fonts had little ornament but many had quatrefoil and heraldic ornaments with shields on the faces of the bowl bearing the arms of donors or benefactors. Good examples are to be seen at Saffron Walden and Halstead, Essex; Holt, Clywyd and Fakenham, Norfolk, Rosettes and fleurettes were also a popular form of decoration.

The most popular type, which might say is a typical Perpendicular font, has the sides panelled. In each panel is a quatrefoil or a quatrefoil within a circle as at Southminster, Essex, and in many instances the stem is also ornamented with panel tracery.

In the fifteenth century figure sculpture was much more largely used on fonts than during the Early English or Decorated periods. Not since the Norman period had such a wealth of human and animal figures been used on fonts in this country. These carved figures were more delicate and life-like than the crudely carved figures of the Norman period, but the figures had a similarity and fell into definite classes which were almost confined to East Anglia. The first class is composed of angelic figures with outstretched wings and may be found at the angles of the bowl beneath its lower rim. (High Wycombe, Buckinghamshire; Darsham, Suffolk and Wymondham, Norfolk). In the second class of font bowl various classes of figures frequently occur, for example angels holding shields, angels with musical instruments, the symbols of the four Evangelist, the Saints, Holy Trinity, the Crucifixion, the baptism of Christ and animal figures. Examples of these may be seen at Staple, Kent, Wymondham, Norfolk, Happisburgh, Norfolk; Little Bromley, Essex; Bradwell, Suffolk; Blakeney, Stalham and Blofield, Norfolk. The third group is to be found in East Anglia and derive their splendour not only from the decoration on the bowl but from the sculptured figures around the stem. Sometimes the figures are of Saints as at Upton, Norfolk, but more commonly alternate lions (sejant) and wild men holding clubs are to be found. The wild men are shown with hairy skins and usually bearing clubs although occasionally holding other weapons. Fine examples are at Happisburgh, Wynmondham and Ludham, Norfolk; Halesworth, Saxmundham, Walberswick and Theberton, Suffolk. There is considerable doubt as to the significance of these figures. One explanation is that the wild men stood for wild and unregenerate humanity and the lions for evil and so were placed round the lower part of the stem to symbolise their subjection in the sacrament of regeneration through the baptism. These wild men also appear in other parts of East Anglian churches, e.g. Caswton, Norfolk, where a wild man is carved above a piscina.

SOUTHMINSTER, ESSEX.
C15 – Quaterfoil decoration.

One of the chief features of the religious art of the twelfth and thirteenth centuries was its symbolic significance which largely dominated the art of the fourteenth century. In the fifteenth century the symbolic treatment became to a great extent academic. Before and after the Constitutions of the Synod of Lambeth, 1281, were issued, episcopal instructions respecting the medieval catechism of the Church were decreed and thus the articles of Christian faith and practice assumed a pictorial form in frescoes on the walls of the churches, in painted windows and also executed in sculpture. These instructions were; the Ten Commandments, the Creed, the Lord's Prayer, the Hail Mary, the Seven

HAPPISBURGH, NORFOLK.
C15 – Symbols of the Evangelists. Lions and wodewoses.

Works of Mercy, the Seven Deadly Sins, the Seven Principal Virtues and the Seven Sacraments.

In 1450 Roger Van der Weyden (1400–1464) a Flemish painter, visited Italy where he became influenced by the work of Simone Martini (1283–1344) an early exponent of Gothic painting, particularly by Martini's *Annunciation* which led to many imitations. In the vault of the church of the Incoronata at Naples are the earliest representations of the Seven Sacraments which were probably painted by a follower of Martini.

Most of Weyden's work was religious and it was following his visit to Italy that he was inspired to paint his well-known work, now in the Picture Gallery at Antwerp, where the Sacraments are depicted in connection with the Crucifixon which has a background of an altar facing the nave in a huge Flemish church. In the side chapels on either side of the great nave six Sacraments are being administered – on the north Baptism, Confirmation and Penance; on the south, Holy Orders, Matrimony and Extreme Unction. Over the figures engaged in the celebration of a Sacrament is an angel holding a scroll and each angel is shown in symbolical colours. The angel of Baptism in white; the angel of Confirmation, yellow; the angel of the Holy Eucharist, green, Penance, scarlet; Extreme Unction, black; Holy Orders, purple and Matrimony, blue.

Within a few years of the painting of this beautiful Femish picture a series of important baptismal fonts were carved in England depicting the crucial point in each of the seven Sacraments of the church, e.g. in Holy Matrimony when the priest is joining the hands of the couple and blessing them. These carvings occupy seven sides of octagonal fonts while the eighth side has either The Crucifixion, the Baptism of Our Lord or some other appropriate subject.

The correct order for the Sacraments is Baptism, Confirmation, Holy Eucharist, Penance, Extreme Unction, Holy Orders and Matrimony. This order is rarely adhered to and varies so greatly that it would appear that each mason and parson did just as he pleased. In a few cases Holy Orders and Confirmation are placed on opposite sides, as each requires the introduction of a bishop. Baptism and Extreme Unction are sometimes portrayed on opposite panels seemingly to indicate that they were the first and last received. On some fonts the panel for the Holy Eucharist is on the east so as to face the altars in the church. Although there does not seem to be any fixed arrangement for the eighth panel it frequently faces west. There are about fifty of these fonts existing and, with only two exceptions, are found in Norfolk and Suffolk.

SLOLEY, NORFOLK – SEVEN SACRAMENT FONT.
showing baptism and matrimony panels

Most of the subjects were badly mutilated by William Dowsing who was appointed by Cromwell to be a Parliamentary Visitor in 1643 to enforce an ordinance for the destruction of monuments of superstition. He was known as 'Smasher' Dowsing and he kept copious accounts of his works of destructions in his diaries. Much of the damage to the beautiful fonts in East Anglia was due to Dowsing especially the font at Southwold, Suffolk, where every piece of the figure sculpture was hacked away. The general features which added greatly to the splendour of Perpendicular fonts was the use of colour in the elaborate decoration of the figure sculpture, traces of which may frequently still be seen (Acle, Norfolk) as well as the large stepped platforms on which the fonts were mounted and which were especially characteristic of East Anglia. These platforms were further enriched with panelling in the rises of the steps (Happisburgh and Acle, Norfolk). During this period brick was coming into general use and was often used in church architecture in the eastern counties. In a few cases where the church was built of brick this material was also used for the font as at Chignal Smealey, Essex.

Wooden fonts are rare but at Marks Tey, Essex, is a fine octagonal font made of oak with ornament resembling a typical panelled font of the fifteenth century. Metal fonts belong to all periods but the majority of them are either early or late. Many date from the Norman period and the latest are of the seventeenth century, (Aston Ingham, Hereford and Worcester and Eythorne, Kent). Some fine Norman figured leaden bowls are to be found at Dorchester, Oxfordshire; Walton-on-the-Hill, Surrey and Wareham, Dorset. It is interesting that during the First World War the vibration caused by the firing of anti-aircraft guns cracked the plaster round the bowl of the font at Halstow, Kent, which when removed revealed a leaden font bowl in good perseveration. Other leaden fonts may be seen at Frampton-on-Severn and Siston, Gloucestershire and Burghill, Hereford and Worcester.

Post Reformation

Several years elapsed before the religious changes brought about by the Reformation affected the font and there were few new fonts between the reign of Elizabeth and the Civil War.

In Queen Elizabeth's reign those who had been exiled on the Continent during the persecutions of Mary's reign returned to this country but could not accept the sacramental system and ceremonial of the English Church. The performance of divine worship and the elevation of the rites of the Church were besieged with confusion and carelessness so that the Church authorities found it difficult to bring decency and order to bear. The Calvinistic custom of baptising in basins grew and Injunctions and Visitation Articles contained references to it in an attempt to check the spread of this custom. By royal command Injunctions were issued under the name of Queen Elizabeth 'that the font be not removed from the accustomed place; and that in parish churches the curates take not upon them to confer baptism in basins but in the font *customably used*.' Despite this Injunction, destruction of fonts and negligent administration grew and there are many instances of demolition recorded in churchwardens' accounts where parishes defied the royal orders.

The Reformation produced varying outlooks regarding baptism, the Lutherans and Anglicans being content to leave the font where it was. The Calvinists, however, believed that public reading and preaching of the Word were the essence of the Sacrament and that the baptism was a bond of fellowship between all the members and therefore a matter of concern to all who participated. John Calvin 1509–1564, in his draft *Ecclesiastical Ordinances,* September and October 1547 declared that, 'the stone or baptismal font is to be near the pulpit, in order that there be better hearing for the recitation of this mystery and practice of baptism.' This had an immediately effect upon the architectural setting of baptism within the Reformed Churches where the font ceased to be placed at the west end, near the entrance, but was placed at he east end close to the holy table and the pulpit. Two other factors arose which affected the setting even more radically. These were the Calvinistic aversion to the font and that many Protestants also regarded it as an article of papal superstition.

These views soon became influenced by the Anglicans and Thomas Becon, chaplain to Cranmer, pointed out in his Catechism that when Philip baptised the eunuch (Acts 8:36) there was neither hallowed font nor holy water, salt, oil, cream, spittle, candle or any other part of papistry. This attitude of mind resulted in the total disappearance of the traditional font within the Reformed Churches. Because it was so disliked for its papist associations, and because it was not now needed for immersion, the Reformed Churches adopted the practice of using shallow basins. The practice grew during the sixteenth century but those in authority in the Church of England defied the Calvanists and on the 10th October 1561, Elizabeth issued a Royal Order to the effect, 'that the Font be not removed from the accustomed place: And that in parish churches the curates take not upon them to confer Baptism in basins but in the Font customably used'. This was later affirmed by the Archbishop Matthew Parker in 1566 and Archbishop John Whitgift in 1583. The battle continued until the Hampton Court Conference in 1604 when Canon 81 ordered, 'that there shall be a font of stone in every church and chapel where baptism is to be ministered, the same to be set up in the ancient usual places'.

In 1640 the King, Charles I had to summon a new parliament which became famous as the 'Long Parliament' as it remained in existence until 1660. Those in opposition to the King quickly gained ascendancy and in 1641 effected a constitutional revolution. It became unlawful for more than three years to elapse without the calling of parliament and for it to be dissolved without its own consent. The courts of Star Chamber and High Commission were abolished and extra-parliamentary taxation was banned. As well as this, two the King's chief ministers were executed, the Earl of Strafford executed in 1641 and Archbishop Laud in 1645. Parliament had deprived the Crown of all the prerogative powers which had been enjoyed by Tudor monarchs. In addition there were two new issues, the Church and the control of the army which arose to divide them into 'root-and-branch' reformers, i.e. parliamentarians and moderates (royalists). In 1642 the wedge between Charles and Parliament had been driven deeper. Rebellion against English rule had broken out in Ireland due, in part, to the fear of the Puritan Long Parliaments's ambition to outlaw property and convert Ireland to some form of Protestant faith. Parliament had already seen its attempts to reform the English church blocked by a royalist House of Lords and because it distrusted Charles's apparent willingness to support its constitutional reforms it refused to vote money and supplies to raise an army to put down the Irish revolt unless the control of the army was placed in its own hands. The King and Parliament were now so divided that the issue could be resolved only by war. With the defeat of the royalists the King was executed in 1649 and so began the Commonwealth, the only republican period in England's history. With the creation of the commonwealth puritanism gained the ascendancy and The Directory of Public Worship, 1644, ordered baptism to be administered, 'in the face of the congregation, where Fonts in the time of Popery were unfitly and superstitiously placed'. The result was the wholesale destruction, desecration and removal of the existing fonts. William Dowsing and his fellow commissioners travelled through Cambridgeshire and Suffolk destroying whatever they thought savoured of popery, which included many fonts.

Many instances occurred where the carved font panels were plastered over to make them appear to be plain and uncarved only to be re-discovered some centuries later. This disguising of some fonts saved them from destruction when the commissioners made their visits. The font at Belchamp St Paul, Essex, has two of its panels plastered over and as the decoration of the remainder is in such good condition it is very probable that all the panels were dealt with accordingly so saving them from destruction. It seems odd, however, that the two blank faces have not been restored by now. On the other hand the font could have originally have been in a corner especially as it would appear that the bowl has been remounted. At Great Maplestead, Essex, the font was completely plastered and painted, the plaster being removed as late as 1930 and traces of colouring may still be seen.

During the Commonwealth the Puritan and Calvinist influence became all pervasive and basins were used for baptism in place of the fonts which had been destroyed. Many churchwardens' accounts for this period show evidence of the wanton vandalism of fonts and the provision of basins. An extract from the churchwardens' accounts for Brinklow church reads, '1653. Brinklow, Warwickshire. Bought a basin to cristen the children, which, cost three shillings sixpence.'

With the restoration of the monarchy the situation was reversed and whereas the records of St Martins, Leicester, for 1645 read: 'For a basin to be used at baptism . . . 5s . . .', the records of the same church for 1661 read: 'Agreed that the font of stone formerly belonging to the church shall be set upon in the ancient place, and that the other now standing near the desk be taken down'.

In 1662 the Act of Uniformity was passed under which no one could hold a living who had not declared his genuine assent and consent to everything contained therein. This meant that basins were not to be used and fonts were to be brought back into use.

The many parishes which had destroyed their fonts now had to have new fonts or, where only the bowls had been destroyed, to mount new bowls on the old pedestals. Occasionally the old font was not destroyed but hidden away and brought out for re-erection. Although most parishes reverted either to their original font or to a new one there were many who still possessed baptismal basins and placed them in the font bowl. It was only in the nineteenth century that a final stop was put to this undignified practice although baptismal basins, of various types, may still be found kept in the font bowl and covered by the lid.

Following the revived interest in Classical learning in the Reformation period there was a change of taste which caused an entire departure from the traditional form of font. The work of Inigo Jones and Sir Christopher Wren established a neo-Classical style architecture and fonts conformed to the new fashion which generally took the shape of small vases standing upon slender pillars, resembling flower vases rather than vessels for baptism. The ancient ceremony of immersion was still set out in the Book of Common Prayer as the normal method of baptising infants but this was quite out of the question due to the size and shallowness of the receptacles (Lambourne End, Essex). Sometimes the bowls were decorated with miniature cherub heads which became popular as an adornment to various items of church furnishings. Good examples of fonts of this class may be seen at Billericay, Essex; Essenden, Herts; St Stephen, Walbrook, London and Warminghurst, Sussex.

By 1840 the Gothic Revival was under way and the Decorated style was the period of architecture which was employed, i.e. between the years 1260 and 1360. The reason given by the Camden Society in 1844 were that during the Norman era the Catholic Church was forming her architectural language but in the Tudor period she was unlearning it. Gothic was deemed to be the Christian architecture and so every part of the church building must have its symbolic meaning. The font was to be put near the door in the west end as it was meant to show that baptism is the door by which a child is brought into the Church. Fonts which were eastward of the centre of the nave were moved, for example, Milton church, near Cambridge, the font was against the chancel arch but was moved in 1844 to the west end.

LAMBOURNE END, ESSEX. C18.

Later, in the third quarter of the nineteenth century, a number of the leading architects, such as, Benjamin Wells, George Street, Arthur W.

Bloomfield, and Augustus Pugin, toured the Continent as part of their training as architects during which they visited many churches observing the detached baptistries, e.g. Florence, Pisa and Padua. Not only did they draw attention to the baptistries but their publications also reached English readers encouraging them to the concept of churches having baptistries. When the building of Truro Cathedral was commenced in 1879, the architect John L. Pearson, provided in his design for a circular baptistry to the west of the south transept which had a porch and was the main entrance. A separate baptistry was provided for Liverpool Cathedral by Gilbert Scott. Parish churches also had less ambitious baptistries, such as, Dodford, Worcestershire; All Saints, Ealing, Greater London and All Saints, Chigwell Row, Essex. This architectural setting of baptism rapidly became popular and, in existing churches where the font had previously been isolated, baptistries were created by defining the space around the font with low balustrades or rails, as at, Holy Trinity, Exmouth, where the area beneath the tower was used as a baptistry. The emphasis placed upon the sacramental life and importance of baptism later resulted in the disregarding of small earthenware basins, pewter plates, china bowls, in fact any old basin or bowl which had crept into use during the opening decades of the nineteenth century, although, as has been said, a few may still be found. This practice grew out of private baptism and consequently the disuse and neglect of the fonts which were occasionally mutilated by their tops being cut off because they were too high, filled with rubbish, candles or brushes, old vases, or degraded to other uses.

The need for a cover to the neo-Gothic font followed logically from the requirement that the font should be designed to conform with the late medieval examples, as already mentioned, although many covers were simply flat lids. The principal idea of the architectural setting of baptism in the twentieth century is that the rite of baptism required not merely articles of furniture but a defined space suitable to its dignity and symbolism. In most modern churches the font is placed at the west end close to the entrance defining baptism as the means of entrance to the Church. The font, in some cases, has not only been placed in a defined space but attempts have been made to enshrine the font by decoration such as a cross hanging above, a fresco on the rear wall, a railing or a glass screen. There is no doubt that an attempt has been made to give dignity and importance to the font in most churches.

Font Projections

A further type of font, although rare in this country, should be mentioned. This type has a small subsidiary bowl either marked off by a division inside the main bowl or attached to it outside, as at Youlgreave, Derbyshire. In some cases the attachment is a small bracket as at Rainham, Essex. There appears to be several reasons for these appendages, In addition to water, the priest required a book, holy oil or chrism and frequently a candle. In order to accommodate these articles some fonts had projections, as at Feniton, Devon, or sometimes a niche or ledge in the adjacent wall, as at Rudford, Gloucestershire.

YOULGREAVE, DERBYSHIRE.
Norman font showing projection.

When affusion replaced submersion some additions to the font were necessary. In England affusion did not become general until well into the sixteenth century (France C14 and Italy C15). The pouring of water over the infants head raised the question of how the child was to be held. According to the Roman rite the consecrated water could not be allowed to spill on to the floor and although it is possible for the child to be held over the font so that the dripping water would go back into it, this practice was not allowed and so receptacles in the form of small basins were used to catch the drippings. As affusion did not become general in England until well into the sixteenth century immersion was still being practised, there are no examples to be found in this country although examples are to be found on the Continent at Cosseuil, near Grenoble, France where there is a font and smaller basin made out of a single block of stone. At Sains, Somme, France a small reservoir was placed against the base of the Norman font and at Chirens, Isere, France a small fifteenth century basin was added to the font. The basins found in England are post Reformation and were used by the Godparents to wash their hands after holding the child during the anointing in case any of the chrism still remained on them. The water used for this purpose had to be disposed of with care and so a small cup-like projection was made on the side of the font bowl with a drain from the bottom which joined with the drain of the font (St Martin, Exeter).

The projection on the side of the Youlgreave font bowl is supported by the head of a salamander, the mythical creature which cannot be consumed by fire and so typifies the Christian who is baptised by the Holy Spirit and with fire. As this projection does not contain a drain it may have supported a basin to catch the drippings from the child's head or have been used to hold a chrismatory, a container for the sanctified holy oils used to anoint the catechumen prior to baptism or for the spoon to rest in. The Rainham font appendage is a small bracket attached to the rim with the remains of a further bracket on the opposite side. These were probably used to hold a small basin or a chrismatory and perhaps a cruet of salt, a candle and napkin all of which would have been used during the baptismal service. At Essendon, Hertfordshire, in addition to the great Classical-shaped earthenware Wedgewood bowl (1780) which stands on a wooden pedestal there is a small gilt basin which, when in use, was placed on a wooden support on the floor and was used for affusion, the large bowl being used for the drippings from the child's head. It is believed that the gilt basin is now kept inside the large bowl.

Lids And Covers

Very early fonts did not have lids and the christening water, having been hallowed, was kept in the font and not freshly put in and emptied after use as it is today. One reason for this was that the hallowed water would be readily available for baptising a newly born baby without delay. This hallowed water was considered to be of great value for black magic and witchcraft and was, therefore, sometimes stolen. J.G.Davies in his book *The Architectural Setting of Baptism* tells us that, 'the Anglo-Saxons used baptismal water in certain of their salves: it was an ingredient in their medieval draughts and love potions'. He goes on to say that consecrated water was used when, in the practice of black magic, a waxen image was baptised in the name of the man or woman who was to be destroyed by melting or stabbing the waxen image.

To overcome these thefts various bishops throughout the country ordered that fonts should be kept locked. In 1220 the Bishop of Durham directed that fonts should be kept locked and sealed because of black magic. Edmund Rich, Archbishop of Canterbury in 1236 ordered that fonts were to be kept locked under seal and that each parish priest should hold the key of his church font because the hallowed water was used in magic. In addition it was ordered that the water be changed every seven days. Again in 1287 Bishop Quivil of Exeter instructed that each church in his diocese should have a well-locked stone font. It is interesting that although every effort appears to have been made to protect the hallowed water in the font nothing was done in respect of the similar hallowed water in the stoup. This may have been because the font water, unlike the stoup water, had acquired something special through being sanctified in the mystical washing away of sin.

The first English Prayer Book of 1549 provided for the water to be changed once a month, the Scottish Prayer Book of 1604 required the renewal of the water every fortnight and the present Book of Common Prayer of 1662 requires that there should be a fresh supply at every baptism.

In 1305 Archbishop Winchelsey of Canterbury ordered that amongst the functions to be provided by the parishioners was a font and lock.

At first the covers were only flat lids secured by a bar and staple and it is probable that they were in general use long before the Order of 1236. At Weobley, Hereford and Worcester, there is one of the very few surviving original locks. It consists of a chain of four links attached to a staple in the rim of the fourteenth-century font. At the other end of the chain is a flat bar of iron about twelve inches in length which passes through the handle of the lid. The end of the iron bar has a slot which engages with a staple in the rim on the opposite side and is secured by a padlock.

SIDBURY, DEVON.
font with square lock-plate, probably the only one in England.
Octagonal boarded cover with moulded rim and ogee ribs, 1620.

Many Norman fonts have holes in their rims or sides showing where the staples have been wrenched out, probably in the sixteenth century. Whether or not these fastenings were inserted prior to the order of 1236 to secure a lid or whether they were put there as a result of the Order we shall probably never know. Not only was the font covered with a lid but between the lid and the rim there was a font cloth made of linen or silk, the cloth being laid over the rim of the font bowl and the lid closed down on to it in order to protect the water from dust.In 1519 the font at Morton, Yorkshire, was reported to be in disrepair as it did not have a staple, lock and key or font cloth.

As the Gothic period advanced so the decorative possibilities of the font were soon appreciated and the results from the fourteenth century, developing further to the fifteenth century, especially in East Anglia, were the beautifully carved spire-like towering tabernacles with delicate architectural detail in miniature in

LITTLE LAVER, ESSEX.
C15 cover.

LITTLE LAVER, ESSEX.
C15 – Counterpoise chain and weight.

the form of open-tracery work. Some good examples, both pre and post Reformation may be found at Worlingworth originally from Bury St Edmunds Abbey, Suffolk; South Weald and Takeley, Essex; Castle Acre, Walpole, St Peter, Norfolk; Ewelme, Oxfordshire and Plymstock, Devon.

These covers were almost always richly painted and gilded, the favourite colours being white, scarlet and green, the tendency being to show increased honour to the font, a practice which persisted for a long time after the Reformation.

A common type of cover consisted of an octagonal lid having a moulded edge and eight radiating trusses rising from the angles and meeting at the top of a central post just below a finial. A variation of this form was boarded over. Examples may be seen at Saffron Walden, Essex; Saxmundham, Suffolk; Bolton Percy, North Yorkshire; Bygrave, Hertfordshire and Knapton, Norfolk.

Following the Reformation in the sixteenth century when the virtues of christening water had been exploded, font covers were prized away by the new Evangelists, the staples and the hasps being broken off. The scars may still be seen.

By the middle of Queen Elizabeth's reign font covers were being destroyed and many entries may be found in church accounts and registers relating to the taking down of the font cover and yet, in some cases, a new font cover was made two or three years later. Again during the Civil War in the seventeenth century both fonts and covers were destroyed only to be replaced at the Restoration. There are few extant covers older than the fourteenth century.

A very large number of font covers has perished for different reasons. Many Gothic covers were of highly complex and intricate designs so that when those that still remained required repair it was either beyond the capabilities of the craftsmen of later years of the pocket of the church to carry out the necessary repairs. Often they were swept away as useless lumber at the 'restorations' of the nineteenth century.

Font covers may be divided into two kinds, those which are moveable and those which are fixed. There are three types of moveable covers, firstly a flat lid which is lifted off by hand. Secondly an octagonal lid which is moulded on the rim and has radiating trusses rising from the angles, meeting in the centre and supporting a finial, often carved and resembling a crown. Sometimes they were in the shape of a pointed cone as at Roydon, Essex. Thirdly the much larger covers which varied considerably in size and weight. These were too heavy to lift by hand and were hung from either the roof or a beam or crane and were counterpoised with a lead, iron or stone weight, as at Little Laver, Essex.

At Salle, Norfolk, the cover hands from a hugh arch-braced and traceried bracket. The font cover at Ufford, Suffolk, is a magnificent specimen of workmanship. It is suspended from a beam and the lower part is arranged so that it will slide up over the upper part. This font cover is so fine that William Dowsing could not refrain from admiring its beauty and stating, 'there is a glorious Cover over the Font, like a Pope's Tripple Crown, and a Pelican on the Top, pecking its breast, all gilt over with Gold'. His appreciation, together with the resistance of some churchwardens in refusing to unlock their churches probably accounts for the survival of this magnificent cover as well as others.

SALLE, NORFOLK.
C15 – Crane and pulley.

FONT COVER, PENTLOW, ESSEX.
Lower stage – C15
Upper stage – renewed.

TRUNCH, NORFOLK.
Canopy *c*1500.
Oak, one of only four in England.

A peculiar custom following the Reformation and chiefly at the beginning of the Jacobean period was the fixed or permanent kind of cover. This type enclosed the font in an ornamental wooden case which rested either permanently on the font or on the floor. The sides, or lower panels, hung on hinges so that they could be opened when the font was required for use. Most of these disappeared in the great period of restoration when many fine fonts were brought to light. Examples of these ornamental cases which rested on the font are at Pentlow, Essex; Hepworth, Suffolk and Marden, Kent. Those which rest on the floor may be seen at Thaxted, Essex where the font is enclosed within wooden panelling, elaborately carved with buttresses and canopies rising to the crocheted finial and at Littlebury, Essex and Stanford in the Vale, Berkshire.

In addition to the moveable and fixed covers there is the ciborium which is a canopy erected to honour the baptismal font. Various types of canopies were used in England comprising a combination of Gothic Classical features such as the one erected in Durham Cathedral in 1663. Eight fluted columns with

Corinthian Capitals rise from stone plinths with two round-headed arches between the tops of the columns and a central pendant. Above are eight baluster-type shafts with window-like tracery of two lights between them having ogee moulding, crockets and finials. The third stage consists of trefoiled windows between carved shafts and crocheted pinnacles surmounted by a crocheted spire and a dove finial.

Another type of canopy was where it hung from the room over the font as at Tuxford, Nottinghamshire where there is a conical Jacobean cover over which is suspended a matching conical canopy of 1673. A further type at Pilton, Devon, is where the canopy is fixed to the wall or to a pillar and is panelled down to the ground having a handsome fretted canopy over the font in the shape of a Jacobean pulpit sounding board. The canopy is used in conjunction with a counterpoised front cover. Other examples may be seen at Astbury, Cheshire, Swimbridge, Devon and Trunch, Norfolk.

20

Windows
Saxon-Norman, C7–1189

Windows of the various periods are extremely interesting, and if original, can be one of the best clues to the date of the church but it must always be remember that a window may have been inserted in a much earlier wall.

In the early days little attention was given to the provision of light. A building was primarily a protection from the external elements, even fresh air was not greatly valued and light to an illiterate community was of little use provided the interior of the building was not so dark that nothing could be seen at all. Windows were considered more of a disadvantage than otherwise as is illustrated by the name given to them as our window is derived from the Anglo-Saxon form of 'wind-eye'.

The windows of small stone buildings, even as late as the Conquest, were boards built with a hole or series of holes in them. The woodwork was set in the very middle of the stonework which was splayed away on either side in order to reduce as much as possible the obstruction to such meagre light as managed to filter through the hole. This method of fitting a window-opening was presumably borrowed from the Byzantines, i.e. the Eastern Roman Empire who employed it frequently in their buildings often using pierced stone slabs instead of boards. Sometimes in this country the apertures were almost filled with stone, thin slabs cut from single stones in which small irregular shaped holes were pierced. It is thought that perhaps the holes were made to fit peculiarly shaped pieces of glass which were available, glass being scarce and not of Anglo-Saxon manufacture. On the other hand it was thought that perhaps they were made during re-building after a Danish raid as a precaution against fire as it would have been easy to throw lighted material through the small apertures. An example may be seen at Barnack, Northants.

When cloth soaked in oil came to be used as more or less translucent draught excluder the hole in the board became enlarged to almost the full area of the wood filling the window opening so as to make the most of the opening for the introduction of light. In addition to oil soaked cloth frames filled in with sheets of horn were used to admit light. In order to reduce draughts windows were placed high up in walls a position which also aided security. Sometimes these windows had wooden shutters for protection from wind and rain and the hooks on which the shutters were hung may still be found as at Sidbury, Devon.

CHICKNEY, ESSEX.
Anglo-Saxon window (exterior).

Early windows, whether round-headed or pointed (13), were kept narrow, no doubt to give security to the glass, if any, which was originally very costly. Few Norman windows were intended to be glazed and interiors were gloomy from necessity, not choice. In the latter part of the twelfth century the manufacture of glass developed and it began to be within reach of most churches and there was no longer any need for windows to be made so small and few. There were, however, still many churches with unglazed windows. Life in the twelfth century, although not entirely peaceful, was much more settled. The Viking raids had finished and there was little fear of invasion. Despite the anarchic period of some nineteen years when Stephen and Maud fought for the throne life was more tolerable and the feudal laws having been enforced the country was generally reasonably safe for the law-abiding citizen. Now it was no longer necessary to place windows very high up the walls or to make them so narrow that a man could not climb through and with the use of glazing draughts were now reduced.

The earliest type of window, common to early Christian churches, was an oblong opening with a semi-circular head. This is the most usual type of Anglo-Saxon as well as Anglo-Norman churches.

Late pre-Conquest windows fell into two types. Firstly a form which may be either very early or very late having the opening flush with the outer face of the wall and splayed within, the jambs slightly sloping towards each other and

CHICKNEY, ESSEX.
Anglo-Saxon window (interior).

having a lintel cut into a semi-circular head from a single block of stone. Secondly some were splayed inside and out.

Triangular headed windows may also be found with single splay and examples of these may be seen at Barnack, Cambridgeshire and Deerhurst, Gloucestershire.

The position of the glass in medieval windows varied considerably, the early windows from the eleventh to the thirteenth century being small and the walls thick. To make the most of the light from these small openings they were widely splayed internally. Glass was scarce and expensive and if it was set near the outside face of the wall a smaller amount would be required and so it was customary for the glass to be almost flush with the wall leaving a very large internal splay. The objection to the glass and walling being all in one plane, or nearly so, was the practical objection that the glass was exposed to the drip from the walling above. As glass became cheaper and more widely used it was set further away from the outer surface of the wall or even centrally, the window being double-splayed both inside and out thus protecting it from drip and admitting more light. Where there was glass it was usually set in wooden frames some of which still survive as at Hadstock, Essex where they are small late Saxon double splayed windows with original oak frames and also at Escombe, East Durham.

Circular windows, as such, were not common but are to be found, e.g. at Barton-on-Humber, Humberside, South Lopham and Coltishall, Norfolk; Bibury, Gloucestershire. and Blundeston, Suffolk. The Normans also used circular windows, although usually larger, but again they were not common. Iffley church, Oxfordshire has a circular window in the west wall. Although it

CASTLE HEDINGHAM, ESSEX.
Late Norman wheel window.

was constructed in the nineteenth century it is believed to have been, so far as possible, a copy of the original circular window. Circular windows of this period are rarely found in side walls. It is thought probable that circular windows with tracery were designed earlier than windows of rectangular form.

Although some of the circular windows of this period were simply large round openings, as in the south transept of Canterbury Cathedral and at Iffley, many were rich in tracery the favourite design being a window with a small centre or 'eye' connected to a ring of tracery around the circumference of the circle by radiating shafts or 'spokes'. This type of window is often called a 'wheel' window. Examples may be found at Fountains, Kirkstall and Byland Abbeys, Yorkshire; Barfreston, Kent and Castle Hedingham, Essex, but they are not common in parish churches. At Castle Hedingham the wheel window in the east wall of the Norman church, was found, during repairs, to have one spoke or mullion made of wood. Was it found to be broken on arrival from the quarry or was it broken during construction and rather than wait for a replacement a wooden mullion was fashioned? Perhaps the story behind the faked mullion will never be discovered. From this type of window developed the beautiful traceried 'rose' windows of Gothic architecture. Examples are at Lincoln Cathedral and Temple Balsall, West Midlands.

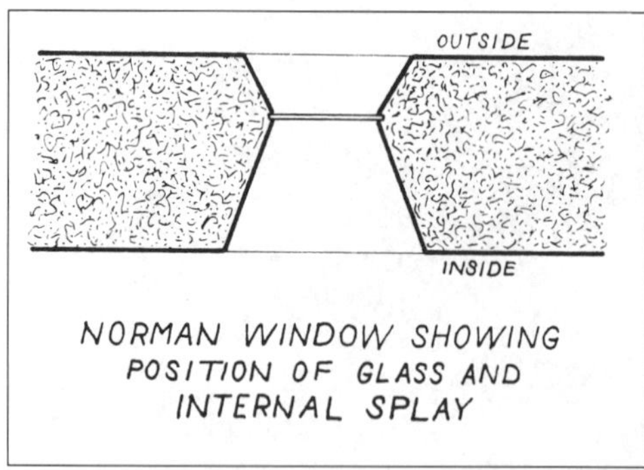

NORMAN WINDOW SHOWING POSITION OF GLASS AND INTERNAL SPLAY

FIGURE 15.

The east wall of the Norman church was sometimes blank as at Notgrove and Aston Blank, Gloucestershire or there might be a single window as may be seen at Elkstone and Hampnet, Gloucestershire. Occasionally groups of several windows occur as at Rainham, Kent.

Following the Conquest the Norman course thick-walling caused the splay to the windows to be on the inside, the wooden shutters or glass filling being kept close to the outer face of the walling (Ford, Sussex). Sometimes the heads of Norman windows were ornamented with, e.g. cheveron or billet moulding and small pillars or shafts with decorated capitals (Waltham Abbey and Copford, Essex).

Examples of Saxon windows: Hadstock and Chickney, Essex; Escombe, Durham; Deerhurst, Gloucestershire, Worth, Sussex, Brixworth, Northamptonshire and Tichborne, Hampshire.

Triangular heads: Barton-on-Humber, Humberside, Barnack, Northants and Bosham, Sussex.

Examples of Norman windows: Barfreston, Kent; Faulkbourne, Waltham Abbey and Copford, Essex; Ifley, Oxfordshire, Kilpeck, Hereford & Worcester, Ovingdean, Sussex and Elkstone, Gloucestershire.

Circular – Barfreston Kent; Castle Hedingham, Essex and Avebury Wiltshire (clerestory).

Early English, 1189–1280

About the middle of the twelfth century the pointed arch made its appearance in England. It had been used in the south of France since the early eleventh century and long before this in Ethiopia, Sicily and later in Spain. The introduction of the pointed arch brought in a tall narrow window having a pointed head which is termed a 'lancet' window. These window, were flush with the outside wall but splayed on the inside. In the Transitional period between the Norman and Early English periods (1145–1189) the head was semi-circular after the Norman style. In the early part of the thirteenth century it became common practice to group together two or more lancet windows thus giving more light to the otherwise dark church interiors. Single lancets were used in the side walls but in the gable-ends, for example, the east wall, the favourite arrangements was a triplet the centre light rising above the other two. Some good examples are at Eastwood, Essex; Brewood, Staffordshire; Foxton, Cambridgeshire; Luton, Bedfordshire; Filey, Yorkshire; Stanton Harcourt, Oxfordshire; Whitcombe, Dorset; North Hayling, Hampshire; Little Snoring, Norfolk; Sandwich (St Clements), Kent and West Kington, Wiltshire. The symbolism attaching to the triplets was that they represented the Trinity, the Three in One.

Sometimes as many as seven are grouped together as in the east walls of Blakeney, Norfolk and Ockham, Surrey, churches. Simple lancets had a label, hood-mould or drip-stone which was a moulding covering the head of the lancet. These labels were used both inside and outside the chuch and were frequently ornamental being of insufficient thickness to be of structural value and were, no doubt, the successors of the architrave moulding used by the Romans in their arches. However, many of the mouldings were undercut and served to throw off the rain-water which ran down the wall and so prevented staining as well as protecting the stonework of the window.

When two lancets, each having its own hood-mould were grouped together, there would be dip in the centre where the two hood-moulds met and where rain-water would collect and spill over on to the window. To avoid this a

FAULKBOURNE, ESSEX.
Norman windows (exterior).

KEMPLEY, GLOUCESTERSHIRE.
Norman window (interior).

hood-mould was constructed to enclose the two lancets. It will be seen that the effect of this was to leave a blank piece of masonry between the heads of the lancets and the hood-mould which would look unsightly. To overcome this the blank masonry was pierced with a circular hole which gave a decorative effect. This treatment is known as 'plate tracery' and was the beginning of all later forms of tracery (Long Wittenham, Berkshire; Tintern Abbey, Gwent; Shrewsbury, St Mary, Shropshire). At first lancets were separated by an amount of wall space but this was soon refined into a slender moulded mullion.

The piercing of the tympanum to form plate-tracery left broad spaces which were gradually reduced by enlarging the piercing and shaping it so as to fill as much of the tympanum as possible. Following this, *circa* 1240, the remaining spaces were pierced so that the stone bar between any two lights was never wider than the mullion. This is called 'Bar-tracery' which throughout the later Middle-Ages was one of the principal decorative elements of churches.

Towards the end of the thirteenth century, *circa* 1280, the upper part of the window contained a number of cusped circles, generally three (Cley-next-the-Sea, Norfolk). Further development took place at the end of the period when the upper part was filled with trefoils, quatrefoils, long-lobed trefoils and multifoils which, although they touch at points, are distinct. This type of tracery is known as 'Geometrical' and was composed of separate stone bars which, as already mentioned, is known as Bar-Tracery.

The splay to the windows of this period is usually quite plain but later in the more elaborate churches there may be a moulded rere-arch or scoinson-arch which supports the wall over the recess of a window as distinct from the outer arch. This rere-arch may have shafts in the jambs as at Thame, Oxfordshire: Examples of Geometrical tracery may be seen at Long Wittenham, Berkshire; Stone, Kent; Edlesborough, Buckinghamshire; and Binham Priory, Norfolk.

Top left: SHREWSBURY, SHROPSHIRE.
C13 window with pointed splay.

Above: AYTHORPE RODING, ESSEX.
Triple lancets in east wall.

Left: WENLOCK PRIORY, SHROPSHIRE.
Plate tracery.

By the end of the thirteenth century there was a fairly equal balance between the piercing and the masonry which throughout the later Middle Ages was one of the principal decorative features. The patterns made by the bars were the geometrical forms already mentioned but later to be superseded by beautiful forms such as flowing tracery.

The Church could now, for the first time, have large windows which might have as many as seven lights below and a large space above for tracery. The larger windows weakened the walls and to overcome this greater protection was given by increasing the size of the buttresses.

Decorated Period, 1200–1377

By the fourteenth century people were beginning to tire of tracery composed of simple geometrical forms. The glazier must have found geometrical tracery extremely frustrating as without a diamond to assist him he had to chip the glass, to the best of his ability, into the awkward apertures left between the geometrical patterns. The glass-painter would also have felt disgusted at being obliged to introduce saints and prophets into apertures ill-fitted to receive them. For both of these craftsmen the new forms of tracery must have come as a welcome relief although they must have still found difficulty.

At the beginning of the fourteenth century, *circa* 1300, a simple form of tracery known as 'Y' tracery was used. This was formed by the mullion dividing two lancets branching into two forming a 'Y' shape (Elmstead, Essex; Westleton, Suffolk and Markham Clinton or West Markham, Nottinghamshire).

The development of the window is one of the main features of the Decorated period and the beauty of the tracery is the greatest joy of the style of window of this period. They grew even larger and required even more and more stonework of mullions and tracery to assist in holding the glazing together against the pressure of the wind. The window heads in this period were slightly less pointed.

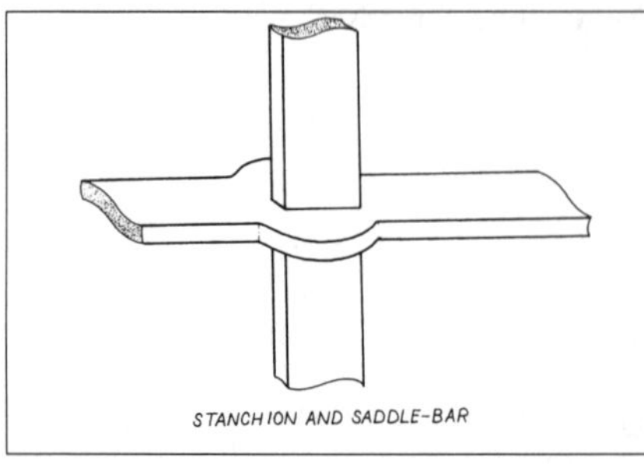

FIGURE 16.

The masons turned their skill to developing various patterns of tracery bars in the heads of the windows. Every light had, perhaps, one or two vertical bars of iron termed 'stanchions' and a series of horizontal iron bars termed 'saddle-bars' which were bedded at either end in the mullions and further secured by the stanchion which passed through them. These bars stiffened the leaded glazing and also provided additional security to

FIGURE 17.
"Y" Tracery.

the church. Each pane of glass was fastened to its neighbour with grooved lead strips known as 'calms' (pronounced 'cams'). The glazed leaded panels were tied to the bars by copper wire strips soldered on to the calms. The shape of the calms was similar to the letter 'H'.

At the end of the thirteenth century not only windows filled with circles and quatrefoils may be found but other forms such as long-lobed pointed trefoils and quatrefoils and long-lobed pointed trefoils having one lobe exaggeratedly long giving the appearance of daggers. All these existed side by side forming Geometrical tracery. These forms extended into the first fifteen years of the fourteenth century and developed into other forms of tracery. One of these early forms was 'Intersecting' tracery where each mullion branched into curved bars which had the same radius as the containing arch and intersected with one another. (Cawston and Great Snoring Norfolk and Bampton, Oxfordshire).

BRADFIELD, NORFOLK.
C14 intersecting cusped tracery.

A further form used between the early to mid-fourteenth century was made up entirely of a network of circles drawn at the top and bottom into ogee shapes, i.e. a double curved line made up of a convex and concave part and forming a net-like appearance. This style of tracery is known as 'Reticulated' tracery. In the thirteenth century attention had been concentrated on the piercings the aim being to give them good form. Now the lines of stonework were the chief consideration, the designer endeavouring to form graceful flowing tracery. (Westhall, Suffolk; Balsham, Cambridgeshire; Stanton, Morley; Norfolk, Wareham, Dorset; Great Baddow, Essex; Ware, Hertfordshire).

Later a further form known as 'Flowing' tracery became popular. This was made up of sinuous lines which flowed from curve to curve. This type of tracery is sometimes known as 'Curvilinear' or 'Undulating' tracery. Although it was used early in the period, it became popular later, and in France the tracery assumed a flame-like appearance and is known as 'Flamboyant' tracery, being used throughout the fifteenth century. Previously the beauty of tracery lay in the form of the openings but now the eye was to follow the curves. The heads of the lights became ogee-shaped and although the tracery patterns kept something of their geometrical character the forms were fulled and rounder and tended to lose structural form branching off into undulating curves of great beauty. They had a peculiar upward tendency which gave them a flame or leaf-like appearance which also tended to make them have a weak look. Examples of flowing-tracery may be found at Little Dunmow, Essex; Besthorpe and Snettisham, Norfolk; Sleaford, Lincolnshire; Patrington and Cottingham, Humberside, Ducklington, Oxfordshire and Ringstead, Northamptonshire. It was this change that Ruskin deplored and he declared that, 'curvilinear tracery undulating like the threads of a cobweb lifted by the wind, lost its essence as a structure of stone'. Reduced to the slenderness of threads it began to be considered as possessing also their flexibility and thereby sacrificed their strength.

BALSHAM, CAMBRIDGESHIRE.
C14 reticulated tracery.

Perpendicular 1377–1547

The wool trade was booming and the merchants were important people now beginning to rival the great landowners as patrons of the arts. This tendency became more marked during the fifteenth century when the aristocracy was impoverished by the long Wars of the Roses, if its members were not killed in battle or executed. The wealth of the land came more and more into the hands of the commoners who, to a large extent, built the Perpendicular churches. The beautiful church of Lavenham, Suffolk, the rebuilding of which was begun by the Lord of the Manor, John de Vere, the thirteenth Earl of Oxford, was completed by the efforts of the clothiers of Lavenham, the Spring family and Simon Branch.

The Black Death of 1349 greatly reduced the number of the population and labour became scarce and wages high. Even small traders and farmers could contribute liberally towards the cost of building and many churches were built by the subscriptions of the parishioners. It was the period following the Black Death that produced a complete change in the tracery of windows, now it was a tracery composed of straight lines. This began at Glouchester Cathedral where the gloomy and massive Norman work was required to be transformed into a more graceful form. More light was called for as well as a vast area for the display of stained glass which was becoming very popular.

WITNEY, OXFORDSHIRE.
C14 Flamboyant or Flowing tracery.

The new windows at Gloucester Cathedral are large having tall mullions which required lateral support obtained by the use of horizontal transoms at frequent intervals. These divided the main lights and provided not only a larger window with resistance against wind pressure but also a large series of panels of varying and graduated size and of rectangular form giving ample opportunities for a picture in stained glass. These panels frequently had short pieces of transom introduced into the tracery and the panels had more pronounced cusps. The windows were varied, square-headed, semi-circular, pointed and commonly four-centred. The arch became depressed so that the tracery in the head was either depleted or usually carried below the springing of the arch. Now that the windows were so much stronger than those of the Decorated period advantage was accordingly taken to increase the size of the windows and some had mullions fifty to sixty feet in height.

All this was a great revolution and was the fashion for windows for a period of almost two hundred years before the Reformation. The stone mullions ran vertically from sill to head and were not more slender taking the place of the flowing-tracery. The mullions and the transoms divided the window into cusped panels having thinner tracery bars and is referred to as 'Panel-tracery' or 'Rectilinear-tracery' because it is composed of straight lines.

NORTHLEACH, GLOUCESTERSHIRE.
Perpendicular window with transom, stanchion and saddle bars.

Now that the mullions were carried straight into the head the glass-painter would be able to see the window as a whole and so gave him every possible scope to decorate it. Figures of Saints could be inserted in the rectangular panels which had been quite impossible with the earlier flowing-tracery. This was the golden age of the glass-painter who was able to produce large pictures which included buildings, landscapes and biblical scenes.

At the end of the fifteenth century tracery became very monotonous and lifeless and finally lost favour with the rest of Gothic architecture in the sixteenth century. There were attempts at revival and in Oxford it lingered on until the seventeenth century and examples are to be seen in several college chapels, for example, Wadham and Jesus College. Examples of Perpendicular-tracery may be seen at Nantwich, Cheshire.; Sleaford, Lincolnshire; Northleach, Gloucestershire; Walpole St Peter, Salle and Cromer, Norfolk; Middleton and Cavendish, Suffolk; Curry Rivel and Crowcombe, Somerset; Ashburton, Devon; Burford, Oxfordshire and East Markham, Nottinghamshire.

Renaissance and Classical, 1547–1830

This period produced large plain windows with again a semi-circular head with a prominent key-stone or with square heads later becoming round-headed. The square-headed window is often found in the side walls, as for example, at Thaxted, Essex.

Glossary

ABACUS. A flat stone forming top of capital.

AFFUSION. The pouring of water over head.

ALB. A full length belted white tunic with narrow sleeves.

AMICE. A white linen neck-cloth.

APSE. A semi-circular termination at one end or both ends of early Christian churches.

ARCADE. A series of arches supported by piers or columns.

ARCHED-BRACES. A pair of curved braces forming and arch usually connecting the rafter or post below with the collar-beam above.

ASHLAR. Masonry of square blocks worked to an even face.

BALUSTER. A turned pillar or pedestal, the profile usually combining convex and concave curves.

BOSS. A square or round projecting ornament often covering the intersections of the ribs in a vault.

BOWTELL. A form of roll moulding usually three-quarters of a circle in section.

BRACE. A diagonal subsidiary timber inserted to strengthen the framing of a roof. It may be straight or arched and used to connect either a tie-beam with the wall below or a collar-beam with the rafters below.

BUTTRESS. A masonry support against overturning pressure upon a wall.

CHASUBLE. A circular or oval cape with central head opening.

CHRISM. Consecrated oil.

CLERESTORY. The upper stage of the main walls of a church pierced by windows, e.g. the windows of the nave above the aisle roof.

COLLAR BEAM. A horizontal transverse timber connecting a pair of rafters or principals between the ridge and the wall-plate.

COLLAR-PURLIN. Single horizontal central timber which carries collar beams and is supported by crown-posts.

COMPOUND PIER. Grouped shafts or solid core surrounded by attached or detached shafts.

CORBEL. A protecting block of stone or timber to support a feature above.

CORBEL TABLE. A row of corbels supporting a parapet or roof.

CROCKET. A carving representing leaves to be found on spires and pinnacles of Gothic architecture.

CROWN POST. A vertical timber standing centrally on a tie-beam and supporting a collar-purlin.

CUSPS. Projecting points defining the foils in Gothic windows, arches and panels.

DADO. Decorative covering of lower part of a wall.

FINIAL. Ornament on the top of a spire, pinnacle, gable, etc.

FLEURETTE OR FLEURON. A decorative carved flower or leaf.

FREESTONE. Any stone which can be easily dressed with the chisel.

FRESCO. Painting on fresh plaster while it is still wet. Only so much of wall or ceiling is plastered with finishing coat as can be painted in one day.

GABLE. Triangular upper portion of a wall to carry a pitched roof.

HAMMER-BEAM. Horizontal brackets projecting at wall-plate level on opposite sides of the wall like a tie-beam with the centre cut away. The inner ends carry vertical timbers called hammer-posts and braces to a collar-beam.

HOOD-MOULD. (Dripstone). A moulding projecting above and outlining an arch, doorway or window.

IMMERSION. Baptism by plunging under water.

IMPOST. A horizontal moulding in the wall on which the end of an arch rests. Sometimes used instead of a capital.

INTRADOS. The inner surface of an arch.

JAMB. The side of an archway, doorway, window or other opening.

KEYSTONE. The central stone in an arch or vault.

KING-POST. A vertical timber standing centrally on a tie or collar-beam and rising to the ridge-piece which it supports.

LABEL. A moulding projecting above and outlining an arch to throw off the rain. May be called, dripstone or hood-mould.

LANCET. A tall narrow single-light window commonly having a pointed head.

LATTEN. A mixed metal resembling brass composed chiefly of copper and zinc.

LIERNES. Subsidiary ribs in crown of vault running between other ribs but not linked to any of the springing points.

LINENFOLD. A wooden panel carved with a pattern resembling linen arranged in vertical folds.

LINTEL. Horizontal beam of stone, timber, metal or concrete bridging an opening.

LONG AND SHORT WORK. The method of forming angles of stone walls in late Saxon period in which flat horizontal stones alternate with tall pillar-like stones.

MOULDING. A concave or convex surface forming a groove or combination of the two of uniform profile throughout its length.

MULLION. A slender vertical member between the lights in a window.

NICHE. A shaped recess in wall or screen etc. usually to received a carved figure.

NIMBUS. A circle surrounding head of a saint. Variation for Deity where it is shown with three rays representing the Trinity.

NOOK-SHAFT. A shaft set at the angle of a pier, respond, buttress or wall.

OGEE. A compound curve partly convex and partly concave.

ORATORY. A small private chapel in a church.

ORDER. One of a series of recessed arches and jambs forming a splayed opening.

ORPHREY. An embroidered band found on chasubles and copes.

PIER. Large masonry support usually for an arch.

PILASTER. A flat representation of a column in shallow relief against a wall.

PINNACLE. A small turret-like termination crowning spires. buttresses, angles and parapets etc.

PISCINA. A drain provided in a wall or pavement near an altar for washing holy vessels.

POLYGONAL. Many sided.

PREDELLA. Horizontal strip below the main representation frequently used for subsidiary scenes.

PRIE-DIEU. A low desk with space for a book above and with a footpiece below for kneeling in prayer.

PROVINCIALE. An explanation, in five books, of the decrees of the province of Canterbury from time of King John C12 to Archibishop Chicele C15. Main source of English medieval canon law.

PURLIN. Horizontal longitudinal roof timber.

PYX. A receptacle of wood, precious metal or ivory for the resorvation of the Blessed Sacrament.

QUOIN. A corner stone.

RAFTERS. Inclined lateral timbers which slope from wall-plate to ridge and support the roof covering.

REBATE. A continuous rectangular notch or groove cut on an edge, so that a plank, door etc. may be fitted into it.

RERE-ARCH. An arch on the inside of a wall spanning the opening or a doorway or window.

ROMANESQUE. The architecture in England and on the Continent in which the influence of Roman buildings and tradition is seen. Style prevalent from 9th to 12th century characteristic by round arches, massive vaulting and thick walls.

ROOD. A crucifix flanked by figures of the Virgin Mary and St John.

SACRISTY. A room for storing sacred vessels and vestments.

SCOINSON-ARCH. See rere-arch.

SEDILIA. Seats for the clergy, generally on the south side of chancel.

SINGLE-FRAMED ROOF. Constructed with no main trusses.

SPANDREL. A space between curve of arch and rectangle enclosing it.

SPLAY. A sloping chamfered surface cut into the walls. An angled reveal frequently applied to windows.

SPRINGING-LINE. The point at which an arch springs from its supports. The bottom stone of the arch which rests on the impost is called a springer.

STALL. A seat supported by arms from others adjoining it. Used especially of seats in church choirs.

STOLE. A decorated band worn round the neck beneath the chasuble often having a device at each end and a cross on the back.

TIE-BEAM. The main horizontal transverse timber which carries the feet of the principal rafters at wall-plate level. When tie-beam rises slightly in the centre it is called 'cambered'.

TRANSOM. A horizontal mullion or cross-bar in a window.

TRUSS. A rigid framework of timbers which is placed laterally across the building to carry the longitudinal roof timbers which support the common rafters.

TRYPTYCH. A wooden reredos consisting of a central painted panel with two folding doors on the inner side of which pictures were painted. Common form of reredos in England in the Middle Ages.

TYMPANUM. The area between the lintel of a doorway and the area above it.

WALL-PLATE. A timber laid longitudinally on top of a wall to receive the ends of the rafters.

WAVE-MOULDING. A compound moulding formed by a convex curve between two concave curves.

WEB. One of the compartments of a groin or rib vault which in the Romanesque period was usually of plastered rubble but in the Gothic period was of coursed stones.

WYVERN. Similar to a dragon but has only two legs.

Select Bibliography

ABBOT CASQUET. *Parish life in Medieval England* (1906)

ANDERSON, M. D. *History and Imagery in British churches* (1971)

ANDREWS, FRANCIS B. *The Medieval Builder and his Methods* (1976)

BOND, FRANCIS. *English Church Architecture* (1913)
Fonts and Font Covers (1908)
The Chancel of English Churches (1910)

BOUQUET, A. C. *Church Brasses, British and Continental* (1956)

BRAUN, HUGH. *An Introduction to English Medieval Architecture.* (1968).

COALES J. (ed) *The Earliest English Brasses* (1987)
Monumental Brass Society.

CROSSLEY, FRED. H. *English Church Monuments* (1921)

DAVIES, J. G. *The Architectural Setting of Baptism.* (1962)

DICKINSON, J. C. *Monastic Life in Medieval England* 1961

ESDAILE, KATHERINE A. *English Church Monuments 1510–1840* (1946)

HARVEY, JOHN. *Medieval Craftsmen* (1975)

HEWETT, CECIL A. *English Historic Carpentry* (1980)

HOWARD, F. E. *Medieval styles of the English Parish Church* (1936)

KNOWLES, DAVID. *Bare Ruined Choirs.* (1976)

PAGE-PHILLIPS, J. *Macklin's Monumental Brasses* (1969)

PAUL, W. N. *Essex Fonts and Font Covers* (1986)

PEVSNER, Sir NIKOLAUS. The buildings of Essex series

RODWELL, WARWICK. *Church Archaelogy.* (1989).

SITWELL, Sacheverell. *Monks, Nuns and Monasteries* (1965)

Index of Places

General Index